Emerging Powers in the WTO

Also by Constantine Michalopoulos

MIGRATION CHRONICLES

DEVELOPING COUNTRIES IN THE WTO

TRADE IN THE NEW INDEPENDENT STATES (*with David G. Tarr*)

AID AND DEVELOPMENT (*with Anne O. Krueger and Vernon W. Ruttan*)

Emerging Powers in the WTO

Developing Countries and Trade in the 21st Century

Constantine Michalopoulos

palgrave
macmillan

Softcover reprint of the hardcover 1st edition 2014 978-1-137-29707-5

First published 2014 by
PALGRAVE MACMILLAN

Palgrave Macmillan in the UK is an imprint of Macmillan Publishers Limited, registered in England, company number 785998, of Houndmills, Basingstoke, Hampshire RG21 6XS.

Palgrave Macmillan in the US is a division of St Martin's Press LLC, 175 Fifth Avenue, New York, NY 10010.

Palgrave Macmillan is the global academic imprint of the above companies and has companies and representatives throughout the world.

Palgrave® and Macmillan® are registered trademarks in the United States, the United Kingdom, Europe and other countries.

ISBN 978-1-349-45201-9 ISBN 978-1-137-29708-2 (eBook)

DOI 10.1057/9781137297082

This book is printed on paper suitable for recycling and made from fully managed and sustained forest sources. Logging, pulping and manufacturing processes are expected to conform to the environmental regulations of the country of origin.

A catalogue record for this book is available from the British Library.
A catalog record for this book is available from the Library of Congress.

Typeset by MPS Limited, Chennai, India.

Transferred to Digital Printing in 2014

To Eveline, a champion of free trade in the fight against poverty and a wonderful oma *in her spare time*

Contents

List of Tables

List of Abbreviations

ACP	African, Caribbean and Pacific Group of States
ACWL	Advisory Centre on WTO Law
AD	Antidumping
AFT	Aid for Trade
AGOA	African Growth and Opportunity Act
AITIC	Agency for International Trade, Information and Cooperation
AMS	Aggregate measure of support
ASEAN	Association of Southeast Asian Nations
BRICS	Brazil, Russia, India, China, South Africa
BWIs	Bretton Woods Institutions
CBD	(UN) Convention on Biological Diversity
COMESA	Common Market for Eastern and Southern Africa
CPs	Contracting Parties
CV	Countervailing
DFID	Department for International Development
DFQF	Duty free and quota free
DSB	Dispute Settlement Body
DSM	Dispute Settlement Mechanism
DTIS	Diagnostic Trade Integration Study
EAC	East African Community
EC	European Community
EIF	Enhanced Integrated Framework
EPZ	Export processing zone
EU	European Union
FAO	Food and Agriculture Organization
FOGS	Functions of the GATT system
FSU	Former Soviet Union

FYROM	Former Yugoslav Republic of Macedonia
GATS	General Agreement on Trade in Services
GATT	General Agreement on Tariffs and Trade
GSP	Generalized system of preferences
GTA	Global Trade Alert
HIPC	Heavily Indebted Poor Countries
HS	Harmonized System
ICTSD	International Center for Trade and Sustainable Development
ILO	International Labor Organization
IMF	International Monetary Fund
IPRs	Intellectual property rights
ISO	International Standards Organization
ITC	International Trade Center
ITO	International Trade Organization
LDCs	Least developed countries
MDGs	Millennium Development Goals
MERCOSUR	Mercado Común del Sur
MFA	Multi-fiber Arrangement
MFN	Most favoured nation
NAFTA	North America Free Trade Area
NAMA	Non-agriculture market access
NTM	Non-tariff measures
ODA	Official Development Assistance
OECD	Organisation for Economic Co-operation and Development
OPEC	Organization of Petroleum Exporting Countries
OTDS	Overall trade-distorting support
PRSP	Poverty Reduction Strategy Paper
PTAs	Preferential trade agreements
QUAD	Canada, EU, Japan, USA (Quadrilaterals)
SAIS	School of Advanced International Studies

SADEC	Southern Africa Development Community
SDT	Special and differential treatment
SG	Safeguard
SITC	Standard International Trade Classification
SPS	Sanitary and phyto-sanitary
SSA	Special Safeguard for Agriculture
SVE	Small and Vulnerable Economies
TBT	Technical barriers to trade
TPR	Trade policy review
TPRM	Trade Policy Review Mechanism
TRIMs	Trade related investment measures
TRIPS	Trade related intellectual property rights
TTIP	Transatlantic Trade and Investment Partnership
UN	United Nations
UNCTAD	United Nations Conference on Trade and Development
UNDP	United Nations Development Program
UPOV	Union for Protection of New Varieties of Plants
USAID	United States Agency for International Development
WIPO	World Intellectual Property Organization
WTF	World Trade Fund
WTO	World Trade Organization

Preface and Acknowledgements

I wrote a very different book, *Developing Countries in the WTO*, more than a decade ago. At that time the World Trade Organization (WTO) had just began to function and developing countries had just started to find their way in the new institution. The international community was thinking about a new Round of multilateral negotiations and a number of chapters were devoted to recommendations about the topics that should be included in such a Round and the positions developing countries should take.

The world has changed. Several developing countries have emerged as powers within the WTO and were active participants in the Doha Round of multilateral negotiations which went nowhere for a long time. The present volume is about these countries and the many others which continue to struggle in international trade, hampered by institutional constraints and continued protection against their products in developed and other developing country markets. It updates several of the chapters of the earlier book, reviews the Doha Round and looks ahead at the future role of the WTO.

The work for this volume was done in 2012–13 when I was a Visiting Scholar at the Paul H. Nitze School of Advanced International Studies (SAIS) of Johns Hopkins University in Washington, DC. I would like to thank Dr Riordan Roett, Director of the Latin American Studies program at SAIS, for making this assignment possible and for his and his staff's support for this project. I am also grateful to Kelley Kornell of SAIS for her help in preparing the volume for publication.

As in the past, I have benefited greatly from the insights and comments of Eveline Herfkens, who also had to bear more of the burden in running our household while I was writing this book. I would also like to thank many friends and former colleagues for their help in completing the project. Bernard Hoekman, formerly of the World Bank and currently Director, Global Economics at the European University Institute, was especially helpful in providing guidance, references and suggestions on practically all aspects of this work, including a thorough review of several chapters. Ricardo Melendez and his staff at the International Center for Trade and Sustainable Development (ICTSD) provided me with a great deal of material and useful perspectives on developing country issues. K. Y. Amoako, President of the African Center for Economic Transformation, has taught me a lot about Africa's development constraints and reviewed a number of chapters. I am grateful to Anne O. Krueger, Senior Research Professor at SAIS and Senior Fellow at Stanford, for her review of the whole manuscript and to Esperanza Duran, former Director of the Agency for International Trade, Information and Co-operation (AITIC) for her comments on several chapters and her permission to use some material from an old article we co-authored on Trade Related Intellectual Property Rights (TRIPs). Richard Eglin and Cato Adrian of the WTO, and David G. Tarr formerly of the World Bank, provided helpful comments on various chapters. Peter Allgeier, former US Deputy Special Trade Represenative and currently President of the Coalition of Service Industries, was helpful in the work on services.

I reserve my greatest and very special thanks to Francis Ng, recently retired from the World Bank, for his immense help with the updating of the material in Chapters 1, 4 and 6 on trends in world trade and trade policy, his overall insights on the quality of various data sources in international trade, and his willingness to have a good deal of the data developed in two jointly authored working papers used in this volume. Neither he nor any of the others who helped with this volume are responsible for any errors and inaccuracies that may remain.

I am grateful to Taiba Batool of Palgrave Macmillan for her support in all aspects of the preparation of the volume for publication. I also wish to thank John Wiley & Sons Ltd for permission to use material from an article I co-authored with Esperanza Duran, 'Intellectual Property Rights and Developing Countries in the WTO Millennium Round', *Journal of World Intellectual Property*, vol. 2, no. 6, November 1999, and my article 'Developing Countries in the WTO', *World Economy*, vol. 22, no. 1, January 1999.

CONSTANTINE MICHALOPOULOS

Introduction: Developing Countries in World Trade

For more than half a century developing countries have made enormous progress in integrating their economies into the international trading system. Growth in their international trade has exceeded growth in output, the product composition of their exports has shifted dramatically in favour of manufactures and away from primary commodities, and since the early 1990s trade in some developing countries has grown exceptionally quickly and far more than trade in developed countries. This includes the least developed countries (LDCs), despite the fact that they continue to rely overwhelmingly on the exports of a few primary commodities.[1]

Integration into the world trading system depends on whether countries and their trading partners establish policies and institutions that are conducive to the mutually beneficial exchange of goods and services, based on specialization and comparative advantage. The effective integration of the developing countries involves not only their own trade policies and institutions but also those of the developed countries, their main trading partners. Integration also requires them to abide by the rules of conduct that govern the multilateral trading system. These rules were established and are being implemented in the context of agreements administered by the World Trade Organization (WTO). Therefore membership of and effective participation in the WTO is an essential element of, and perhaps even a necessary condition for, full integration in the world trading system.[2]

The draft charter of the International Trade Organization (ITO) – which together with the International Monetary Fund (IMF) and the World Bank was intended to be one of the three pillars of international economic cooperation after World War II but never came into being – contained specific exceptions to general trade rules when applied in the

[1] These are the 48 developing countries formally designated as 'least developed' by the United Nations based on a number of criteria, including per capita income and the structure of production.

[2] WTO members can be countries or customs territories, such as Hong Kong (now part of China) which joined the WTO when it was a British colony. Similarly, the European Community is a member but there are separate delegations from each of the 27 constituent states. For purposes of simplicity, in this volume the term 'country' is used whatever the legal status of the member.

context of development. The General Agreement on Tariffs and Trade (GATT), which was signed as an interim agreement in the aftermath of the failure of the effort to launch the ITO but lasted almost 50 years, contained no explicit provisions pertaining to development.

Almost half of the original GATT membership consisted of developing countries. Over time, these countries succeeded in incorporating a variety of development-related provisions in GATT. Nevertheless, for a variety of reasons (discussed in detail in Chapter 2), the developing countries did not feel that GATT as an institution was responsive to their special needs in trade. As a consequence, in the 1960s they lobbied for and succeeded in establishing a new global institution, the United Nations Conference on Trade and Development (UNCTAD). Throughout the 1960s and 1970s, developing countries viewed UNCTAD rather than GATT as the main institution through which to promote their trade interests. Their representation in GATT reflected this priority: many were not Contracting Parties, and the participation of those that were was passive. They did not engage in a significant way in the mutual exchange of trade liberalization concessions on a reciprocal basis in GATT negotiations, but focused on securing measures of special and more favourable treatment for their exports and in the rules governing protection against foreign imports.

Beginning with the GATT Uruguay round of multilateral trade negotiations in the mid-1980s, the developing countries' attitude towards participation in GATT and, subsequently, in the WTO changed significantly: many developing countries played a very active role in the Uruguay round negotiations, and a large number decided to become members of GATT and later the WTO during and at the end of the round. This change of attitude reflects a number of complex and interrelated developments.

The trade policies in many developing countries had been liberalized, favouring an outward orientation and lower protection. Several countries in East Asia had become major trading powers, especially as exporters of manufactures. And, there was a growing appreciation of the importance of observing international rules in the conduct of trade, as well as the need to safeguard trading interests through effective participation in the activities of the new organization and in the making of general rules that govern international trade – as opposed to focusing on special rules and exceptional treatment for developing countries.

The WTO incorporates the fundamental provisions of GATT regarding the trade of goods, such as the most favoured nation principle, as well as the principle of special and differential treatment for developing countries and LDCs. But the establishment of the WTO has also resulted in further changes that have placed additional demands on developing countries in respect of effective participation. First, the WTO covers a variety of new areas – such as services, standards and intellectual property rights – in which new rules governing the conduct of international trade have been agreed and whose implementation requires additional institutional capacity on the part of member governments. Second, the WTO has been engaging in a number of on-going negotiations in the liberalization of different sectors which involve continuous active participation by members. Third, the new WTO Dispute Settlement Mechanism (DSM) enables developing countries to address grievances, but it also poses tremendous challenges because of their very limited institutional capacity to initiate action against developed countries.

The participation of developing countries in the WTO has increased by comparison with their earlier participation in GATT. This is especially true for a number of middle and higher income developing countries.

In the years following the Uruguay Round Agreements many developing countries were concerned that aspects of the agreements of interest to them were not being implemented as expected. In particular, they questioned whether developed countries lived up to their commitments on market access as well as their promises to provide developing countries with technical and other assistance to strengthen their institutional capacity and to cushion the adjustment costs resulting from a more rational and liberal international economic system. Failure to address these concerns and developing country dissatisfaction with WTO processes contributed to the failure of the third WTO ministerial meeting in Seattle in 1999, convened to agree on an agenda for the launching of a new round of multilateral trade negotiations.

A new WTO round was launched with great fanfare in Doha, Qatar in 2001. Its negotiating content, pointedly labelled the 'Doha Development Agenda' was intended to address developing country issues. The Agenda, however, also contained a number of topics such as competition, the environment and labour standards which most developing countries for a variety of good reasons wanted to exclude from the negotiations. This they achieved in the next WTO ministerial meeting in Cancun, Mexico. The actual negotiations for the Doha Round did not start in earnest until after the Hong Kong ministerial meeting in 2005. Developing countries especially Brazil and India have played a major role in them. They and a number of others, including South Africa and China, have become the emerging powers in the WTO. Unfortunately, nothing has come from these negotiations after many years of sometimes intensive discussions.

Developing countries have also been involved in negotiations on many regional agreements, both among each other and with developed countries. Perhaps the most important have been those pushed on the African, Caribbean and Pacific Group of States (ACP) by their EU partners. These negotiations have also failed to produce concrete results in most instances.

Despite the failure of the multilateral trade negotiations and the limited success of concluding regional arrangements, the trade of developing countries has flourished in the last decade. Stimulated by rapid income growth in China, Brazil and other middle income countries, developing countries' exports of goods and services were able to overcome the major financial crisis of 2008; by 2010 they were more than triple their levels in 2000.

And yet, in the second decade of the new millennium, developing countries' policies towards further integration into the multilateral trading system are clouded with uncertainty. Global economic prospects are undermined by on-going financial difficulties in the eurozone and slowdowns in other developed countries, as well as in India and China. There is a general unease that globalization will benefit only a few countries and that at the same time it will move forward at a faster pace than the institutions in most other countries can cope with. Developed countries are seeking to establish more and more preferential trade agreements with each other and with higher income developing countries. At the same time, there is awareness that exogenous forces involving technological change are pushing globalization and growth inexorably forward, and hence there is a fear of being left behind – of becoming more marginalized. Within countries, faster growth has helped reduced poverty but in most cases it has also increased income inequalities.

In the currently unsettled international environment, it would seem useful to take stock of developing-country policies and institutions, and their integration into the multilateral trading system, the challenges they face and what they and the international community can do to address them.

In this volume I attempt such a stock taking after a decade of failed WTO multilateral trade negotiations. I then consider what needs to be done to strengthen the institutional capacity of developing countries to participate in both the WTO and the trading system, as well as how the system can be modified in order to reflect better the interests and strengths of emerging powers. The focus is on merchandise trade and to a lesser extent on trade in services, but special attention is devoted to the implications for developing countries of the rules established in the WTO on Trade Related Intellectual Property Rights (TRIPS).

The book is organized as follows. Chapter 1 presents a summary of developing countries' trade performance in goods and services between

1980 and 2010. This includes a review of indicators of integration into the trading system (for example, the ratio of trade to GDP) and trade structure (for example, the importance of value chains), as well as an analysis of the differing performance of various developing-country groupings (by region and income group). In Chapter 2 I review the evolution of thinking on trade policies suitable for development and how this is reflected in GATT/WTO rules and in the concept of 'special and differential' treatment for developing countries.

Chapter 3 is devoted to the requirements and procedures for WTO accession – often quite cumbersome for poorer developing countries. Chapters 4–6 are devoted to an analysis of the trade policies and institutions in developing and developed countries. In Chapters 4 and 5 I discuss developing-country trade policies and institutions respectively, including a discussion of aid for trade activities and issues. In Chapter 6 I analyse issues of developed-country policies which affect developing-country market access in goods and services. In Chapter 7 I explore the special challenges the TRIPS agreement poses for development.

The next two chapters address aspects of developing countries' participation in the WTO including their participation in the DSM (Chapter 8) and in the Doha Round of multilateral trade negotiations and what needs to be done to conclude it (Chapter 9). Chapter 10 deals with the future role of the WTO, how to take into account the emerging developing-country interests and strengths, and the links between international trade policies for development and other national and international development policies including the links among the WTO, the IMF and the World Bank. The final chapter summarizes the main conclusions and recommendations of the analysis and presents a 12-point action programme aimed at strengthening the WTO and the role developing countries play in it.

1
Trends in the Trade of Developing Countries, 1980–2010

Introduction

The period covered by this study, 1980–2012, witnessed a rapid expansion of world trade and an even more rapid expansion of developing countries' trade, especially in the last decade (see Appendix A for a description of developing country and group coverage). The share of trade in developing countries in total world merchandise trade (exports plus imports) was appreciably higher at the end of the period than at the beginning: 27 per cent as opposed to 39 per cent (see Tables 1.1 and 1.2). There was a sharp decline in world trade in 2009, though this was offset by an even larger increase in 2010. Trade growth has decelerated in 2011–12, with exports growing at about 2 per cent in 2012 compared with 5 per cent in 2011; and there are many uncertainties about 2013. Yet, this does not affect these broad overall trends.

A similar picture emerges if one also considers trade in services. While the data on services are much less complete than for merchandise trade, there is little doubt about the overall trends: services trade grew even faster than merchandise trade; and there was a rise in the share of developing countries' exports. As a consequence of these trends the role developing countries play in the international trading system has changed radically; and this has been reflected in their participation in the moribund Doha Development Round negotiations.

GDP growth during this period was much less than the growth in trade for developed and developing countries alike. Using the ratio of total trade to GDP as an indicator of integration into world trade, on average developing countries were more integrated at the end of 2010 than 20 years earlier. This was the result of another long-term trend in evidence over the past 50 years and an important dimension of the globalization process.

Table 1.1 World merchandise exports by country group and region, 1980–2010

Country group	1980		1990		2000		2010	
	Exports ($ bill)	Share in %	Exports ($ bill)	Share in %	Exports ($ bill)	Share in %	Exports ($ bill)	Share in %
By income level								
Developed economies	1,314	66.6	2,653	76.4	4,418	68.4	8,909	58.5
Developing economies	597	30.2	837	24.1	2,035	31.5	6,268	41.2
High income developing economies	254	12.9	363	10.5	854	13.2	2,108	13.8
Upper middle income economies	211	10.7	332	9.5	873	13.5	3,175	20.8
Lower middle income economies	120	6.1	128	3.7	285	4.4	908	6.0
Low income economies	12	0.6	14	0.4	23	0.4	77	0.5
Of which least developed countries	15	0.8	18	0.5	36	0.6	162	1.1
Developing economies, excl. China and India	570	28.9	757	21.8	1,744	27.0	4,471	29.4
Upper middle income, excl. China	193	9.8	269	7.8	624	9.7	1,597	10.5
Lower middle income, excl. India	112	5.7	110	3.2	243	3.8	689	4.5
By region								
World	1,973	100.0	3,473	100.0	6,456	100.0	15,228	100.0
Developing economies	597	30.2	837	24.1	2,035	31.5	6,268	41.2
Asia	165	8.3	459	13.2	1,285	19.9	4,005	26.3
Latin America and Caribbean	104	5.3	145	4.2	362	5.6	886	5.8
Europe, Middle East and North Africa	250	12.7	165	4.8	293	4.5	1,035	6.8
Sub-Saharan Africa	78	3.9	68	2.0	94	1.5	341	2.2
BRICS 5 countries	72	3.7	203	5.8	482	7.5	2,481	16.3
OPEC 12 members	280	14.2	174	5.0	311	4.8	1,077	7.1

Source: UN COMTRADE database.

Table 1.2 World merchandise imports by country group and region, 1980–2010

Country group	1980		1990		2000		2010	
	Imports ($ bill)	Share in %	Imports ($ bill)	Share in %	Imports ($ bill)	Share in %	Imports ($ bill)	Share in %
By income level								
Developed economies	1,465	72.9	2,775	78.2	4,792	72.0	9,508	62.0
Developing economies	485	24.2	784	22.1	1,863	28.0	5,764	37.6
High income developing economies	153	7.6	327	9.2	749	11.3	1,726	11.3
Upper middle income economies	202	10.1	298	8.4	808	12.1	2,859	18.7
Lower middle income economies	112	5.6	136	3.8	269	4.0	1,051	6.9
Low income economies	18	0.9	23	0.6	37	0.6	129	0.8
Of which least developed countries	25	1.2	26	0.7	43	0.6	170	1.1
Developing economies, excl. China and India	451	22.4	707	19.9	1,586	23.8	4,019	26.2
Upper middle income, excl. China	182	9.1	245	6.9	582	8.7	1,464	9.6
Lower middle income, excl. India	97	4.8	113	3.2	217	3.3	700	4.6
By region								
World	2,009	100.0	3,550	100.0	6,659	100.0	15,326	100.0
Developing economies	485	24.2	784	22.1	1,863	28.0	5,764	37.6
Asia	181	9.0	476	13.4	1,216	18.3	3,873	25.3
Latin America and Caribbean	116	5.8	123	3.5	384	5.8	891	5.8
Europe, Middle East and North Africa	122	6.1	127	3.6	181	2.7	693	4.5
Sub-Saharan Africa	66	3.3	58	1.6	82	1.2	307	2.0
Memo:								
BRICS 5 countries	79	3.9	168	4.7	410	6.2	2,280	14.9
OPEC 12 members	122	6.1	100	2.8	148	2.2	595	3.9

Source: UN COMTRADE database.

These overall trends, however, disguise very different patterns during some of the sub-periods and among different developing countries and groups. Broadly speaking, the data show that, except for Asia, the 1980s were pretty much a 'lost' decade for many different developing countries and groups. By comparison, during the 1990s and 2000s trade for practically all major groupings of developing countries grew faster than trade of developed countries and, in many cases, very rapidly indeed. The Least Developed Countries (LDCs) deserve special mention: while growth in their merchandise trade was much slower than that of developing countries as a whole for the first 20 years (1980–2000) it was the most rapid during the decade 2001–10. As a result, for the first time in many decades these countries showed an increase in their small share of total world trade.

Trends in merchandise trade

The merchandise exports of developing countries grew at an annual rate of 8.2 per cent for the period 1980–2010 compared with 6.6 per cent for developed countries (see Table 1.3). But the performance was very different in the 1980s compared with the 1990s and 2000s. In the 1980s, developing-country exports grew only at 3.4 per cent while exports of developed countries expanded at over 7 per cent per annum. This reflects in large part the slower growth of the world economy during this period as well as the debt problems encountered by many groups of developing countries, especially in Latin America and Africa.

In the last two decades the situation was reversed with the export growth of developing countries at more than 10 per cent per annum compared with about 6 per cent for the developed countries. The trends in merchandise imports parallel those in exports both for developed and developing countries alike. But in both periods, the developing countries' imports grew faster than their exports. Table 1.3 also shows the performance of different regions and groupings of developing countries.

China's exceptional trade performance throughout the period, and India's in the last two decades, are well known. What is not always understood is that other groups of developing countries' trade also grew very rapidly during the past 20 years, especially since 2000. Indeed, since the beginning of the 21st century, growth in the trade of all major developing country groupings, whether classified by income level or by region, was faster than that of developed countries. For the 30 years from 1980 to 2010, only the developing countries in sub-Saharan Africa and the group of developing countries in Europe, Middle and

Table 1.3 Growth in world merchandise trade by country group and region, 1980–2010

Country group	Annual export growth (%)				Annual import growth (%)			
	1980–90	1990–2000	2000–10	1980–2010	1980–90	1990–2000	2000–10	1980–2010
By income level								
Developed economies	7.3	5.2	7.3	6.6	6.6	5.6	7.1	6.4
Developing economies	3.4	9.3	11.9	8.2	4.9	9.0	12.0	8.6
High income developing economies	3.7	8.9	9.5	7.3	7.9	8.7	8.7	8.4
Upper middle income economies	4.6	10.2	13.8	9.5	4.0	10.5	13.5	9.2
Lower middle income economies	0.7	8.3	12.3	7.0	2.0	7.0	14.6	7.7
Low income economies	1.2	5.2	12.8	6.3	2.1	5.0	13.3	6.7
Of which least developed countries	1.9	7.1	16.2	8.2	0.4	5.3	14.6	6.6
Developing economies, excl. China and India	2.9	8.7	9.9	7.1	4.6	8.4	9.7	7.6
Upper middle income, excl. China	3.4	8.8	9.9	7.3	3.0	9.1	9.7	7.2
Lower middle income, excl. India	–0.1	8.2	11.0	6.3	1.5	6.8	12.4	6.8
By region								
World	5.8	6.4	9.0	7.0	5.9	6.5	8.7	7.0
Developing economies	3.4	9.3	11.9	8.2	4.9	9.0	12.0	8.6
Asia	10.8	10.8	12.0	11.2	10.2	9.8	12.3	10.8
Latin America and Caribbean	3.3	9.6	9.4	7.4	0.6	12.0	8.8	7.0
Europe, Middle East and North Africa	–4.1	5.9	13.4	4.8	0.4	3.6	14.4	6.0
Sub-Saharan Africa	–1.3	3.3	13.7	5.1	–1.4	3.6	14.2	5.2
BRICS 5 countries	10.8	9.1	17.8	12.5	7.8	9.3	18.7	11.8
OPEC 12 members	–4.6	5.9	13.2	4.6	–2.0	3.9	15.0	5.4

Source: UN COMTRADE database.

North Africa – whose exports are dominated by oil – experienced trade growth slower than that of developed countries. In practically all cases and periods, Asia as a region has shown the greatest growth, with Latin America second. But sub-Saharan Africa, Europe, the Middle East and North Africa grew fastest in the last decade.

As noted in many studies, the trade performance of the various groups of developing countries depends very much on the composition of their exports as between manufactures, primary commodities and foodstuffs on the one hand and the direction of their trade on the other. Overall, the growth of developing countries' manufacturing exports and imports has exceeded that of developed countries for practically all groupings of developing countries for the last two decades and for the period as a whole (see Table 1.4). The same holds true for non-manufacturing trade – except that in this case LDC exports of raw materials and minerals lagged behind those of developed countries in the 1990s. In the 2000s, however, increased demand and rising prices of raw materials led to a very rapid (14.6 per cent per annum) increase of LDC non-manufacturing trade.

In the 1980s and 1990s, with the exception of China, trade grew fastest for the higher and middle-income developing countries and more slowly for the lower income countries and the LDCs. This relationship, however, did not hold up in the 2000s when LDC exports expanded very rapidly, indeed more rapidly than any other group, except for the upper-middle income economies whose performance is dominated by China.

Within manufacturing, developing country export growth was especially rapid in machinery and transport as well as chemicals. Practically all developing country groups shared in this growth (see Table 1.5), which was especially rapid in the upper-middle income countries, even when excluding China, as well as Brazil, Russia, India, China and South Africa (the BRICS) and Latin America.

The growth of manufactured exports in the developing world was in part prompted by the development of value chains, which took advantage of labour-cost differentials. Developing countries benefited from large investments by both multinationals and local entrepreneurs in assembly or production of final consumer goods based on the importation of intermediates. It is difficult to estimate how much of this happened in different parts of the developing world. One proxy for intermediates is given by an indicator consisting of 75 parts and component products at the Standard International Trade Classification (SITC) two to five-digit level (for a list of parts and component products, see Michalopoulos and Ng, 2013a, Appendix B, Table 3).

Table 1.4 Growth in manufacturing and non-manufacturing trade by country group and region, 1980–2010

Country group	Annual growth in manufacturing trade (%)				Annual growth in non-manufacturing trade (%)			
	1980–90	1990–2000	2000–10	1980–2010	1980–90	1990–2000	2000–10	1980–2010
By income level								
Developed economies	9.1	5.7	6.2	7.0	3.3	4.2	10.0	5.8
Developing economies	11.0	11.5	11.1	11.2	1.7	7.3	13.8	7.5
High income developing economies	14.9	9.6	8.1	10.8	0.6	7.3	13.0	6.9
Upper middle income economies	7.8	14.6	13.2	11.8	1.6	7.1	14.5	7.6
Lower middle income economies	8.7	9.8	12.7	10.4	3.5	7.9	13.5	8.2
Low income economies	5.8	7.0	12.4	8.4	2.5	4.3	14.1	6.8
Of which least developed countries	5.7	8.0	12.8	8.8	6.1	2.6	14.6	7.7
Developing economies, excl. China and India	11.1	10.9	8.5	10.1	1.5	6.9	12.3	6.8
Upper middle income, excl. China	6.7	13.8	8.1	9.5	1.5	6.3	12.1	6.5
Lower middle income, excl. India	8.4	10.1	10.9	9.8	3.4	7.8	11.2	7.4
By region								
World	9.7	7.1	7.8	8.2	2.7	6.0	11.2	6.6
Developing economies	11.0	11.5	11.1	11.2	1.7	7.3	13.8	7.5
Asia	15.5	11.4	11.5	12.8	5.1	7.2	15.8	9.3
Latin America and Caribbean	3.7	16.6	7.6	9.2	2.4	7.0	11.9	7.0
Europe, Middle East and North Africa	3.3	6.0	15.1	8.0	–3.5	9.4	12.1	5.8
Sub-Saharan Africa	5.2	4.3	13.0	7.4	3.0	2.7	12.3	5.9
BRICS 5 countries	11.6	10.9	18.3	13.6	8.3	3.9	18.7	10.1
OPEC 12 members	1.8	5.7	15.9	7.7	–2.8	8.9	11.5	5.7

Note: The classification of manufacturing products in exports and imports is defined as SITC 5+6+7+8–68 in revision 3.
Source: UN COMTRADE database.

Table 1.5 Growth in sectoral exports by country group and region, 1980–2010 (annual average, %)

Country group	Agric. & feed	Ores & metals	Fuels	All manuf.	Chemical products	Textiles & clothing	Machinery & transport	Other manuf.
By income group								
Developed economies	5.1	6.3	8.1	6.5	8.0	4.2	6.5	6.1
Developing economies	7.9	10.1	6.6	14.6	15.8	10.3	17.2	13.2
High income developing economies	6.4	11.5	4.9	12.1	15.5	5.5	14.7	10.6
Upper middle income economies	8.8	11.3	9.6	18.5	16.7	15.5	21.7	16.3
Lower middle income economies	7.1	7.9	8.3	13.5	14.4	10.7	16.8	12.9
Low income economies	5.6	4.8	6.6	9.5	9.1	6.5	9.6	11.2
Of which least developed countries	5.7	7.4	7.9	9.0	10.0	6.5	11.2	9.3
Developing econ, excl. China & India	7.5	9.7	6.4	12.8	14.8	7.4	15.5	11.2
Upper middle income, excl. China	8.1	10.8	9.3	14.1	14.1	8.6	17.5	11.8
Lower middle income, excl. India	6.9	6.8	7.7	14.6	13.5	11.5	19.0	13.3
By region								
World	5.9	7.4	7.2	8.1	8.8	6.7	8.3	7.5
Developing economies	7.9	10.1	6.6	14.6	15.8	10.3	17.2	13.2
Asia	7.5	9.2	8.3	14.7	16.9	10.6	17.2	13.6
Latin America & Caribbean	9.7	12.6	11.5	16.6	14.8	9.4	20.6	14.5
Europe, Middle East & North Africa	8.9	7.9	5.2	14.1	15.3	8.1	13.9	16.5
Sub-Saharan Africa	4.8	8.7	10.0	8.0	8.1	5.2	11.7	6.7
BRICS 5 countries	12.1	14.0	21.6	19.2	18.5	16.6	24.8	16.7
OPEC 12 members	10.4	14.3	5.7	16.9	21.1	16.9	14.8	16.6

Notes: The classification of product groups is defined in SITC revision 2 as agriculture & feed (0+1+2+4–27–28), ores & metals (27+28+68), fuels (3), all manufactures (5+6+7+8–68), chemical products (5), textiles & clothing (26+65+84), machinery & transport (7) and other manufactures (6+8–65–68–84). Export data in sectoral breakdown are based on 161 countries available from the UN COMTRADE database. Where the aggregate merchandise export data is based on a total of 192 countries, data available in Table 3 from World Development indicators database.

Source: UN COMTRADE database.

Table 1.6 Growth and share of parts and components in manufacturing imports by country group and region, 1980–2010

Country group	Share of parts and components in manufacturing imports (%)				Annual growth in parts and component imports (%)				Annual growth in manufacturing imports (%)		
	1980	1990	2000	2010	1980–90	1990–2000	2000–10	1980–2010	1980–90	1990–2000	2000–10
By income level											
Developed economies	22.1	23.1	27.4	24.1	10.6	7.9	4.9	7.8	10.1	6.0	6.3
Developing economies	22.9	29.5	38.7	35.6	11.3	13.5	9.9	11.6	8.5	10.5	10.8
High income developing economies	27.9	31.0	40.4	39.8	13.3	12.3	7.9	11.1	12.0	9.4	8.0
Upper middle income economies	20.3	30.2	39.0	35.9	10.2	16.0	11.2	12.4	6.0	13.1	12.1
Lower middle income economies	19.2	23.6	32.3	26.3	8.9	10.5	12.3	10.6	6.7	7.1	14.6
Low income economies	25.8	23.9	27.6	23.8	5.7	7.1	10.6	7.8	6.5	5.6	12.2
Of which least developed economies	25.4	24.1	27.7	23.8	6.2	7.6	11.0	8.3	6.8	6.2	12.7
Developing economies, excl. China and India	24.8	28.9	38.7	34.7	10.2	13.4	7.8	10.4	8.5	10.1	9.0
Upper middle income, excl. China	23.7	27.7	38.2	31.7	6.9	16.1	6.7	9.8	5.2	12.4	8.7
Lower middle income, excl. India	20.1	24.0	34.6	28.1	8.2	11.3	10.5	10.0	6.4	7.3	12.8
By region											
World	22.6	24.3	30.5	28.4	11.0	9.7	7.0	9.3	10.3	7.3	7.8
Developing economies	22.9	29.5	38.7	35.6	11.3	13.5	9.9	11.6	8.5	10.5	10.8
Asia	22.9	32.4	42.7	40.7	17.7	13.6	10.3	13.8	13.6	10.5	10.8
Latin America and Caribbean	21.9	20.5	33.2	29.6	1.8	21.8	7.1	9.9	2.5	16.1	8.4
Europe, Middle East and North Africa	24.3	26.9	27.1	20.6	2.4	5.9	11.5	6.5	1.3	5.8	14.5
Sub-Saharan Africa	21.8	22.9	22.9	20.9	6.4	2.3	13.4	7.3	5.9	2.3	14.4
BRICS 5 countries	13.3	28.2	35.6	34.3	18.8	12.3	17.5	16.1	10.2	9.6	17.9
OPEC 12 members	23.0	25.8	24.8	20.0	1.5	5.0	12.8	6.3	0.3	5.4	15.2

Note: The classification of parts and components items is based on 75 products at SITC 2 to 5-digit level in revision 2, including textiles & clothing (65+61), machinery & transport equipment (7), metal manufacturing (69), other miscellaneous manufactured goods (8). For details see Aminian et al., 2009.

Source: Based on UN COMTRADE statistics.

In 1980 the share of parts and components in total manufacturing imports was only slightly higher in developed countries than in developing ones. In the next two decades this share grew in both groups of countries, but much faster in developing countries. The aggregate share of parts and components in total imports fell in both developed and developing countries in the decade 2001–10. At the end of 2010 the shares were higher the higher the developing-country income grouping.

But not all groups of developing countries followed this pattern over time: for example, low income economies and the least developed ones did not see an increase in the share of parts and components until the decade of the 1990s. Sub-Saharan Africa, Europe, the Middle East and North Africa as well as the LDCs actually had lower ratios of parts and components in their imports at the end of the 30 years than at the beginning. By contrast, the BRICS raised their share drastically – more than doubling in the decade of the 1980s – and maintained their growth, almost uninterruptedly until 2010. China increased its income sixfold from value chains between 1995 and 2009, India fivefold, Brazil threefold (OECD, WTO, UNCTAD, 2013). Lower-income economies, sub-Saharan Africa and the LDCs have benefited much less. They have failed to diversify and continued to specialize in the primary product phase of the supply chains.

A significant portion of the growth in developing countries' exports of manufactures as well as of commodities is the result of expanding trade among the developing countries themselves. China's growth has been instrumental in this but trade among developing countries has grown rapidly in other regions as well. Part of this growth may be the result of preferential regional arrangements, but part of it can be explained by the fact that during most of the 1990s and 2000s growth in incomes in most developing countries' groupings outpaced that of developed countries. Table 1.7 shows that South–South trade grew faster than any other trade over the last 30 years. Indeed the share of this trade in total world trade quadrupled over this period.

The improvement in the export performance of developing countries during the 1990s was due mainly to increased demand in the commodities they exported and to a much lesser extent to diversification or increases in the market shares of their traditional exports. While this is true for the developing countries as a whole, different regions had different experiences. Both Asia and Latin America improved their competitive position, but, by contrast, sub-Saharan Africa experienced slow growth in world trade for its export basket, reflecting the continued decline in primary commodity prices and slow demand growth for these commodities. The same was true for the least developed (World Bank, 2000).

Table 1.7 World market shares and trade growth in developed and developing countries, 1980–2010

Reporter	**Partner**	**World trade market share (%)**				**Annual trade growth (%)**			
		1980	**1990**	**2000**	**2010**	**1980–90**	**1990–2000**	**2000–10**	**1980–2010**
Developed econ (48)	Developed econ (48)	55.8	61.4	53.7	42.9	8.2	5.4	6.4	6.7
Developed econ (48)	Developing econs	27.2	18.5	18.5	19.6	3.1	6.9	9.4	6.4
Developed econ (48)	World	82.9	79.9	72.2	62.5	6.8	5.8	7.2	6.6
Developing econ (ROW)	Developed econ (48)	11.4	11.8	15.5	15.8	7.6	9.7	9.0	8.8
Developing econ (ROW)	Developing econs	5.6	8.2	12.3	21.7	11.3	11.2	15.2	12.5
Developing econ (ROW)	World	17.1	20.1	27.8	37.5	8.9	10.4	12.1	10.5
World	Developed econ (48)	67.2	73.3	69.2	58.7	8.1	6.2	7.0	7.1
World	Developing econs	32.8	26.7	30.8	41.3	5.0	8.4	12.0	8.4
World	World	100.0	100.0	100.0	100.0	7.2	6.8	8.8	7.6

Source: UN COMTRADE database.

In the decade of the 2000s, the trends of the 1990s continued in many ways – except, of course, for the increase in African exports of raw materials, a relatively rapid growth of Latin America exports of foodstuffs and an expansion of exports of fuels from developed countries and the BRICS (see Michalopoulos and Ng, 2013(a), Appendix Tables 1 and 2). During this period practically all developing income groups and regions improved their competitiveness with respect to developed countries overall and in most sectors (Hanson, 2011).

The overall weak export performance of the LDCs in the 1980s and 1990s was largely due to their dependence upon a small range of primary commodities (usually two or three), for the bulk of their export earnings. On average the top three LDC export commodities account for over 70 per cent of each country's exports, and with the exception of Bangladesh, few countries have any significant exports of manufactures. On average, manufactures, mainly textiles and clothing, constituted about 20 per cent of total LDC exports in the 1990s (WTO, 1997b). Although these exports grew substantially over this period, it was not possible to overcome the weak performance of primary commodities, which accounted for the bulk of LDC merchandise exports.

The situation changed drastically in the 2000s: both the volume and the prices of LDC primary commodity exports rose very rapidly and, while their manufacturing exports also increased, the share of primary commodities in their total exports rose from 58 per cent in 2000 to 75 per cent in 2011, while clothing fell from 18 per cent in 2000 to 11 per cent in 2011. China was the main force in this growth, and sub-Saharan LDCs were the main beneficiaries: China's share of LDC exports rose from 9 per cent in 2000 to 22 per cent in 2011, while the share of developed countries decreased by almost the exact same percentage (Ancharaz, 2012).

Trade in services

Data on trade in services are far weaker than data on merchandise trade. Indeed many countries do not report data on certain service categories (Goswami et al., 2012; Mattoo, 2005; Whichard, 1999), and data are simply not available for a number of countries for certain periods (e.g. countries of the former Soviet Union in the period before 1995). Nonetheless, it is clear that growth of world trade in services in the 30 years from 1980 to 2010 was faster than that for goods. Service exports for developing countries grew faster than those of developed countries for the period as a whole (9.7 compared to 7.7 per cent) and for the last 20 years; their growth was only marginally lower in the 1980s. The same trends hold true for service imports except that the differences are less pronounced (see Tables 1.8–1.10).

The regional growth patterns in services trade were similar to those in goods. The Asian developing countries' trade grew the fastest; sub-Saharan Africa's was the slowest; and Latin America, Europe, the Middle East, and North Africa was in-between (see Table 1.10). Growth over the period as a whole was associated with the per capita income levels of the various developing country groups, especially if you take India out of the lower-middle income group.

Different developing countries have been successful in exporting different kinds of services: India is well known for its exports of software and business services. Latin America, Brazil, Costa Rica, Chile, Mexico and Uruguay are among the successful cases of exporters of information technology, communication and distribution services. Kenya and South Africa are among sub-Saharan Africa countries exporting professional services to Europe; and a range of different countries in Asia, Latin America, the Middle East and North Africa are exporters of health services (Goswami et al., 2012).

Table 1.11 shows the growth rates of service exports by main sector for different developing country groupings. The growth in financial and insurance services in the 1990s for countries in Asia and the BRICS during the last decade is especially noteworthy. Similarly there was very large growth in the export of information technology exports in the period 2000–10 in practically all developing country groups except for sub-Saharan Africa.

The picture regarding service imports is very similar to that of service exports with only one interesting difference: LDC service imports for the period as a whole as well as for all sub-periods tended to grow much faster than for non-LDC low income economies. This is probably due to very rapid expansion of service imports by Bangladesh.

The overall conclusion that emerges from these findings is that the patterns of growth both for exports and imports of merchandise trade and commercial services have been very similar for different developing country groupings whether by region or by income level. There is a particularly striking similarity in their growth performance in the 2000s which far outpaces that of developed countries during this period.

Integration in world trade

A key indicator of a country's integration into world trade is the ratio of the total trade in both goods and services (exports plus imports) to

Table 1.8 World commercial service exports and shares by country group and region, 1980–2010

Country group	1980		1990		2000		2010	
	Exports ($ bill)	Share (%)	Exports ($ bill)	Share (%)	Exports ($ bill)	Share (%)	Exports ($ bill)	Share (%)
By income level								
Developed economies	290	75.0	669	80.6	1,182	77.1	2,650	70.0
Developing economies	63	16.2	141	17.0	303	19.7	1,000	26.4
High income developing economies	23	5.9	63	7.6	118	7.7	360	9.5
Upper middle income economies	25	6.5	48	5.8	126	8.2	390	10.3
Lower middle income economies	13	3.2	27	3.2	54	3.5	234	6.2
Low income economies	2	0.5	3	0.4	5	0.4	16	0.4
Of which least developed countries	2	0.5	3	0.4	6	0.4	17	0.4
Developing economies, excl. China and India	57	14.9	131	15.8	256	16.7	707	18.7
Upper middle income, excl. China	23	5.9	42	5.1	96	6.2	220	5.8
Lower middle income, excl. India	10	2.5	22	2.7	37	2.4	111	2.9
By region								
World	387	100.0	830	100.0	1,535	100.0	3,784	100.0
Developing economies	63	16.2	141	17.0	303	19.7	1,000	26.4
Asia	26	6.6	87	10.5	196	12.8	742	19.6
Latin America and Caribbean	16	4.3	28	3.4	56	3.6	115	3.0
Europe, Middle East and North Africa	13	3.4	16	2.0	36	2.3	105	2.8
Sub-Saharan Africa	8	1.9	10	1.2	15	1.0	38	1.0
BRICS 5 countries	9	2.4	26	3.1	70	4.5	382	10.1
OPEC 12 members	10	2.5	8	0.9	15	1.0	30	0.8

Source: Based on World Bank World Development Indicator database.

Table 1.9 World commercial service imports and shares by country group and region, 1980–2010

Country group	1980		1990		2000		2010	
	Imports ($ bill)	Share (%)	Imports ($ bill)	Share (in)	Imports ($ bill)	Share (in)	Imports ($ bill)	Share (in %)
By income level								
Developed economies	275	66.6	661	78.7	1,102	74.2	2,263	65.5
Developing economies	106	25.6	163	19.4	352	23.7	1,098	31.8
High income developing economies	29	6.9	62	7.4	111	7.5	325	9.4
Upper middle income economies	47	11.4	60	7.2	152	10.3	478	13.8
Lower middle income economies	26	6.2	35	4.2	80	5.4	271	7.8
Low income economies	5	1.1	6	0.7	9	0.6	23	0.7
Of which least developed countries	6	1.4	8	1.0	12	0.8	44	1.3
Developing economies, excl. China and India	101	24.4	153	18.2	297	20.0	789	22.8
Upper middle income, excl. China	45	10.9	56	6.7	117	7.8	286	8.3
Lower middle income, excl. India	23	5.5	29	3.5	61	4.1	155	4.5
By region								
World	413	100.0	839	100.0	1,486	100.0	3,456	100.0
Developing economies	106	25.6	163	19.4	352	23.7	1,098	31.8
Asia	27	6.5	80	9.5	209	14.1	705	20.4
Latin America and Caribbean	28	6.7	34	4.0	69	4.7	156	4.5
Europe, Middle East and North Africa	33	7.9	31	3.6	48	3.2	147	4.3
Sub-Saharan Africa	18	4.4	19	2.2	25	1.7	89	2.6
BRICS 5 countries	12	3.0	36	4.3	92	6.2	458	13.2
OPEC 12 members	38	9.1	28	3.3	38	2.6	137	4.0

Source: Based on World Bank World Development Indicator database.

Table 1.10 Growth in world commercial service exports and imports by country group and region, 1980–2010

	Annual export growth (%)				Annual import growth (%)			
Country group	1980–90	1990–2000	2000–10	1980–2010	1980–90	1990–2000	2000–10	1980–2010
By income level								
Developed economies	8.7	5.9	8.4	7.7	9.2	5.3	7.5	7.3
Developing economies	8.4	7.9	12.7	9.7	4.4	8.0	12.0	8.1
High income developing economies	10.7	6.4	11.8	9.6	8.0	6.1	11.3	8.4
Upper middle income economies	6.6	10.1	12.0	9.5	2.5	9.8	12.1	8.0
Lower middle income economies	7.9	7.2	15.9	10.3	3.2	8.5	13.0	8.2
Low income economies	4.8	5.8	11.0	7.2	2.6	3.9	10.7	5.6
Of which least developed countries	3.6	6.5	11.4	7.1	3.2	4.3	13.7	7.0
Memo:								
Developing econonomies, excl. China and India	8.6	7.0	10.7	8.7	4.2	6.9	10.3	7.1
Upper middle income, excl. China	6.3	8.5	8.7	7.8	2.2	7.6	9.4	6.4
Lower middle income, excl. India	8.6	5.5	11.5	8.5	2.6	7.6	9.8	6.6
By region								
World	7.9	6.3	9.4	7.9	7.3	5.9	8.8	7.3
Developing economies	8.4	7.9	12.7	9.7	4.4	8.0	12.0	8.1
Asia	13.0	8.4	14.2	11.9	11.4	10.1	12.9	11.5
Latin America and Caribbean	5.4	7.1	7.6	6.7	2.0	7.5	8.5	5.9
Europe, Middle East and North Africa	2.2	8.2	11.3	7.2	–0.6	4.6	11.9	5.2
Sub-Saharan Africa	2.5	4.7	9.7	5.6	0.2	3.0	13.5	5.4
Memo:								
BRICS 5 countries	10.5	10.4	18.6	13.1	11.1	9.9	17.4	12.8
OPEC 12 members	–2.4	6.7	7.3	3.8	–3.1	3.3	13.6	4.4

Source: Based on World Bank World Development Indicator database.

Table 1.11 Growth in sectoral exports of commercial services by country group and region 1980–2010

Country Group	Annual % Growth Rate in Service Exports (%)															
	Transport Service Exports				Travel Service Exports				Insurance & Financial Service Exp				Info, Tech & Other Service Exports			
	1980–90	1990–00	2000–10	1980–10	1980–90	1990–00	2000–10	1980–10	1980–90	1990–00	2000–10	1980–10	1980–90	1990–00	2000–10	1980–10
By income level																
Developed economies	4.1	5.2	7.2	5.5	10.5	5.9	4.9	7.1	18.6	10.5	11.4	13.4	7.5	8.9	10.6	9.0
Developing economies	4.7	10.1	11.8	8.8	8.1	9.1	11.3	9.5	1.4	19.8	15.2	11.9	5.1	12.5	16.3	11.2
High income Developing	3.9	19.6	10.4	11.1	8.4	7.9	14.8	10.3	2.4	49.6	15.5	20.9	1.4	14.5	13.5	9.6
Upper Middle income	5.8	5.0	12.5	7.7	8.3	9.5	9.9	9.2	1.0	10.2	11.2	7.3	4.9	14.9	16.8	12.1
Lower Middle income	3.7	3.6	15.1	7.4	7.2	9.9	10.9	9.3	2.5	11.8	23.2	12.2	11.5	7.6	20.0	12.9
Low income	1.4	3.4	12.5	5.7	6.7	6.6	10.8	8.1	9.1	2.5	18.1	9.7	5.4	5.2	9.5	6.7
Of which: Least developed co.	1.6	3.2	10.8	5.1	6.0	9.6	12.5	9.4	9.3	10.8	4.1	8.0	4.7	6.0	5.2	5.3
Memo:																
Developing econ, excl. China & India	4.3	10.8	10.0	8.3	8.5	7.7	11.2	9.1	1.1	21.2	13.5	11.6	4.5	10.9	12.6	9.3
Upper middle income, excl. China	5.4	5.3	7.6	6.1	8.2	6.9	9.5	8.2	1.0	11.3	8.7	6.9	4.0	12.3	11.1	9.1

(*continued*)

Table 1.11 Continued

Country Group	Annual % Growth Rate in Service Exports (%)															
	Transport Service Exports				Travel Service Exports				Insurance & Financial Service Exp				Info, Tech & Other Service Exports			
	1980–90	1990–00	2000–10	1980–10	1980–90	1990–00	2000–10	1980–10	1980–90	1990–00	2000–10	1980–10	1980–90	1990–00	2000–10	1980–10
Lower middle income, excl. India	3.1	2.8	12.8	6.2	10.0	10.2	9.9	10.0	–0.1	9.5	10.2	6.4	12.2	2.2	12.5	8.9
By region																
World	5.0	4.8	8.3	6.0	10.6	5.1	7.1	7.6	12.6	9.4	12.0	11.3	7.7	8.3	11.3	9.1
Developing economies	4.7	10.1	11.8	8.8	8.1	9.1	11.3	9.5	1.4	19.8	15.2	11.9	5.1	12.5	16.3	11.2
Asia	8.0	14.8	12.4	11.7	13.0	11.1	12.3	12.1	3.1	33.5	16.9	17.2	8.7	14.6	17.5	13.5
Latin America & Caribbean	4.7	3.8	8.3	5.6	7.3	6.8	5.8	6.6	0.3	12.2	5.9	6.0	3.4	11.1	10.7	8.3
Europe, Middle East, & N. Africa	2.6	3.9	12.3	6.2	0.7	9.6	16.1	8.6	8.4	12.4	29.0	16.3	–4.3	3.6	17.6	5.2
Sub-Saharan Africa	–1.9	2.6	10.1	3.5	4.6	4.6	11.7	6.9	1.2	3.2	8.8	4.3	7.3	5.9	2.8	5.3
Memo:																
BRICS-5	6.1	7.5	19.3	10.8	5.6	15.5	11.7	10.9	2.6	9.2	23.2	11.4	8.6	20.7	22.4	17.1
OPEC-12	–4.5	4.0	11.9	3.6	–8.5	5.3	20.2	5.0	–8.6	11.4	19.2	6.7	–8.8	3.1	12.6	1.9

Source: Based on World Bank World Development Indicator database.

GDP. Essentially it shows how much of a country's economy is directly affected by international trade. This indicator is especially useful in determining the links between a country's economy and international trade over time, but it has to be used with caution when making comparisons between countries. This is because large countries tend to have smaller ratios of trade to GDP than small economies. Also, the existence of large enclave-type export sectors in some developing countries may give the false impression that the economy is well integrated into the world trading system, while in practice the bulk of economic activity may be subsistence domestic production.

Tables 1.12 and 1.13 show the evolution of this indicator of integration in developing countries, grouped by income level and over time for the period 1980–2010. After stagnating during the 1980s (and declining for some groups), the trade/GDP ratio recovered, rose rapidly and was substantially higher for all developing country income groupings by the end of the 1990s and increased further in the last decade. Since 2000 the ratio is higher for all developing country groups than for developed countries.

The other striking and sobering fact from Table 1.12 is that, despite recent progress, sub-Saharan Africa had the lowest growth of trade and output than all other regions for the 30 years from 1980 to 2010.

One study (Frankel and Romer, 1999) using earlier data estimated that the ratio of trade to GDP is strongly and positively related to growth in incomes: an increase in the ratio by 1 per cent can raise the level of income by anywhere between 0.5 and 2 per cent. It is unclear whether the experience of the last decade would support this finding, as a number of very large countries with relatively low ratios of trade to GDP grew very rapidly – as did some small and poor countries.

Interestingly, with the exception of the high-income developing countries, the data show an inverse relationship between the level of per capita income and the share of trade to GDP. As noted earlier, however, inter-country comparisons of this indicator are risky: some of the most rapid growth in the LDCs resulted from booming commodity exports, which had little impact on the rest of their economies. The only thing that can be stated definitively is the very strong evidence of globalization at every developing-country income level and grouping.

Policy issues

This strong overall trade performance – with some important exceptions, for example sub-Saharan Africa in manufactures – raises a lot of

Table 1.12 Growth rates in total trade (X + M) and output by country group and region, 1980–2010

Country group	**Annual trade (g + s) growth (%)**				**Annual GDP growth (%)**			
	1980–90	1990–2000	2000–10	1980–2010	1980–90	1990–2000	2000–10	1980–2010
By income level								
Developed economies	7.8	5.2	7.3	6.8	8.4	3.4	5.3	5.7
Developing economies	5.4	9.4	12.0	8.9	5.0	6.5	11.6	7.7
High income developing economies	6.6	9.6	9.4	8.5	7.1	7.9	7.1	7.3
Upper middle income economies	5.4	10.1	13.4	9.6	4.9	7.0	12.7	8.1
Lower middle income economies	3.4	7.7	14.0	8.2	3.8	4.4	12.8	6.9
Low income economies	3.1	4.1	12.0	6.3	4.1	1.5	9.9	5.1
Of which least developed countries	2.7	5.8	14.6	7.6	4.2	1.7	12.8	6.1
Memo:								
Developing economies, excl. China and India	5.2	8.7	9.9	7.9	4.8	5.7	9.4	6.6
Upper middle income, excl. China	4.8	8.2	9.7	7.6	4.6	5.1	9.7	6.5
Lower middle income, excl. India	3.0	7.2	11.5	7.2	2.7	4.8	12.4	6.6
By region								
World	6.5	6.2	8.8	7.2	7.1	3.9	6.9	6.0
Developing economies	5.4	9.4	12.0	8.9	5.0	6.5	11.6	7.7
Asia	10.1	10.8	12.3	11.1	7.9	7.8	12.8	9.5
Latin America and Caribbean	3.9	9.8	9.2	7.6	4.1	6.3	9.3	6.6
Europe, Middle East and North Africa	0.1	5.4	13.5	6.2	2.1	4.8	10.9	5.9
Sub-Saharan Africa	0.0	3.9	12.9	5.5	1.3	1.3	12.5	4.9
BRICS 5 countries	10.6	8.6	18.2	12.4	9.8	4.3	15.7	9.8
OPEC 12 members	–1.9	6.2	14.2	6.0	–0.6	5.0	12.1	5.4

Source: Computations based on World Bank World Development Indicator database.

Table 1.13 World total trade (X + M) and share in output by country group, 1980–2010

Country group	World trade (g + s) in $ billion				Output (GDP) in $ billion				Total trade as % of GDP			
	1980	1990	2000	2010	1980	1990	2000	2010	1980	1990	2000	2010
Developed economies	3,198	6,775	11,275	22,758	8,206	18,329	25,491	42,813	39.0	37.0	44.2	53.2
Developing economies	1,094	1,856	4,561	14,108	2,188	3,569	6,700	19,995	50.0	52.0	68.1	70.6
High income developing economies	401	762	1,914	4,693	365	723	1,543	3,057	110.1	105.4	124.1	153.5
Upper middle income economies	437	740	1,935	6,822	1,198	1,935	3,801	12,517	36.5	38.2	50.9	54.5
Lower middle income economies	220	307	642	2,374	542	788	1,212	4,050	40.6	39.0	53.0	58.6
Low income economies	35	47	70	219	83	124	144	370	41.4	37.9	48.7	59.1
Of which least developed countries	41	53	93	366	95	143	169	562	43.0	37.1	55.3	65.1
World	4,671	8,747	15,989	37,198	11,021	21,977	32,329	63,136	42.4	39.8	49.5	58.9
Developing economies, excl. China and India	1,024	1,702	3,905	9,998	1,809	2,886	5,026	12,380	56.6	59.0	77.7	80.8
Upper middle income, excl. China	395	636	1,404	3,549	1,008	1,578	2,603	6,587	39.3	40.3	54.0	53.9
Lower middle income, excl. India	192	257	516	1,537	352	461	737	2,366	54.4	55.8	70.0	65.0
BRICS 5 countries	168	459	1,043	5,563	695	1,774	2,710	11,609	24.2	25.8	38.5	47.9

Source: World Bank World Development Indicator database.

questions about the factors responsible, the implications for the architecture of the trading system and its sustainability.

How much of this growth was due to the developing countries' own policies? To what extent did improved market access result from the implementation of multilateral trade liberalization following the Uruguay Round Agreements as well as the establishment of numerous regional preferential arrangements? Following the 2008 crisis, protectionism has reared its ugly head again – but much less than had been feared (Dadush et al., 2011; Wolfe, 2011).

To what extent does the robust developing-country performance reflect the strengthening of their capacity to export, even though weaknesses in trade institutions and infrastructure continue to be a problem in many low-income developing countries and the least developed countries? And what is the impact of this growth on poverty and income inequality? Partly as a consequence of strong trade performance, in the last decade the role developing countries play in global trade relations has changed dramatically. They have also become increasingly assertive in global trade negotiations in the WTO. What does this mean for the future of the WTO? Finally, to what extent are these trends sustainable? The slowdown in China's and India's growth, Europe's continued problems with the euro and the US's slow recovery pose obvious dangers. Commodity trade booms are often followed by busts. While protectionism has not been as bad as was feared, the cumulative effect of protective measures may have an impact over time.

All these issues create obvious risks for the sustainability of the surge in developing country trade. But we should not allow these risks to overshadow what has been accomplished in the last 30 years. The world tomorrow will be very different from the world of the 1980s and developing countries will play a much more important role in the future trading system because of what they have accomplished already.

Overall averages disguise stagnation in many countries. On the other hand, the successful performance of many countries, several of which are low income, suggests that marginalization, stagnation and poverty are not inevitable. Countries can integrate into the world economy, grow and alleviate poverty. The key questions have to do with the policies and institutions, both in the countries themselves and in the international environment that can support this objective; and in this context, we can ask what role is played by international trade and the WTO.

2
Trade and Development in GATT and the WTO

Introduction

The increasing integration of developing countries in the world economy since the start of the 1980s has occurred in the context of a changing international and institutional environment in respect of the rules affecting developing-country participation in international trade. In particular, the establishment of the WTO in 1995 introduced profound changes to the institutional and legal setting for the conduct of trade. The rules affecting developing-country participation in the multilateral trade system have reflected, sometimes with a considerable lag, the evolution in the thinking about the role of trade in development.

This chapter reviews how development concerns have been addressed within GATT and subsequently the WTO. I will trace the evolution of developing-country participation in these organizations and link this to changes in the types of international trade policies that are deemed to be conducive to development. Particular attention is paid to the concept of differential and more favourable treatment for developing countries in respect of their rights and obligations in GATT/WTO and to its changing content and emphasis over time.

In the first section I review the main principles and practices of developing-country participation in GATT, from the time of its establishment through to the mid-1980s, and I link them to the concerns about the relationship between trade and development that prevailed during this period. In the subsequent section I discuss developing-country participation in the Uruguay Round as well as the Round's significance for the treatment of development issues within the WTO. The last sections focus on the special treatment issues in favour of developing countries in general and the LDCs in particular, the manner in which they have been addressed in the WTO and in the Doha Round.

Principles and practices of developing countries in GATT, 1947–86

Trade and development in the early days of GATT[1]

The draft charter of the ITO, which was never ratified, provided for exceptions to be made to the general trade rules when dealing with issues of development. For example, one provision allowed Contracting Parties to use protective measures during the establishment, development or reconstruction of particular industries or branches of agriculture, provided they obtained the permission of the other Contracting Parties.[2] When GATT was established in 1947, 11 of the original 23 Contracting Parties would have been considered developing countries.[3] At the time, however, there was no formal recognition of developing countries as a group, nor were there any special provisions or exceptions in the agreement in respect of their rights or obligations. The fundamental principle was that all rights and obligations should apply equally to all Contracting Parties with no exceptions (GATT, 1948).

Today, developing countries account for over two-thirds of the 159 strong WTO membership, and the WTO agreements contain a very extensive set of provisions on the rights and obligations of developing countries and LDCs. Despite this, there is still no official definition of what constitutes a 'developing country'. Rather, countries use the designation on the basis of self-selection. As a consequence, Singapore with a per capita income of $46,241 in 2011, and Kenya with a per capita income of $808 (World Bank, 2012), are both supposed to benefit from the same provisions. On the other hand, there is an official UN list of 48 LDCs of which 34 are currently members of the WTO.

The original GATT contained no explicit provisions for developing countries, though they soon started to voice their concern about the special challenges they faced in international trade. Their starting point was that sustainable increases in income and output could only be brought about by increased industrialization. In most countries there

1 This section of the study draws in part on material from WTO, 1999a.
2 This provision was introduced as an amendment to GATT in 1948.
3 These were Brazil, Burma, Ceylon, Chile, China, Cuba, India, Lebanon, Pakistan, Rhodesia and Syria.

was a consensus that liberal trade policies would not promote industrialization and development because of the prevailing patterns of international specialization. Developing countries tended to specialize in raw materials and primary commodity exports and were dependent on imports for manufactures, especially the capital goods and intermediate inputs needed for investment and industrialization. It was felt that liberal trade policies would stymie the development of infant industries, while the continued dependence on primary commodity and raw material exports would result in volatile export earnings and deteriorating terms of trade (Prebisch, 1950; Singer, 1950). Moreover, it was thought that the development process was inherently associated with balance of payments difficulties, which could be addressed in the short term through trade controls. The trade strategy that emerged from this thinking and that was practiced by most developing countries at the time had three main strands: (1) the promotion of industrialization through import substitution behind protective tariff and non-tariff barriers; (2) the promotion of manufactured exports in order to diversify the export structure, in part through export subsidies, which were perceived as necessary to offset the advantages enjoyed by established developed-country producers; and (3) the use of trade controls in response to actual or potential balance of payments difficulties.

The trade strategies pursued by developing countries during this early period gave rise to requests for changes to be made to the multilateral trading system in four main areas: improved market access for developing-country exports of manufactures to developed markets (through the provision of trade preferences) in order to overcome the disadvantages developing countries faced when attempting to break into these markets; less than full reciprocity in trade relations between developing countries and developed countries, in order to permit developing countries to maintain protective measures that were deemed necessary to promote development; for the same reason, flexibility in the application of rules by developing-country members of GATT, and later WTO; and stabilization of the world commodity markets.

GATT and developing countries, 1954–86

Throughout this early period, developing countries sought to emphasize the uniqueness of their development problems and challenges and their need to be treated differently and more favourably in GATT, in part by being permitted not to liberalize their own trade and in part by being awarded preferential access to developed-country markets. In the 1954–55 GATT review session, for the first time provisions were adopted to address the needs of developing countries as a group within GATT. Reflecting the argument that developing-country members were likely to face balance-of-payments instability over an extended period of time, Article XVIII (B) was revised to include a specific provision to allow countries at 'an early stage of their development' to adopt quantitative restrictions on imports whenever monetary reserves were deemed to be inadequate in terms of the country's long-term development strategy.[4] Article XVIII (C) was revised to allow for the imposition of trade restrictions (both tariffs and quantitative restrictions) to support infant industries with a view to improving living standards. A provision granting the right of veto to certain affected Contracting Parties (CPs) was deleted, thus facilitating the imposition of quantitative restrictions (GATT, 1954).

Commodity issues were first addressed in GATT as early as 1956 when the CPs adopted a joint resolution which called for an annual review of trends and developments in commodity trade, and the convening of an intergovernmental meeting, if it was felt that international joint action would usefully contribute to the solution of the problem. In 1958, the Haberler report – by an expert panel appointed at the 1957 GATT Ministerial – concluded, in quaint and guarded language, that 'there is some substance in the feeling of disquiet among primary producing countries that the present rules and conventions about commercial policies are relatively unfavorable to them'. The report recommended (1) stabilization programmes to address commodity price fluctuations through buffer stocks, and (2) a reduction in developed countries' internal taxes on primary products such as coffee, tea and tobacco as these taxes served to constrain consumption and import demand (GATT, 1958).

In 1961, GATT adopted another declaration on the promotion of trade of less developed countries, which inter alia called for preferential market access for developing countries not covered by the preferential tariff systems (such as the Commonwealth preferences) or by preferences in customs unions or free trade areas which were subsequently established. This was the first mention in GATT of what would later on become the Generalized System of Preferences (GSP) for developing countries.

In 1964, GATT adopted a specific legal framework within which the concerns of developing countries could be addressed: Part IV dealt

[4] The *Report of the Review Working Party on Quantitative Restrictions* (GATT, 1955) argued that the safeguard provisions of Article XII, paras 1 and 2, were not adequate in the case of developing-country members, for whom insufficient reserves were deemed to be a more chronic problem.

specifically with trade and development and consisted of three new Articles. Article XXXVI stated that CPs should provide 'in the largest possible measure' more favourable and acceptable market access conditions for products of export interest to developing countries, notably primary products and processed or manufactured products. Paragraph 8 of the Article addressed the principle of less-than-full reciprocity by specifying that developing-country members 'should not be expected' to make contributions that would be inconsistent with their level of development in the process of trade negotiations.[5] Article XXXVII called for the 'highest priority' to be given to the elimination of restrictions that served to 'differentiate unreasonably' between primary and processed products. Article XXXVIII called for joint action by the CPs through international arrangements to improve market access for products of export interest to developing countries. The Committee on Trade and Development was established and mandated to review the application of Part IV provisions, carry out or arrange any consultations required for the application of these provisions, and consider extensions and modifications to Part IV suggested by CPs with a view to furthering the objectives of trade and development.

A pattern appears to have evolved during these early years: the CPs accommodated the developing countries desire not to liberalize their import regimes, partly on infant industry grounds and partly for balance of payments reasons, but on the question of improved access to developed-country markets and commodity price stabilization, no action was taken or legally binding commitments made. None of the provisions of Part IV legally bound developed countries to undertake specific actions in favour of developing-country CPs. The Committee on Trade and Development was then, and still is, primarily a forum to discuss developing-country issues but not to negotiate legal commitments in their favour. During this period, many developing countries were not party to GATT, and those that were participated minimally in its deliberations.

Partly because developing countries felt that their trade concerns were not being effectively addressed in GATT, they successfully lobbied for the establishment of a separate organization to deal explicitly with problems of trade and development. This organization, the United Nations Conference on Trade and Development (UNCTAD) came into being in 1964, and was the main institution through which developing

[5] The Decision on Tropical Products approved the objective of duty free access for tropical products in developed-country markets (GATT, 1964).

countries pursued their international trade agenda during this period. The establishment of a system of preferences for developing-country manufactured exports to be used in developed-country markets, and the stabilization of commodity trade, were important topics on the agenda of the new institution during the 1960s and 1970s.

In 1968, the developing countries succeeded in establishing a GSP under the auspices of UNCTAD. The system was established on a voluntary basis by the developed countries, meaning they were not legally bound under GATT to maintain it; but a GATT waiver from most favoured nation (MFN) obligations was granted in 1971, initially for a period of ten years (GATT, 1972), along with another waiver allowing developing country CPs to grant preferences amongst themselves.

While pursuing the GSP, developing countries were at the same time benefiting from significant gains in market access that were the product of tariff reductions implemented on an MFN basis for all the parties to GATT, leading in effect to the creation of a two-track market access. The stability and predictability of market access resulting from the practice of binding tariffs in GATT was a further gain: in general, developed countries' tariff bindings throughout the history of GATT and the WTO have corresponded to the rates actually applied.

Both the Kennedy Round of GATT negotiations, which ended in 1967, and the Tokyo Round, which ended in 1979, resulted in cuts on tariffs on industrial goods on the basis of an agreed formula.[6] However, the average reduction in tariffs following each Round was less favourable to developing countries than to developed ones: 26 per cent, compared with an average of 36 per cent, on goods of export interest to developed countries after the Kennedy Round (UNCTAD, 1968) and 26 per cent, compared to 33 per cent, after the Tokyo Round (GATT, 1979). This was because many such goods were either exempt from formula cuts or subject to lower-than-formula cuts. On the other hand a number of developed countries extended to developing countries non-reciprocal reductions in the duties on tropical products.

The relatively less favourable outcome of the two GATT Rounds for the developing countries was in part attributable to their limited participation in the negotiating of concessions (Hudec, 1987; Kemper, 1980). The basic formula having being agreed, it was the developed countries

[6] The formula for the Kennedy Round required a cut of 50 per cent on tariffs on industrial goods. The so called 'Swiss' formula for the Tokyo Round reduced tariffs to a level z, where $z = 14x/(x + 14)$, where x is the pre-round tariff. It thereby generated greater reductions in higher tariffs than lower ones.

that negotiated exceptions to the cuts specified in the formula. Final concessions were then extended to all CPs by virtue of the MFN provisions of GATT.

In the Kennedy and Tokyo Rounds, developing countries placed at least as much emphasis on discussing the extent and the manner in which they should undertake the rights and obligations of the multilateral trading system, as on the negotiating specific concessions and commitments. The principal result of these 'Framework Discussions' of the Tokyo Round was the Enabling Clause of 1979. The clause established the principle of differential and more favourable treatment, reciprocity and fuller participation of developing countries (GATT, 1980). It provided for: (1) preferential market access of developing countries to developed-country markets on a non-reciprocal, non-discriminatory basis; (2) more favourable treatment for developing countries in respect of other GATT rules on non-tariff barriers; (3) the introduction of preferential trade regimes between developing countries; and (4) special treatment of LDCs in the context of specific measures for developing countries.

The adoption of the Enabling Clause thus established a stronger legal basis for the special and differential treatment of developing countries within the rules of the multilateral trading system. While the clause formally embodied the concept of special and differential treatment, it did so in discretionary and permissive, rather than legally binding, terms.

In terms of concrete measures in favour of developing countries, the Enabling Clause transformed the ten-year waivers for the GSP and for trade preferences among developing countries into permanent waivers. In this regard, the clause did not create any new legally binding obligations for developed country CPs; rather, it made possible the introduction of preferential and non-reciprocal market access schemes, with the extent of preferences and the level of reciprocity being left to the discretion of each country that extended them. In bringing together the key elements of preferential market access, non-reciprocity and flexibility in the implementation of rules and commitments, the Enabling Clause was a summation, rather than an extension, of the efforts made since 1954 to address the concerns of developing countries within the multilateral trading system.

The permissiveness of special and differential treatment was also reflected in the non-participation of developing countries in a number of agreements negotiated during the Tokyo Round on such matters as export subsidies, countervailing duties, technical barriers to trade and government procurement. Although these agreements contained specific special measures for developing countries, most of them chose not to join, arguing that they had not been invited to do so until late in the negotiations, which had been conducted without their full participation – a complaint that will be repeated frequently in later years.

As a counterweight to the provisions of the Enabling Clause for special and differential treatment and relaxation of Article XVIII disciplines,[7] the CPs agreed to the principle of 'graduation'. The idea of graduation was the expectation that the capacity of developing countries to undertake negotiated conditions and to make contributions – within the framework of rights and obligations of the multilateral trading system – would increase with the improvement over time of their economic status and trade situation. This provided the formal basis for developed countries to phase out non-reciprocal preferential market access measures to CPs that over time were deemed to have attained a sufficient level of progress (GATT, 1980, p. 205). Because the preferences permitted by the Enabling Clause were permissive and non-binding, and because of the 'fuller participation' clause, developing countries had no legal recourse within GATT against unilateral termination of preferences by developed countries.

Finally, following a series of negotiations in UNCTAD, the Common Fund for Commodities was established in 1980 and went into effect in 1989. The Fund comprised two accounts each with different objectives: the first was intended to finance international buffer stocks and internationally coordinated national stocks, and the second was to finance measures for commodity development and promote coordination and consultation on commodity issues.

Rethinking trade and development in the 1980s

It could be argued that by the beginning of the 1980s developing countries had achieved their objectives in establishing international trade rules that were responsive to their perceived needs for development:

- They had ample flexibility under the existing GATT rules to provide protection on infant industry or balance of payments grounds.
- They did not have to liberalize their trade on a reciprocal basis in the context of multilateral trade negotiations.
- They could support their exports through subsidies, although they remained open to the risk of countervailing duties.

---

7 The requirement for advance warning was removed (GATT, 1980, p. 209).

- They had preferential access to developed country markets under the GSP.
- They had a new fund to support commodity stabilization schemes.

Yet, all was not well with the international rules governing developing-country trade. There were two main problems. First, access to developed-country markets was far more difficult than one might suspect given the existence of GSP and the extensive reductions of tariffs on manufactures negotiated in previous GATT Rounds. Second, as the developing countries appeared to have successfully secured a set of trading rules that would be beneficial to their development, the intellectual underpinnings of these rules started to be extensively questioned.

There were many serious problems with market access. First, while the tariffs on manufactured imports to developed countries had been reduced considerably, non-tariff barriers had tended to increase, especially on products of interest to developing countries. This was especially true in the case of textiles and clothing (under the Multi-fiber Arrangement – MFA) and in respect of the so called 'voluntary' export restraints imposed by developed countries on emerging developing-country suppliers in such products as shoes, iron and steel, and non-ferrous metals. Second, despite the tariff reductions, tariff escalation was substantial, restraining developing-country entry into the processed goods markets and thereby inhibiting their industrialization efforts. Third, the agricultural sector remained essentially outside GATT, permitting developed-country exporters to constrain imports and subsidize exports at will, including on a number of products of export interest to developing countries.

The GSP turned out to be less than it had been touted at its inception. It was important for some products, for some countries and for some of the time. But it was not serving to strengthen the integration of developing countries into the world trading system. Because it was a voluntary scheme, it meant that developing country suppliers were less certain about market conditions than under the contractual arrangements involving bound tariffs in GATT. At the same time the benefits of preferences seemed to be accruing primarily to the more advanced developing countries, which needed them the least. According to Karsenty and Laird (1987), early on four beneficiaries – Brazil, Hong Kong, Korea and Taiwan – enjoyed more than 50 per cent of all GSP benefits. But, perhaps most importantly, a number of products of great export interest to developing countries, such as textiles, were either excluded from preferential treatment or severely limited. In addition the margin of preference was eroded as a consequence of the MFN tariff reductions agreed in successive multilateral trade negotiations.[8]

Recourse by developed countries to 'graduating' higher-income or more competitive developing counties from the GSP (along with occasional recourse to political or non-trade-related graduation criteria) increased the relative importance of reciprocal liberalization with 'bound' concessions. Over time other preferential systems also emerged and were applied to different developing-country groupings in various developed-country markets, such as the so-called Lomé preferences extended to African, Caribbean and Pacific (ACP) countries in the EU markets. These systems offered deeper and more secure preferences than the GSP. Indeed, it appeared that developed countries saw measures such as the GSP as a substitute for thoroughgoing action to liberalize trade (Leutweiler et al., 1985).

At the same time a serious rethinking of trade policies appropriate for development was taking place in many developing countries. In the early 1970s many had begun seriously to question the effectiveness of infant industry protection – supported by trade controls and foreign exchange restrictions – as a vehicle for industrialization and long-term sustainable development. Various potential perils in persisting with import substitution strategies had been identified. Trade barriers designed to protect infant industries created disincentives to export, since high rates of effective protection distorted relative prices in favour of import-competing production. As a result, many infant industries remained inefficient and failed to achieve export competitiveness.[9]

In cases where selective incentives were provided, the overall trade regime often proved too complex to administer. The use of quantitative restrictions and exchange controls increased the scope for rent-seeking activities (Krueger, 1974). The inefficiency and waste implicit in some import-substitution policies led to increased vulnerability to external shocks, even in countries that had achieved rapid rates of growth in real income in the earlier stages of import substitution. At the same time,

---

[8] The trade-weighted preferential margin on imports (agricultural and industrial) into the EC, the US and Japan fell by 27.3 per cent after the Tokyo Round (UNCTAD, 1980).

[9] Several intensive studies of developing-country trade regimes during this period reached these conclusions. The two most important were a five-volume effort sponsored by the OECD, whose findings are summarized in Little et al. (1970), and a 12-volume study under the auspices of the National Bureau of Economic Research whose findings are summarized in Bhagwati (1978) and Krueger (1978).

industrialization policies based on import substitution typically discriminated against the agricultural sector, contributing to increased rural poverty (Krueger et al., 1988). Moreover, the use of fiscal and monetary instruments was far superior to trade and exchange control measures to address external imbalances as the former do not entail the resource misallocation costs typically associated with latter. Consequently there seemed to be little justification for the use of trade restrictions to address balance-of-payments difficulties (Bhagwati, 1978).

The experiences of the 1960s and 1970s also seemed to suggest that countries that had pursued more open trade policies – for example those that broadly balanced incentives for import-substitution production with incentives for export manufacturing – enjoyed strong growth in both exports and per capita income. On the other hand, countries that had persisted with import substitution behind high trade barriers had broadly experienced slow growth or a decline in per capita income.

While the direction of causality between trade and income growth is controversial, there is no doubt that a large number of developing countries opted for more open trade regimes in the 1980s and many countries undertook autonomous trade liberalization involving fewer trade restrictions in the belief that such regimes were more conducive to the attainment of their development objectives. Many developing countries introduced stabilization and adjustment programmes during this period (supported by the World Bank and/or the IMF) which frequently involved the conversion of quantitative restrictions into tariffs, tariff reductions, the phasing out of selective export subsidies and the liberalization of foreign exchange markets.[10]

All this was done outside GATT and involved no changes in the formal commitments of developing countries in that context. Indeed it was argued that the emphasis within GATT on the provisions for special and differential treatment – as embodied, inter alia, in the Enabling Clause – created scope within the multilateral trading system for the implementation, and in some cases entrenchment, of development strategies with deleterious consequences: the provisions for special and differential treatment may have introduced a bias in favour of protection and against exports in the formulation of commercial policy.

---

[10] 'In the broad swing of the pendulum, developing countries have been shifting from severe and destructive protection to free trade fever' (Dornbush, 1992); 'the 1980s have seen the beginnings of a change of heart among developing country policy makers with regard to trade policy. The import substitution consensus of the previous decades, with its preference for high levels of tariff and non-tariff barriers, has all but evaporated' (Rodrik, 1992).

At the same time as developing countries were starting to take steps to liberalize their trade policies in the 1980s, there was growing recognition of the value of participating actively in multilateral negotiations with a view to securing market access in areas of export interest through the agreement of reciprocal commitments and concessions. This was in turn connected to the recognition that, partly as a consequence of the emphasis on non-reciprocity, the MFN tariff concessions agreed in the Kennedy and Tokyo Rounds were on the whole less favourable for products of export interest to developing countries than were concessions relating to products of interest to developed countries.

Finally, attitudes regarding the usefulness of buffer stocks and commodity agreements as instruments for commodity market stabilization started to be questioned. Many developing countries continued to depend heavily on a few primary commodity exports and the terms of trade of primary commodity exporters continued to deteriorate (Sapsford and Balasubramanyam, 1999). But efforts to use such agreements to reverse or slow the deterioration in terms of trade through supply management failed. By the early 1990s new market-based approaches to guard against price fluctuations started to be explored and, by 1996, the economic provisions in all the major commodity agreements had either lapsed or failed (ITF, 1999). While the Common Fund provided technical assistance to increase the productivity and supply response of primary commodity-producing developing countries, no funds from its first account were ever used to support buffer-stock management of commodity agreements.

As a consequence of the waning interest in GSP and commodity stabilization, and of the emerging consensus that the liberalization of policies was more conducive to development as well as the rising importance of reciprocal liberalization as a means of attaining greater market access, GATT's importance as an institution within which developing countries wanted to pursue trade objectives started to rise. This was manifested in the decision by a number of developing countries, especially in Latin America (for example, Mexico) to join GATT. It was against this background that the Uruguay Round was launched – symbolically enough, in a developing country – in 1986. The Round, which did not conclude until eight years later, brought about a fundamental restructuring of the rules guiding the international trading system as well as a significant change in the role played by developing countries within the system.

The Uruguay Round and the development dimension of the WTO

The Uruguay Round led to the establishment of the WTO which has three main functions: (1) the undertaking of multilateral trade negotiations;

(2) the establishment of rules for the conduct of international trade; (3) dispute settlement. The WTO agreements resulted in the strengthening and deepening of the multilateral trading system in ways that offered to developing countries the possibility of greater integration. This was achieved through the extension of trade rules to cover services, trade-related intellectual property rights and investment measures, as well as through the establishment of a strengthened dispute settlement mechanism. One of the issues that emerged in the late 1990s, however, was precisely whether this potential was being realized.

Two aspects of the Uruguay Round agreements were of great potential importance to developing countries. First, the market access negotiations covered areas of interest not previously subject to GATT disciplines, such as agriculture and textiles and clothing. Moreover, the agreement on safeguards benefited developing members' market access through the elimination of voluntary export restraints, which had acted as significant barriers in the case of goods such as footwear and leather products. And, of course, the negotiations on tariffs resulted in further reductions in tariffs on industrial imports with the average trade weighted tariff rate on such imports from developing countries falling by 34 per cent. Second, the strengthening of the dispute settlement mechanism by introducing greater certainty about the adoption of quasi-judicial decisions by dispute settlement panels was of great potential benefit to developing countries: it offered judicial protection against the larger and more powerful developed countries and a better chance of prevailing in a bilateral trade dispute with them than would be the case outside the WTO.

At the end of the Uruguay Round a number of studies were undertaken which attempted to estimate, through quantitative model simulations, some of the net benefits that might accrue to developing countries. Invariably, these studies concluded that large gains might be made by developing countries in the aggregate, although the distribution of benefits was expected to favour countries in Latin America and East Asia, while countries in Africa would benefit little, if at all. This was partly due to the fact that the African countries had engaged in less trade liberalization, and partly because they could be expected to suffer from the likely increase in the prices of food imports following the reduction of agricultural export subsidies in developed countries. Moreover, the expected dynamic benefits resulting from increased trade and incomes worldwide dwarfed the estimated static effects of trade liberalization (Harrison et al., 1996).

At the same time, by participating in the Uruguay Round agreements in services, trade-related intellectual property rights (TRIPs) and trade-related investment measures (TRIMs), developing countries would have to conform to rules and policy disciplines in areas where they had previously enjoyed complete latitude. The same was true of the new agreements on subsidies, technical barriers to trade (TBT), customs valuation, sanitary and phyto-sanitary measures (SPS), all of which converted previous multilateral agreements, in which few developing countries participated, into general developing-country commitments to abide with multilaterally agreed rules, albeit within a framework of certain special provisions (see p. 38). Tighter discipline was also introduced on actions taken under Article XVIII (B) that ran counter to trade liberalization. The agreed 'Understanding about the Article' encouraged the use of price-based measures, extended the documentation and notification requirements, and provided procedures for the phasing out of restrictions. These modifications were at least partly informed by the developments in economic policy described earlier, most notably in respect of the greater effectiveness of fiscal and monetary instruments in meeting balance-of-payments shocks.

The Uruguay Round also saw an evolution in the developing countries' attitude towards the special and differential treatment provisions. The Round continued to be guided by the general principles agreed in previous negotiating Rounds, and these were even extended in a number of ways. But without formally relinquishing the principle of non-reciprocity, developing countries eschewed past practices and participated more actively in the reciprocal liberalization in goods and services. In particular, as part of the agreement on agriculture, they agreed to bind all their tariffs in that sector, and they also increased their share of bound industrial tariffs from 14 to 59 per cent. But the level of the vast majority of these bindings was much higher than the applied levels, leaving developing countries considerable scope to increase their tariffs should they so decide (see Chapter 4).

In other areas the special treatment provisions on market access through the GSP were maintained. Flexibility was also maintained by permitting developing countries to engage in certain agriculture support practices that were not allowed to other countries, and similarly regarding export subsidies. Moreover, the Uruguay Round agreements introduced new elements of special and differential treatment by providing transitional time frames and technical assistance in the implementation of the various agreements reached in the WTO. The basic reason for the extension of special treatment through these two new elements was simply that developing countries did not have the institutional capacity to implement the commitments demanded of them in some of the new areas covered by the WTO. They would not have signed the agreements had they not been promised both additional time and technical assistance to build the necessary capacity.[11]

The conceptual justification for special and differential treatment

The legal texts of the agreements embodied in the WTO contain a very large number of provisions on the differential and more favourable treatment of developing countries and the LDCs which, for example, benefit from longer transition periods in the implementation of certain agreements such as TRIPS. Thus, while a lot has been made of the fact that the developing countries participated in the Uruguay Round agreements on the same basis as other members, the agreements are replete with special provisions for them (GATT, 1995). Some provisions are in the nature of exhortations, the implementation of which is difficult to evaluate; others, although also of a general nature, underpin programmes such as the GSP; still others are very specific and relate to a particular aspect of developed or developing-country policy.

There are several conceptual premises underlying the provision of special and differential treatment as reflected in the WTO agreements. The fundamental one is that developing countries are intrinsically disadvantaged when participating in international trade and therefore any multilateral agreement involving them and developed countries must take this weakness into account when specifying their rights and responsibilities. A related premise is that the trade policies aimed at maximizing sustainable development in developing countries necessarily differ from those of developed economies, and hence policy disciplines applying to the latter should not apply to the former. The final premise is that it is in the interest of developed countries to assist developing countries to integrate fully into the international trading system.

Based on these premises, the new provisions in the WTO agreements fall into two broad categories: (1) positive actions by developed-country members or international institutions; and (2) exceptions to the overall rules for developing countries and, sometimes, additional exceptions for the LDCs.

Positive steps to be taken by developed countries

Developed countries have agreed to take three kinds of actions to support developing countries' participation in international trade: (1) to

[11] Participants in the final negotiations for establishing the WTO have indicated that there was a tacit understanding that transition periods in the implementation of some of these agreements were linked to transition periods in the implementation of the agreement on textiles and clothing.

provide preferential access to their markets; (2) to provide technical and other assistance to permit them to meet their WTO obligations and enhance the benefits developing countries can derive from international trade; and (3) to implement the overall agreements in ways that are beneficial or least damaging to the interests of developing countries and LDCs.

Preferential market access

As noted earlier, in recognition of the importance of developing countries diversifying their exports into manufacturing, and the difficulties that they may face in breaking into international markets for such products, developed countries have provided tariff preferences for manufactured exports from developing countries under the GSP and, within that context, for special treatment of the LDCs. As already discussed, the key issue regarding these programmes is whether in practice they will significantly enhance market access prospects for developing countries.

Technical and other assistance

The WTO agreements contain numerous references to provision by developed-country members and international institutions of technical assistance to developing countries and LDCs. The main purpose of such assistance is to strengthen the institutional capacity of the latter countries in a way that will enable them to meet the obligations under the agreements. The main areas in which technical assistance is envisaged include TBT, SPS, Customs Valuation, Pre-shipment Inspection, Dispute Settlement, Trade Policy Reviews (TPRs) and TRIPs.[12] In most cases, the relevant articles call for such assistance to be provided upon request by the developing country or LDC on terms and conditions appropriate to the countries involved.

The conceptual underpinning of these provisions reflects the emerging analytical consensus that institutional capacity constraints significantly impede the effective integration of poorer countries and LDCs into the multilateral trading system. While it may be relatively easy to promulgate policies to liberalize trade, it is far more difficult to develop the capacity to take advantage of the opportunities international trade provides that are critical for the economic transformation of these countries. Weaknesses in the human and physical infrastructure and the institutions that deal

---

[12] See inter alia SPS Article 9.1; TBT Articles 11, 12.7; Implementation of GATT Article VII–Article 20.3; The Agreement on Pre-shipment Inspection, Article 1.2; TRIPS Article 67; DSB Article 27.2; the Trade Policy Review Mechanism (TPRM).

with international trade are key impediments in the capacity of developing countries to benefit from international trade and technical support by developed countries and international institutions (as well as longer transition periods; see pp. 42–3) that have been recommended to address these problems (see UNCTAD/WTO, 1996). Concern has also been raised regarding the high costs and affordability of implementing the Uruguay Round Agreements (Finger and Schuler, 2000) and whether technical assistance alone will be sufficient to provide the physical and human capital costs needed to build capacity in areas where developing countries have assumed WTO commitments (see pp. 119–20).

Pursuant to the mandate provided by the relevant articles and decisions, such as the 'Decision on Measures in Favor of LDCs', a range of technical assistance activities and programmes are being provided to developing countries and LDCs by international organizations, in particular the WTO, UNCTAD and the International Trade Center (ITC) and the World Bank. During the 2000s the Aid for Trade and the Enhanced Integrated Fund for LDCs have been the most visible international initiatives in support of developing country integration in international trade (see pp. 123–7). The main question that arises in this respect concerns the overall adequacy and effectiveness of these efforts.

Implementation of the WTO provisions in a manner favourable to developing-country members

The WTO agreements contain many references in the preambles and in the substantive provisions of the various texts that commit members to implement the agreements in ways that take into account the interests of developing countries and LDCs. Some of these references are of a general nature and are expressed in broad 'best efforts' terms, but in a few cases there are more explicit provisions on how developing countries should be treated more favourably or in ways that will least damage their interests. Examples of the general preambular statements include 'the need for positive efforts designed to ensure that developing countries and especially the least developed secure a share in the growth in international trade commensurate with the needs of their economic development' (Preamble of the Agreement for establishing the WTO); 'members shall give particular attention to the provisions of this agreement (the TBT) concerning developing country Members' rights and obligations' (Article 12.2); and 'special regard must be given by developed country Members to the special situation of developing country Members when considering the application of antidumping measures' (Article 15).

While a strong case can be made that these provisions are not legally enforceable (Kessie, 2000) developing countries have questioned whether the developed countries have lived up to the spirit of their commitments (see p. 179).

Differential commitments and obligations by developing countries

There are two fundamental ways in which developing countries and LDCs have accepted differential obligations under the WTO agreements: (1) they enjoy the freedom to undertake policies that limit access to their markets or provide support to domestic producers or exporters in ways which are not allowed to other members, which can be viewed as exemptions from WTO disciplines so as to take into account particular developing country circumstances; (2) they are provided with more time to meet their obligations or commitments under the agreements. In some cases, more favourable treatment involves a combination of (1) and (2).

Exemption from disciplines

The most general and fundamental way in which developing countries continue to be exempted from WTO disciplines in respect of market access policies is through the principle of non-reciprocity in trade negotiations whereby developed countries reduce or remove tariffs and other barriers to trade. This principle is recognized in GATT Article XXXVI and in the 'Enabling Clause'. Consistent with these provisions, many developing countries have not bound tariffs on their industrial products to the same extent as developed countries or have agreed to bind at levels that are substantially higher than the applied levels. Similar provisions for non-reciprocity are included in GATS, Article XIX (2) which states that 'there shall be appropriate flexibility for individual developing countries Members for opening fewer sectors, liberalizing fewer types of transactions, progressively extending market access in line with their development situation'.

Protection of domestic industry

A second way in which developing countries have greater flexibility in providing protection to domestic industry is through the provisions of GATT Article XVIII, which enables developing countries to (1) provide the tariff protection required to establish a particular industry and (2) apply quantitative restrictions for balance of payments purposes. Since the establishment of the WTO there have been very few instances of these provisions being invoked.

The Agreement on Agriculture contains a variety of measures that exempt developing countries and, to even a greater extent, LDCs from disciplines and obligations that apply generally, and it extends longer timetables or more modest reductions in government support and subsidies than are required from other members. For example, investment subsidies or input subsidies to low-income producers are exempted from the calculation of aggregate measures of support; reductions in export subsidies are either set lower or may take place over a longer period of time; and there are specific provisions for the operation of government stockholding programmes aimed at enhancing food security as well as less demanding minimum-access provisions for primary agricultural products that are the predominant staple in the traditional diet of the developing country in question. A number of developing countries have notified the WTO that they are implementing programmes that take into account the specific exemptions contained in these provisions.

There are similar exemptions from disciplines in the Agreement on Subsidies and Countervailing Measures. This agreement permits LDCs and countries with a per capita income of less than $1,000 to retain certain kinds of export subsidy that are otherwise prohibited; and for other developing countries it extends the period over which subsidies can be provided. Again, a number of developing countries have invoked these provisions by notifying the WTO that they are maintaining their export subsidy programmes.

Finally, the agreements contain a number of other provisions that allow developing countries greater flexibility in meeting certain requirements. For example, the Enabling Clause allows greater flexibility in determining adherence to the GATT provisions on the formation of free trade areas and customs unions among developing countries; the agreement on TRIMS permits temporary deviations for developing countries that are applying balance of payments measures; and the dispute settlement agreement provides for special procedures for LDCs.

Flexibility has thus emerged as the most widespread instrument of special and differential treatment. It could be argued that flexibility, as applied in the WTO, is not the negation of reciprocity. Commitments were agreed on a reciprocal basis, and flexibility applies to the differential application of such commitments. However, the Uruguay Round agreements, by placing flexibility in the context of reciprocity, mark a significant shift away from the concept of non-reciprocity in the handling of development issues within the multilateral trading system. While there is little reason to question the overall principle of policy space and flexibility, there is a question as to whether the magnitude of the latitude permitted, for example, in respect of tariff bindings, results in policies that are more suited to development.

Time extensions

The final way in which special and differential treatment is conferred on developing countries and LDCs in the WTO is the extension of the time in which certain obligations under the agreements must be implemented. Such flexibility is provided in practically all the WTO Agreements, with the exception of the Agreements on Anti-Dumping Procedures and on Pre-shipment Inspection. Time extensions were allowed, especially under the TBT, SPS and TRIPS agreements. Flexibility in transition times has also allowed the conclusion of a number of agreements on a multilateral basis, such as those on Customs Valuation, Import Licensing, Subsidies and Safeguards, which had been dealt with only on a plurilateral basis prior to the Uruguay Round. In addition there are provisions in the Subsidies and Countervailing Duties Agreement and in the Agreement on Agriculture that permit developing countries to continue to subsidize exports for a certain period and in a variety of ways that are prohibited to other members. In the majority of cases, flexibility takes the form of a slower rate of implementation of commitments agreed. For instance, the agreement on subsidies and countervailing duties permits a transition period of eight years, while the TRIPS agreement permits a transition period of five years. In the case of the Agreement on Textiles and Clothing, flexibility took the form of an accelerated phasing out of MFA quotas for developing countries.

Transition-time flexibility, like the other types of flexibility discussed in the previous section, is thus a mechanism for providing special and differential treatment in the context of reciprocal and multilateral commitments.[13] And a strong case can be made that the special provisions extended to the developing countries – unlike the provisions calling for developed-country actions – are legally enforceable (Kessie, 2000).

The main justification for granting additional time for the implementation of agreed measures relates to the weak institutional capacity of developing countries and LDCs. It is assumed, that, given extra time and technical assistance (which is often also expected to be provided in these areas), developing countries and LDCs will be able to strengthen their institutions sufficiently to implement the agreements. In the case

[13] However, developing countries seeking to accede to the WTO do not benefit automatically from transitional provisions (Drabek and Laird, 1998).

of subsidies, the presumption is that additional time would enable countries to introduce alternative means of support (for agriculture or exports in general) that are acceptable under the agreement.

The main issues that arise in connection with this aspect of special and differential treatment are the adequacy of the time extensions and the cost to build the institutional capacity needed for full implementation of the obligations laid down in the agreements. The Uruguay Round negotiators do not appear to have consulted anybody involved in institution building in developing countries about the transition periods agreed upon. The extensions have already expired and there is little evidence that many countries have made sufficient progress with institution building to permit them to implement their obligations leading to requests for further extensions.

Special measures for LDCs

The Enabling Clause of 1979 provided the basis for special treatment of LDCs 'in the context of any general or specific measures in favor of developing countries'. The Uruguay Round agreements contain 17 provisions that apply specifically to LDC members, in addition to those applicable to all developing countries. These include a longer transition period than that granted to developing countries under the TRIPS, TRIMS and SPS Agreements. In addition the agreements on agriculture and subsidies exempt LDCs from all reduction commitments, with the subsidies agreement allowing for an extended phasing out of subsidies once export competitiveness is established.

A number of initiatives have also been adopted for LDC members since the establishment of the WTO. For example, the 'Decision on Measures in Favor of Least Developed Countries' (1994) allows LDC members to limit commitments and concessions to an extent that is compatible with their individual development, financial and trade needs, and which is consistent with administrative and institutional capabilities.

The High Level Meeting on LDCs in October 1997 formalized the twin-track approach in respect of special and differential treatment of these countries in the WTO, with one track emphasizing their limited commitments to liberalization, and the other track emphasizing the increased commitment by developed countries in respect of market access and technical assistance. In that context, a number of WTO members announced measures for improved and preferential market access for LDCs. With regard to technical assistance, an 'Integrated Framework for Trade Related Technical Assistance to Support Least Developed Countries in their Trade Related Activities' has been developed, involving the IMF, ITC, UNCTAD, the United Nations Development Program (UNDP), the World Bank and the WTO. This Integrated Framework seeks to address shortcomings in technical and institutional capacity, particularly in the areas of trade policy, human resources, export supply capability and regulatory regimes. After a lot of international discussion a new WTO unit was established to implement the mandate of this programme in 2007 (see pp. 125–7).

The key issues to be addressed in connection with the special provisions for the LDCs are much the same as with developing countries as a whole. Are the commitments for preferential market access and treatment offered by developed countries meaningful in light of the constraints these countries face in integrating in the world trading system? Is the international technical assistance provided to these countries adequate and effective? And will the flexibility offered to these countries in meeting their WTO commitments assist them in achieving their long-term trade and development objectives?

The Doha Round

This review of GATT and WTO provisions shows that since the 1950s developing countries succeeded in establishing the principle that the trade rules applying to them and the LDCs will differ in many ways from those that apply to other WTO members. While increasing their commitment to various aspects of participation in the international trading system, they have ensured that this participation is guided by the principle of special and differential treatment, which itself has been amplified in a number of ways, especially with regard to the provision of technical assistance and securing extra time for the implementation of their WTO commitments. These additional aspects of special and differential treatment reflect the increasing recognition that the integration of developing countries into the international trading system is constrained by their institutional weaknesses which will require additional time and technical assistance to overcome. In light of the even poorer capacities of LDCs, they have been given even greater flexibility in the implementation of their commitments.

In the late 1990s, the developing countries claimed that the developed countries had not lived up to their commitments in the Uruguay Round in general, and specifically with regard to the provision of special and differential treatment. When the Doha Round was launched, a key developing country objective was to ensure that the principles established regarding special and differential treatment during previous Rounds were safeguarded and that the commitments made by developed countries were implemented effectively. Thus, the Doha Ministerial declaration specifically focused on developing country issues and called for a variety of actions as part of what came to be known as the Doha Development Agenda. The preamble of the declaration recognizes that 'the majority of WTO members are developing countries. We seek to place their needs and interests at the heart of the Work Program adopted in this Declaration'. Separate sections of the Declaration dealt with developing country issues including technical cooperation and capacity building, LDCs and special and differential treatment (WTO, 2001a).

Under technical cooperation the declaration underscores 'the urgent necessity for the effective coordinated delivery of technical assistance with bilateral donors ... within a coherent policy framework and timetable'. In the section on LDCs the members 'commit themselves to the objective of duty free, quota-free market access for products originating from LDCs' and 'to work to facilitate and accelerate negotiations with acceding LDCs'.

Members also agreed to review all special and differential provisions 'with a view to strengthening them and making them more precise, effective and operational'. In this connection several steps were undertaken: first, a list of special and differential provisions in specific agreements was developed which related to particular concerns of developing country members and LDCs. Second, all the different formulas considered in the negotiations on tariff reductions explicitly involved smaller reductions in the tariffs of developing countries, while the LDCs were completely exempted from reducing their tariffs. Third, an effort to deal with specific developing country concerns was made in specific negotiations, as for example in the discussions on modifying the provisions of the special safeguard in agriculture, or separately in connection with the revision of the agreement on TRIPS.

The Doha Round (discussed in detail in Chapter 9) has not yet been completed after protracted and arduous negotiations over more than ten years. Over the course of the negotiations, developing country trade expanded rapidly and changed in character.The rapid expansion of value chains means that activities rather industries tend to define a country's specialization. An important question for the Round and for the future of the WTO is the nature of the special and differential treatment that is conducive to development in light of the changing character of international trade. The next four chapters provide some answers to this question.

3
WTO Accession Issues

Introduction

In previous chapters I have noted how the decision of many developing countries to integrate themselves more fully into the world trading system led several of them to join GATT in the 1980s and later the WTO. There is no way of making the rules of the international system benefit a country's interest, unless the country is a member of and, as will be stressed in Chapter 8, is effectively represented in the WTO.

WTO accession is a far more complex, difficult and lengthy process than was the case during GATT.[1] As of 31 December 2012, 24 countries were at various stages of their membership negotiations. At the time *Developing Countries in the WTO* (Michalopoulos, 2001) was published, there were 28 countries in the queue. In the intervening years only 12 countries have managed to become members; eight new countries have applied. Of the current applicants six, including Belarus, Kazakhstan and Uzbekistan, applied for accession after the collapse of the Soviet Union in the early 1990s. About half of the remainder are LDCs (see Table 3.1). Indeed there is hardly any country of any size that is neither in the WTO nor applying to accede.[2]

---

[1] There were 23 original GATT signatories. But 64 developing countries that were previously colonies became CPs when they gained their independence through a much less stringent process than that required of countries or territories seeking GATT accession (Cattaneo and Braga, 2009).

[2] Afghanistan, Iran, Iraq, Libya and Tajikistan, all of which were listed as uninterested for 'political reasons' in Michalopoulos (2001), have since applied to accede; and Tajikistan has recently become a member.

In this chapter I analyse the WTO accession process. I first briefly summarize the main benefits that countries can expect from WTO membership, before discussing the process and strategies for accession as well as the main issues that have arisen in the case of developing countries and other applicants. I then review the progress made on accession by various countries, as well as the causes of the delays, which have been common in the accession of most countries. Finally I draw the main conclusions from the analysis and present a number of recommendations aimed at facilitating and expediting the process of accession for those countries which have already applied and those which have not.

The benefits of WTO membership

Apart from the obvious benefit of participating in the activities of an institution within which the global rules for trade are set, WTO membership provides additional benefits in four main areas: (1) strengthening of domestic policies and institutions for the conduct of international trade in goods and services, which is needed before accession into the WTO can be accomplished; (2) helping establish more liberal trade regimes; (3) improving the ease and security of market access to major export markets; and (4) gaining access to a dispute settlement mechanism for trade issues.[3]

Domestic policies and institutions

While there are significant differences between the institutional and policy environments of the countries applying to accede, it is remarkable how similar the opportunities and challenges that WTO membership are for individual countries or groups. In economies previously under central planning, the government controlled trade through ministries and state trading enterprises. The institutions governing other aspects of the international exchange of goods and services, such as intellectual property rights, standards, phyto-sanitary provisions and procurement were either different or non-existent. LDCs applying for accession face similar challenges in establishing the institutions needed to implement their WTO commitments. Perhaps the most important of these challenges is the introduction of laws and institutions for the

[3] See Cattaneo and Braga (2009). These authors also suggest another benefit, namely that membership reduces the cost of engaging in multilateral negotiations. Against this, however, one needs to weigh the costs of the many changes that countries have to make in their policies and institutions to make them consistent with WTO provisions.

operation of private enterprises and markets free from government controls other than those explicitly provided under WTO regulations regarding, for example, health, intellectual property rights and state trading practices.

Equally important to a country's economy is the greater stability in commercial policy that comes from adherence to WTO rules and legally binding agreements. Stability is important both to domestic producers and to exporters from other countries wishing to access that country's markets. There is little doubt that adherence to WTO provisions, for example by binding tariffs and specifying conditions of establishment of FDI in the agreement on services, improves the efficiency and productivity of acceding countries.

Trade liberalization

The WTO membership process typically results in pressures from existing members to reduce trade barriers through reductions in the level of applied tariffs, elimination of non-tariff barriers and liberalizing services trade as a price of admission, which benefits both the country itself and the rest of the world. The process also offered the opportunity for some relatively new members such as the Baltic countries to lock into relatively liberal trade regimes.[4] For these countries, membership provided the opportunity to lock in these regimes by assuming legally binding obligations regarding tariff levels. This not only permitted them to enjoy the benefits of liberal trade but also gave them a first line of defence against the domestic protectionist pressures that are inevitably present in all market economies.

Market access

There are two main dimensions of market access that are important to acceding economies. The first is the extension of permanent and unconditional MFN status that comes with WTO membership. At present, economies that are not members of the WTO enjoy voluntary MFN treatment by major trading partners. But there is no guarantee that they will continue to receive such treatment. For example the US extension of MFN to Russia and several other formerly centrally planned economies used to be contingent on these countries' adherence to the provisions of

---

[4] Actually Latvia's liberal policies on audio-visual services caused problems with the more protectionist EU and delayed its accession. Estonia ran into the same difficulties on account of its very liberal agricultural trade policies.

the Jackson-Vanik amendment to the 1974 Trade Act regarding freedom of emigration.[5]

Second, there is substantial evidence, as will be discussed in Chapter 6, that the incidence of anti-dumping actions (both investigations and definitive measures) is much higher against non-WTO members than against members. Also, for countries which are considered as 'non-market economies' by major trading partners such as the EU and the US, WTO membership could help improve market access, by making the processes used in anti-dumping cases against them more transparent.

Dispute settlement

Access to an impartial and binding dispute settlement mechanism whose decisions have a significant chance of being enforced is a very important potential benefit for the acceding economies, many of which are small and heavily dependent on international trade. The dispute settlement mechanism has proven successful in providing the opportunity for a member to satisfactorily address its grievances when the practices of other members damage its trade. The problems developing countries face in accessing this mechanism have been noted, but membership provides opportunities that, with proper assistance, can be beneficial to new members, especially in their relationship with large trading partners.

The accession process and strategies

The process of accession to the WTO is demanding and takes a long time for most countries. It can be divided into an introductory phase of formalities and three substantive phases. The three substantive phases involve: (1) preparation of a 'Memorandum on the Foreign Trade

[5] Belarus (and until recently China) is subject to annual waivers; the rest have been found to be in full compliance and receive 'permanent' conditional MFN. When however, Armenia, Georgia, Mongolia, the Kyrgyz Republic, Moldova and Russia became WTO members the US exercised its right of non-application under WTO's Article XIII – which means that it did not provide these countries with unconditional MFN – or for that matter with any other WTO rights and thus de facto had not accepted their accession. Subsequently, legislation was enacted permitting the US to notify the WTO that it has accepted membership of these countries – except for Moldova (Tarr and Volchkova, 2010). In the case of China, the US had to address this important issue through amended legislation *before* membership negotiations were concluded.

Regime' in which the applicant provides full details of its policies and institutions that have a bearing on the conduct of international trade; (2) the fact-finding phase; (3) the negotiation phase. The last two phases, while conceptually separate, in practice tend to overlap. Throughout the applicant has to meet the requirements and provisions of the WTO and the demands from existing members. With very few exceptions the negotiations are one-sided: the applicant is required to demonstrate how it intends to meet the existing WTO provisions – it cannot seek to change them. Moreover, the existing members can ask the applicant to reduce the level of protection in its markets; but the reverse is not usually possible.

The formalities

The first step taken by an applicant country is to send a letter from the government to the Director General of the WTO expressing its desire to accede to the Organization. The request is then considered by the WTO General Council, which consists of representatives of all the member countries and meets frequently during the course of the year. The General Council routinely sets up working parties with appropriate terms of reference to consider individual accession applications. The Council nominates the chairman,[6] but participation is open to all members of the WTO. In the case of large countries such as China or Russia, a large number of countries participated; in the case of smaller countries, participation is limited to QUAD countries, plus Australia, New Zealand, Switzerland, a few of the larger developing countries and neighbouring countries that are significant trading partners. This phase can be quite short and normally takes no more time than that needed to find a chairman for the working party and to translate and distribute the accession request for the next meeting of the General Council.

The memorandum

The first substantive phase is the preparation of a 'Memorandum on the Foreign Trade Regime' in which the applicant explains its policies and institutions. This can be a very demanding task because of the range

---

[6] Usually an ambassador or a permanent representative to the WTO. A chairman may not be appointed until much later and is needed only when the Working Party meets, which may take a while. Countries often request and obtain observer status at the WTO to familiarize themselves with it prior to a formal request for accession.

of issues that the memorandum has to address and the degree of detail required. The issues include much more than simply trade in goods and services – although the latter encompasses issues such as the financial sector, insurance, telecommunications, professional services and is itself a large enough task. The other issues range over various aspects of macroeconomics (especially that related to foreign exchange management and controls), foreign investment policy, the protection of intellectual and other property rights, and enterprise privatization. The preparation of this report is the responsibility solely of the applicant, as is any delay in its preparation.

The greater the extent to which the memorandum is incomplete in its details or the legislation and practices described are inconsistent with the WTO provisions, the more protracted the subsequent question and answer period becomes. On some occasions members have asked the WTO Secretariat to review draft memoranda before they are circulated so as to prevent incomplete documentation from being circulated. But the Secretariat does not assume any responsibility for the contents of memoranda and has limited power to persuade sovereign governments to be more comprehensive or transparent.

Fact finding

Once a memorandum has been circulated to WTO members, the accession process enters the second, often time consuming, stage, in which members ask questions about and obtain clarifications on the applicant's policies and institutions, either based on the memorandum or on independent evidence gathered by the members. This typically takes several months, but in the case of Russia, it took more than a year. The working party does not usually meet until the memorandum and the initial questions and answers have been distributed. The subsequent questions, answers and clarifications can occupy several working party meetings and sometimes take several years.

The purpose of this detailed review is to clarify what part of the applicant's legislation and institutions may be considered in conformity with the provisions of the WTO and what part is not. The process is so time consuming in part because the review is exhaustive in its details. The applicant is requested to submit for consideration by the working party all relevant legislation on a variety of issues covered by the WTO which is reviewed in detail for its consistency with the provisions of WTO agreements. The purpose of the initial fact-finding is to gain a critical mass of information on the economic and trade regime of the applicant so that negotiations on market access can take place in a meaningful context. Delays during this phase are frequent: if a member country feels that the answers submitted to a question or the actions taken to remedy an inconsistency are inadequate, it simply returns the question for resubmission.

The issues raised in each accession vary somewhat according to the country, but some common themes emerge in the discussions that are worth highlighting. First, there is a general requirement for the laws and regulations of the acceding country to be in conformity with the WTO provisions. These extend far beyond the obvious such as customs law, tariff schedules and related regulations on imports and exports. They include such items as laws on joint stock companies, the central bank and credit institutions, the licensing of economic activity, domestic taxation, regulations on food and alcoholic beverages, veterinary medicine, quarantine, patent and copyright protection and consumer protection. The list of laws of a small country reviewed by a typical working party may run into two single-spaced pages and involve more than 75 laws and regulations.

Second, in the context of laws and the operation of government institutions, there are two broad issues that typically receive special attention in countries with previously centrally planned economies: the degree of privatization of the economy and the extent to which government agencies involved in the regulation of economic activity do so on the basis of transparent rules and criteria as opposed to administrative discretion. A key issue in respect of enterprises that are expected to remain state-owned is whether they operate under market conditions or enjoy special monopoly rights and privileges.

Third, there are issues that relate to the jurisdiction and capacity of national agencies to implement policies on which commitments are being made. The fundamental concern is one of governance: whether the government agencies have the authority and capacity to implement the commitments they are making in the context of WTO accession in the case of the laws and regulations that concern the conduct of international trade. A related concern is the role and jurisdiction of local authorities and whether they have the right and opportunity to nullify the commitments made by the national authorities in the context of accession negotiations.

Negotiations

At some point during the question and answer phase, frequently before all the points raised by the working party have been answered, the applicant is requested to submit its initial schedule of 'offers' in goods and services. This consists of the following:

- A detailed schedule of the tariffs the applicant proposes to impose on goods and the level at which the tariffs are bound.
- The applicant's commitments (and limitations) on maintaining access to its market for services. These include the so-called 'horizontal commitments' involving market access to and national treatment in all service sectors, and commitments and limitations in respect of the different modes of supply in the covered service sectors and subsectors.[7]
- The level of support it plans to provide to its agricultural sector relative to a base reference period (usually three representative years before the application for accession) and other aspects of its support for agricultural trade (for example, export subsidies).

Once these offers are tabled, the accession process enters its final phase, which involves bilateral negotiations on proposed tariff levels and degree of openness in the service sector. The timing of the offers varies considerably, and sometimes they are tabled very early in the fact-finding phase, as for example in the case of Georgia. The bilateral negotiations often take place in parallel with formal meetings of the working party which continues to deal with fact finding about the foreign trade regime. The negotiations phase can also be lengthy, depending on the degree of openness the applicant proposes and the demands for market access made by members. Finally, the multilateral phase of the negotiations often focuses on systemic issues such as adjustment periods for non-adherence to the TRIMS or TRIPS agreements or the level of agricultural subsidies.

When these negotiations are being finalized and the applicant has provided assurance that the legislation and institutions that will permit compliance with the WTO provisions are in place, a draft report on accession is prepared by the Secretariat for consideration by the working party. This report includes all commitments including institutional commitments and the schedule of agreed commitments on goods and services. After approval from the working party, the report is forwarded to the General Council. Following a favourable decision by the General Council (usually a formality), the country is invited to sign a protocol of accession. After the protocol is signed it has to be approved by the

---

[7] All service commitments are typically more general and open ended than in the sphere of goods. For a discussion see Hoekman (1996).

country's legislative body. Membership formally starts 30 days after the WTO has been notified that the domestic ratification procedures have been completed.

Progress in accession

Progress to date

In mid-2013, 24 working parties formally existed to consider the accession applications of prospective members to the WTO (Table 3.1). Most of these had been established for some time. Nine of the 24 are active. The oldest are those of Algeria, established in 1987, and Belarus, established in 1993. *Developing Countries in the WTO* (Michalopoulos, 2001) estimated that in 2001 on average the working parties had been in place for 67 months. In 2012 the average life of the existing working parties was almost double at 131 months, i.e. more than ten years!

The fastest WTO accession was that of the Kyrgyz Republic at two years and ten months. The longest so far is that of Russia at almost 20 years. But the record will be exceeded when Belarus eventually becomes a member.

Table 3.1 shows that some countries apply to accede then do nothing for a number of years, e.g. Algeria and Uzbekistan, only to pick up the process later on, do a little bit more and then abandon the process again. Others (Comoros and Equatorial Guinea) have applied, had a working party established and then done nothing to follow up. Several others such as Azerbaijan, Kazakhstan, Serbia and Yemen have been involved in the accession process for a long time with revised offers on goods and services having been made or the drafting of the working party report under discussion. For these countries, accession to the WTO could be imminent, provided agreement can be reached with WTO members on remaining points of contention.

Some of the applicants are LDCs which face immense institutional and human constraints in coping with the demands of accession. Vanuatu, whose institutional weaknesses have been extensively documented (Gay, 2005) finally became a member in 2012, 17 years after it applied. The problems faced by this small island LDC are characteristic of other LDCs seeking accession.

Why does it take so long?

To understand why it takes so long to accede to the WTO, one has to look more closely at the various phases of the accession process and investigate the reasons why delays may occur.

Table 3.1 Timetable of accessions to the WTO as of December 2012

Government	Establishment of working party	Memorandum	Tariff offers	Service offers	Draft working party report
Afghanistan	12/04	03/09	11/12	06/12	11/12
Algeria	06/87	07/96	11/07	11/07	06/06
Andorra	10/97	02/99	09/99	09/99	–
Azerbaijan	07/97	04/99	11/12	10/11	11/12 (FS)
Bahamas	08/01	04/09	03/12	03/12	–
Belarus	10/93	01/96	03/06	09/06	11/12 (FS)
Bhutan	10/99	02/03	11/07	11/07	12/07
Bosnia-Herzegovina	08/99	10/02	02/07	02/07	09/12
Comoros	10/07	–	–	–	–
Equatorial Guinea	02/08	–	–	–	–
Ethiopia	02/03	01/07	02/12	–	03/12 (FS)
Iran	05/05	11/09	–	–	–
Iraq	12/04	09/05	–	–	–
Kazakhstan	02/96	09/96	09/12	06/04	11/12
Lebanon	04/99	06/01	06/04	06/04	10/09
Liberia	10/07	04/11	–	–	–
Libya	07/04	–	–	–	–
Sao Tome / Principe	05/05	–	–	–	–
Serbia	02/05	03/05	11/08	11/08	10/12
Seychelles	07/95	08/96	09/12	05/12	06/12
Sudan	10/94	01/99	10/06	10/06	09/04 (FS)
Syria	05/10	–	–	–	–
Uzbekistan	12/94	09/98	09/05	09/05	–
Yemen	07/00	11/02	08/08	08/12	08/12

Source: WTO (2012d).

Weak follow-up

There are several cases (Comoros, Equatorial Guinea, Libya, Sao Tome and Principe) where the countries have applied for accession and a working party has been set up, but have failed to prepare a memorandum on their policies. In other cases (Sudan and Uzbekistan) the memoranda on foreign trade policy have been prepared after long delays, but the negotiations have been suspended for more than five years.

In the case of Algeria, the working party was set up in 1987, but the government did not produce a memorandum until 1996. There were numerous working party meetings between 1998 and 2008, but nothing since.

Political issues

There are a few cases where political issues between the applicant and one or more WTO members have introduced delays in the process. Arguably, this has to some extent been the case with China (and Chinese Taipei which was linked to it); the accession of the former Yugoslav republic of Macedonia (FYROM) whose accession was delayed over a dispute over its name with Greece; and the accession of Russia may well have been delayed somewhat by politically motivated objections from Georgia. The latter signed its bilateral agreement with Russia in 2004, but subsequently blocked the meetings of Russia's working party for several years, which was forced to meet informally (Tarr and Volchkova, 2010). It is a moot point whether Georgia's actions delayed accession since there were many other unresolved issues as well, but the conflict clearly spilled over into the WTO negotiations and was only resolved with the mediation of the Swiss representative.

Inherent time-consuming processes

Even in the absence of the above problems, the process of accession is inherently time consuming. The preparation of the Memorandum presents serious difficulties to governments, especially concerning LDCs that lack the necessary human or material resources to address the relevant issues, which have to be analysed in detail. In some cases, there is a lack of familiarity with the concepts and legal and economic issues involved. This was especially the case in the early 1990s for the formerly centrally planned economies, most of which had to seek assistance from outside experts (funded by bilateral aid agencies), the WTO itself and the World Bank. Despite this assistance, it has taken on average about 30 months to prepare the initial Memorandum (even excluding the extreme case of Algeria).

The fact-finding process is also time consuming because institutional weaknesses in applicant countries can mean that it takes a long time to ascertain the consistency between the existing legislation and regulations and WTO requirements as well as to design and put in place the required amendments, new legislation or regulations. This is compounded by the range and extent of the legislation needed, and by the fact that legislative processes are themselves time consuming. At the same time, the discussions between the applicant and the working party on points of detail can be protracted: on average it takes nine months from the time of circulation of the memorandum for the first questions and answers on it to be distributed.

The fact-finding process can also stretch over several years. In part, this can again be due to weaknesses in the institutional capacity of the applicant. The WTO Secretariat can assist only in a very limited way in the accession process: the WTO budget allocation is very limited. The five staff in the WTO Accession Division (first established in 1995 – GATT had no explicit secretariat resources for the processing of new members) are hard pushed to service even the procedural needs and paperwork generated by more than 20 or more active accession working parties. At the same time, the members themselves do not apply large resources in support of the accession process.[8] Finally, delays occur because fact finding about policies merges into negotiations about how existing policies need to be changed to ensure conformity with the WTO.

Negotiations

The negotiating phase can be, and frequently has been, the most time-consuming phase in the accession process. The negotiations are partly about whether the applicant's policies and institutions are consistent with various aspects of the WTO agreements and partly about specific tariff bindings and commitments in agriculture, goods and services. Delays can be caused by both sides. The applicant may be unwilling to make the necessary liberalization commitments and slow the process by, for example, not offering to liberalize its non-tariff barriers or proposing to bind tariffs at levels much higher than the current applied ones; and WTO members may be unsatisfied with the level of liberalization proposed or unwilling to accept delays in bringing the applicant's laws and institutions into line with WTO provisions.

Applicants' strategies and tactics

Within the rules and disciplines of the WTO, each applicant has considerable discretion in respect of how restrictive or liberal its trade

[8] In the early 1990s the EU had six staff in Brussels and the US had a similar number in Washington to deal with the accession issues arising in more than 20 active working parties. Many WTO members, however, notably the EU, the US and Switzerland, support the accession process through technical assistance from their aid programmes.

regime will be. There are no specific rules on the maximum level at which an applicant has to bind its tariffs, how many services it will liberalize, whether or not to establish anti-dumping legislation, or how fast it will liberalize its agricultural trade. Regrettably, not all pressures are in favour of liberalizing commitments. Estonia, an applicant with very liberal trade policies, had no plans to establish anti-dumping legislation at accession but was pressured by the EU, the US and others to do so. Applicants thus have a strategic choice to make during the negotiating phase: how liberal their trade regime will be, subject to the overall WTO disciplines.

One strategy that some countries have pursued in their accession negotiations offers the minimum degree of liberalization necessary to ensure accession. The logic of this strategy is that, for the most part, improvements in market access cannot be negotiated during accession, so it is desirable to try to maintain significant levels of protection for use as bargaining chips to obtain improved access in future negotiating rounds. Some of the countries that have used this strategy, for example China, Ukraine and Russia (Gabunia, 1998), also feel that significant levels of protection are necessary during the transition period in which restructuring of inefficient enterprises is undertaken. Similar issues arise in services. Many developing economies feel that their service sector is underdeveloped and would like to limit the commitments they make to open it up to foreign competition. This is a particular issue in areas such as financial services and telecommunications, sectors in which they frequently face requests from WTO members to establish liberal policies on commercial presence. The latter would permit foreign service suppliers to establish subsidiaries or joint ventures based on the principle of national treatment which prohibits discrimination against foreign service providers and thus has a direct bearing on foreign direct investment.

However, the minimum liberalization accession strategy can have negative effects. Individual countries, especially small developing economies, have little leverage in market access negotiations; hence any benefits they might obtain through such a strategy may be very small. At the same time, maintaining protection through relatively high tariffs and protected agriculture and service sectors simply means that they impose costs to their own economies by foregoing the benefits of a more liberal trade regime, which in the first instance accrue to the country itself.

On the other hand, if countries bind their tariffs at levels higher than those currently applied and assume few commitments on agriculture and services, both of which are possible under WTO rules, they are subject to another risk: they create an opening for domestic interests to exert political pressure for additional protection in the future.

A different strategy has been pursued by many of the previously centrally planned economies that have become WTO members including Albania, Estonia, Georgia, the Kyrgyz Republic, Latvia and Mongolia.[9] In most of these cases the governments in question have adopted a liberal trade strategy as part of the accession process including: binding tariffs at the prevailing levels and agreeing to reduce and bind tariffs at these unusually low levels as part of the negotiations; agreeing to a liberal trade regime in agriculture and services; and considering at an early date after accession to participate in such agreements as the government procurement code, which serves to increase competition and transparency in the operation of their markets.

The fundamental benefits of such a strategy are economic: it provides countries with liberal trade and investment. But it has a number of other advantages: it tends to facilitate the negotiating part of the accession process; it provides governments with political cover against domestic protectionist interests which may otherwise succeed in subverting the existing liberal trade regime; and the legally binding WTO commitments make it more difficult for future governments to reverse the liberalization. Increased protection to safeguard against serious injury to domestic industry is permitted under WTO rules, though it is supposed to be decided on the basis of a detailed and transparent investigation to demonstrate injury, which is then notified to the WTO and subjected to the scrutiny of other members. This is far more difficult to do than for a powerful domestic industry to seek government support to raise tariffs beyond the applied level but below the higher bound level, which a government can do almost without any constraint. The point about the WTO is not that it prohibits protection, but rather that it permits it only according to certain rules, and that obeying these rules makes protection more transparent as well as more difficult to initiate and spread.

WTO member attitudes and policies

The demands made on newly acceding countries are greater, in a variety of ways, than the disciplines on existing members. This is what has come to be known as 'WTO-Plus' commitments of new members (Charnowitz, 2008). The following areas are ones in which members typically request that acceding countries make commitments in excess

[9] The trade regimes in Croatia and Jordan are somewhat less liberal.

of what many existing members at similar levels of development have agreed to:

- *Tariffs.* Until recently (see changes below with respect to LDCs) all acceding countries were requested to bind all tariffs, although a large portion of the tariff schedule of many developing countries is still unbound. Ceiling bindings have been accepted, but there is pressure for these to be close to the applied rates, and in many cases (Albania, China, Russia) for substantial reductions (Tarr and Volchkova, 2010). For example, applied tariffs in Russia will come down to about 7.6 per cent from about 11 per cent or an even greater percentage fall on a weighted average basis.
- *Agriculture.* In addition to binding their tariff schedule, commitments are expected on aggregate measures of support and export subsidies. Since many acceding countries have not provided substantial support to agriculture, but rather penalized it, the requests they faced for reductions in aggregate measures of support were often difficult to meet.
- *Services.* Typically, acceding countries have been asked to make commitments to liberalize far more sub-sectors than countries at similar levels of development liberalized during the Uruguay Round (Cattaneo and Braga, 2009).
- *Rules and disciplines.* Acceding countries are typically requested to meet all commitments at entry (for example with regard to TRIPs, customs valuation, standards or sanitary and phyto-sanitary regulations) without time limits, such as those available to existing members at similar levels of development and regardless of whether institutional weakness makes it difficult for them to fulfil such commitments. Such weakness relates broadly to aspects of the operations of a market economy, where it will take time to establish the proper institutional infrastructure to enable them to discharge their responsibilities properly under the WTO agreements (see p. 42). When such weaknesses are brought out in the negotiations, applicants are advised to seek technical assistance (available from a variety of bilateral and multilateral donors) and are asked to present details of the particular aspects of the relevant WTO provisions in which weaknesses exist, as well as how and over what time period it proposes to remedy them. Countries such as China and Russia, however, have used their strong geopolitical position to negotiate substantial transition periods, for example in implementing TRIMS commitments.
- *Multilateral agreements.* There is pressure on countries to examine the provisions of the multilateral agreements on, for example, government

procurement and civil aviation at the time of accession and sign up to the agreement soon after. Russia agreed to negotiate participation in the Government Procurement Agreement three years after accession.

- *Market economy issues.* The WTO agreements have no explicit requirement for member states to be market economies.[10] On the other hand, the requirement for new members to have a fundamentally market economy is pushed de facto by existing members as part of the leverage they have in the accession process. Pressure has been exerted on all acceding countries, including China, where an explicit understanding has been reached with regard to the existence of state trading in specific sectors.

At the same time the Quad countries have been unwilling to modify their own anti-dumping procedures in respect of applying the designation of 'non-market economy' to countries that have become WTO members. This designation is used to apply different, less transparent and potentially discriminatory practices in the determination of anti-dumping and, in the case of EU safeguard actions, against imports from a number of these countries, including many former Soviet Union countries and China (Michalopoulos and Winters, 1997). It has been a major cause of trade friction between many of these economies and the US and the EU.

The justification for such practices can be found in Article 2.7 of the Antidumping Agreement which refers to the second Supplementary Provision in paragraph 1 of Article VI in Annex I to GATT 1994 which permits different treatment 'in the case of imports from a country which has complete or substantially complete monopoly of its trade and where all domestic prices are fixed by the State' (Palmeter, 1998, p. 116; Grimmett, 2012).[11] Such practices were perhaps fully justified when practically all trade was controlled by state trading enterprises or ministries and prices were fixed by the state and hence could not be taken to reflect 'normal value'. Countries, however, have made great progress in introducing market forces and eliminating state trading in recent years. It would very difficult to argue that, for example, China at present has 'a substantially complete monopoly on trade' or that all domestic prices are fixed by the

[10] GATT Article XVII calls for notification of enterprises engaging in state trading practices. However, Article XVII had never been intended to address problems that come up when the bulk of external trade was controlled by the state. Indeed the old GATT accommodated several countries, for example Hungary and Poland, which at the time had centrally planned economies.

[11] This interpretation was supported by recent findings of the WTO Dispute Settlement Body (Grimmett, 2012, p. 15).

state. Hence, continuation of traditional EU and US anti-dumping practices in the new setting does not appear to be justified (Michalopoulos and Winters, 1997). However, because the anti-dumping provisions of GATT accept national legislation and practices as decisive, it is possible to have the odd situation where a country acceding to the WTO is still designated as a non-market economy for anti-dumping purposes.[12]

Special country-specific commitments

Saudi Arabia, for example, did not commit to applying secondary and tertiary boycotts on firms trading with Israel. Russia committed to maximum export taxes on natural gas and an export tax/quota system on timber.

The difficulties encountered by LDCs in meeting WTO requirements led to the establishment of guidelines in 2002 – which however did not appear to have eased their accession. Among the 48 LDCs listed by the United Nations, 34 have become members (WTO, 2012a). At the time of the establishment of the WTO in 1995, 28 LDCs became members and did not have to go through the difficult accession process. Since 1995, only six LDCs have become members (Cambodia, Nepal, Cape Verde, Samoa, Vanuatu and Laos). Another eight LDCs are at various stages in the process, including one (Yemen) that has essentially completed the negotiations. Thus new guidelines were established in mid-2012 which are relevant to 13 LDCs – seven that have already applied but whose negotiations are still at early stages, and six that have not.

The key elements of the new guidelines are as follows:

- All agricultural tariffs must be bound with an average rate no higher than 50 per cent.
- 95 per cent of tariff lines of industrial goods must be bound at an average rate no higher than 35 per cent. Countries would be permitted higher average bound rates and longer transition periods, if they bind all of their tariffs.
- Service sector liberalization will not be requested in excess of liberalization commitments made by existing LDCs that are WTO members.
- Technical assistance is to be provided to help LDCs with accession.

The guidelines do little to ease the institutional capacity problems that pose the most severe obstacles in LDC accession especially in areas such as TRIPS, TRIMS and SPS. They contain a provision that 'requests for additional transition periods, beyond those foreseen under the WTO

[12] Besides China, Vietnam agreed at accession to have countries treat it as a non-market economy until 2019.

agreements, would be favorably considered on a case by case basis'. This promises nothing more than has already been the practice with individual LDCs and disregards the fact that the transition periods under the WTO agreements are woefully inadequate.

The guidelines contain no concrete technical assistance commitments by developed countries that are WTO members, nor do they ease the pressure LDCs face in participating in multilateral agreements. They only ease the negotiating pressure to liberalize trade policy and permit LDCs to maintain certain levels of protection in agriculture, industry and services. But the levels of protection 'permitted' continue to be significantly lower than those applied by developing countries that are already members. Thus, the 'payment' to enter the WTO 'club' continues to be much stiffer than that exacted from existing members.

On the other side of the ledger the accession negotiations have resulted in what some have called 'WTO-minus' commitments (Cattaneo and Braga, 2009). Many countries have negotiated such commitments, including China, Russia, Taiwan and some of the LDCs. They all amount to an extension of the time frame (i.e. transition periods) when the member is to adhere to the WTO disciplines rather than permanent exceptions.

The Chinese and Russian accessions share some common characteristics but are in many respects unique and cannot be used as precedents for other countries. First, China has used the process of WTO accession to stimulate and make irreversible substantial trade liberalization and more broad-based reform. Second, China's strength as a major market and place of investment permitted it to negotiate far more extensive and longer transition periods both in liberalizing its trade regime and in introducing market based institutions and making other changes in its laws and administrative procedures. Unlike most other accession countries, China obtained transition periods for eliminating non-tariff barriers both to exports and imports in a number of areas. In services, while China's liberalization commitments have been very extensive, they are supposed to take place over several years. Similarly, the country's transition periods for the implementation of TRIMS, TBT and other institutional changes have been more lengthy and extensive than those provided to other acceding countries, most of which have been expected to meet these requirements at the time of accession. Finally, China has not been forced to accede to multilateral agreements, such as those on government procurement.

On the other hand, China's strength both as a major exporter and a feared competitor has resulted in provisions which treat it less favourably than other developing countries on market access and other issues:

- A transitional safeguard mechanism has been agreed, which permits WTO members to introduce temporary restraints on imports of Chinese products with less evidence of damage to their domestic industry than is the case for imports from other WTO members.
- While quantitative restraints on imports of Chinese textile and clothing under the Agreement on Textiles and Clothing were to be terminated as with other countries in 2005, a special negotiated safeguard permitting temporary (one year at a time) restrictions on Chinese exports was in place until 2008.
- The anti-dumping provisions of the protocol of accession continue to permit the use of somewhat arbitrary methods of calculation of damage caused by Chinese exports when they are supposed to involve 'non-market economy' sectors, and the onus of proving that the sector is operating on market economy principles falls on the Chinese exporter.
- While China is supposed to be treated as a 'developing economy' as far as certain aspects of the Subsidies and Countervailing Agreement is concerned, it has committed itself not to use certain other provisions that call for more favourable treatment of developing countries (WTO, 2001c).

By comparison, Russia's accession involved very lengthy negotiations but resulted in relatively few exceptions to the usual accession packages as Russia agreed to implement most commitments required for membership at entry. The major difference with other accessions was the WTO members' agreement that Russia maintain tariff quotas in a number of agricultural and industrial products for several years, stretching out to 2019 for motor cars and 2020 for pork products, and implement the tariff reductions it has agreed to over several years. It also has substantial transition periods regarding many of its service sector commitments, such as branches in insurance and, as noted earlier, has undertaken a number of commitments regarding the imposition of export taxes. Unlike China, Russia has agreed to consider participating in the multilateral agreement on procurement.

Is all the trouble to become a member worth it?

There have been many prospective studies which have shown that a country considering to accede would gain significant economic benefits from becoming a member. A great number of these studies were undertaken in the context of the protracted negotiations of China and Russia (Hertel et al., 2004; Jensen et al., 2007; Rutherford and Tarr, 2008). Fewer efforts have been made to analyse the benefits of new members retrospectively. One of the difficulties in making a balanced assessment is that it is very difficult to quantify the costs of discriminatory practices for non-members as well as the cost of lacking an effective, all be it flawed, dispute settlement mechanism.

Still there have been some partial attempts: Rose (2004) argued that WTO membership does not necessarily result in more trade. On the other side there have been several studies (Subramanian and Wei, 2007; Tomz et al., 2007) showing that the WTO had a strong positive impact on trade. Perhaps the most convincing argument about the benefits to be derived from WTO membership is that no member has ever considered quitting the organization.

Lessons of experience and issues for the future

The most important lesson gained from the accession experience is that the negotiations and their dynamics vary from case to case. Thus, it is difficult to generalize. The recent accession of Russia means that there is now no large country left outside the WTO. Its accession is likely to precipitate action by Kazakhstan and Belarus – both members of a customs union with Russia, whose governments had been reluctant to enter final accession negotiations in advance of Russia – and a number of other former Soviet Union countries, such as Azerbaijan. The remaining countries in the accession queue are either LDCs or politically difficult cases, mostly in the Middle East and North Africa, such as Iran, Syria, Iraq, Algeria and Libya.

The recent decision on LDC accession sets the parameters for these countries' future accession as there is virtually no chance that there will be a further review of their accession difficulties in the near future. As noted above, this decision has major shortcomings. While the WTO members' insistence on the existence of a relatively more liberal commercial policy at entry is likely to serve both acceding countries long-term development interests and WTO members' commercial objectives, their insistence on negotiating, case by case, transition periods in areas such as customs valuation, TRIPS, standards and sanitary and phyto-sanitary measures – where obvious institutional weaknesses are present – raises serious problems. Applicant countries, because of their desire for membership, may end up agreeing to obligations that, later on, their weak institutional capacity would make difficult to implement, leaving them open to subsequent complaints. Fortunately, as we will see in Chapter 8, the likelihood that LDCs would be the target of complaints is very small, as their markets are not large enough to warrant action under the WTO's dispute settlement. Thus, these countries' negotiations are likely to plod along until they achieve membership, in principle with similar commitments and responsibilities as all other members. In practice they are likely to play a marginal role in the organization, which is commensurate with their smaller role in world trade.

For the other countries, experience suggests that the smaller the country and the more liberal its regime, the faster the accession process. This is because smaller countries realize that the costs of protection are high in small economies and because the small size of their economies poses fewer market access problems for the major WTO members.

It is politically difficult to adopt a liberal trade strategy at accession, especially when major WTO trading partners take advantage of opportunities to limit market access that are perfectly legal under the WTO, for example maintaining high levels of protection in agriculture. While recognizing the political difficulties involved, there are strong indications that if the countries that are currently applying for WTO membership adopt a liberal trade strategy at entry, they will maximize the benefits and opportunities for integration in the international community that WTO membership offers.

It is fair to ask whether countries should not maintain some flexibility when making their initial offers, as they are bound to face some liberalization demands by existing members, almost irrespective of the level of protection they initially propose. However, while there is merit to this point, it should not be pushed too far. None of the current applicants have the negotiating clout of China or Russia. Experience suggests that countries that make an initial offer to bind their tariffs at levels that are significantly different from the applied levels encounter serious difficulties in accession, although the practice is quite widespread among existing developing-country members, many of which have failed to bind a large portion of their tariff schedule. When such an initial offer is put on the table, working party members may refuse to consider it or enter negotiations on that basis, as has happened with several former Soviet Union (FSU) countries and applicants for accession. Rather, they inform the country that it must submit a revised offer with bound rates that are closer to the applied ones before serious negotiations can begin.

Acceding countries should keep in mind that, to the members of WTO negotiating their accession, it is almost irrelevant what their trade and investment regime does to their own economies. They are only concerned about the impact of these regimes on their export and investment opportunities in the acceding countries' markets. Unlike membership of the United Nations – which occurs basically automatically – or membership in the Bretton Woods institutions,[13] a major factor contributing to the delays associated with WTO negotiations is that the particular commercial interests in all countries dominate the political economy of international trade policy. Thus while at a general policy level WTO members might agree that accession of a country to the WTO is of paramount importance to their national interest – and for some countries, such as China and Russia, to the very operation of the international trade system – accession cannot occur until the particular commercial interests in all countries are satisfied; and that takes time.

UNCTAD, the World Bank, the EU, Switzerland, the US, China and the WTO all have technical assistance programmes for various aspects of the accession process, especially the preparation of the initial memorandum. Anecdotal reports about these programmes suggest a somewhat uneven performance. Most countries report very helpful contributions by foreign consultants and advisors in the preparation of the Memorandum. In some cases, however, advice provided by outside experts has actually slowed the accession process, because the consultants suggested and the country agreed to a 'bargaining' strategy of bindings of tariffs at high levels and limited offers on services. At the same time, as with assistance for other purposes, there have been problems of coordination among the various donors as well as between the bilateral aid agencies providing the assistance and their colleagues in the trade ministries who are negotiating the accession.[14]

Because the pool of the remaining countries outside the 'Club' is slowly becoming small, accession issues are likely to be less prominent in the future than they have been in the past. One of the most interesting questions for the future, however, will be the way that the new members, in particular China and Russia, will influence the way the WTO functions.

---

[13] Michalopoulos (2001) contains a detailed comparison of the accession experience of FSU countries into the World Bank, the IMF and the WTO in the 1990s.

[14] Based on the author's personal observations in World Bank missions to several countries applying for accession, such as China, Kazakhstan, Russia, the Kyrgyz Republic, FYROM and Yemen.

4
Developing-Country Trade Policies

Introduction

The remarkable expansion of developing countries' trade in the period 1980–2010 and especially in the last two decades, as discussed in Chapter 1, was fuelled in part by their introduction of more outward looking trade regimes that involved less domestic protection, and in part by favourable developments in the access they enjoyed in developed-country markets. Institutional deficiencies and supply capacity and logistics constraints continued to plague many lower income countries and LDCs. But the spread of offshore production and the increased role of value chains played an important part in the growth of many countries' trade. In this chapter I examine the evolution of developing countries' policies that affected merchandise and services trade.[1]

No effort will be made to discuss other policies that affect trade performance, including exchange rate or macroeconomic policies or domestic subsidies and taxes. It is important to note, however, that all evidence on this issue points to a significant improvement in developing-country policies that affect exchange rate management. At the same time there is evidence that military conflicts, both domestic and international, undermined trade performance in a number of developing countries, especially in Africa, during the 1980s and 1990s (World Bank, 2000).

Trade policies that affect merchandise imports

The analysis in this section documents the great progress made by many developing-country WTO members in liberalizing their trade regimes since

[1] The material in this chapter is based on Michalopoulos and Ng (2013b).

the early 1990s (see also Drabek and Laird, 1998; Finger and Schuknecht, 1999). This liberalization has had several dimensions: (1) applied tariffs have been lowered; (2) the overall use of formal non-tariff barriers to trade has decreased in many countries; (3) services have been liberalized in many sectors; and (4) in general, the incidence of government intervention in trade has declined. The analysis also throws light on a number of outstanding issues in the reform agenda and some new challenges which have emerged. For example, unilateral liberalization has increased the gaps between tariff bindings and applied tariffs, increasing the uncertainty to exporters wishing to access these countries' markets as well as the opportunities for resurgent protectionism. Also, while the overall use of non-tariff measures has declined, the use of trade remedies, such as anti-dumping, as well as TBT and SPS controls on imports is on the increase.

The analysis of trade policies is based in part on information from 50 developing countries for which trade policy reviews (TPRs) had been conducted under GATT and the WTO.[2] The group includes 15 economies in Latin America and the Caribbean, 17 in Asia, 13 in sub-Saharan Africa and five in Europe, the Middle East and North Africa.[3] They account for over 95 per cent of the total trade of the developing members of the WTO. Their policies and problems can be taken to represent the developing countries as a whole. For 40 of these countries the TPRs go back to 1990 and give us a perspective on the evolution of their policies over more than 20 years.[4]

Tariffs

The simple average applied MFN tariff level and the standard deviation in the applied tariff level for the latest year available, as well as the average level of binding, the average difference between applied

---

[2] With the exception of Vietnam.

[3] For a list of countries see Appendix A.

[4] GATT/WTO published findings of TPRs, conducted on a regular basis since the beginning of the 1990s, which are a useful source of information regarding the evolution of developing-country policies (Cadot, Malouche and Saez, 2012, p. 12). The objective of the review mechanism is to 'contribute to improved adherence by all WTO Members to rules, disciplines and commitments under the Multilateral Trade Agreements by achieving greater transparency and understanding of the trade policies and practices of members' (WTO, 1995, p. 434). The reviews contain detailed information on policies and institutions affecting trade on a consistent basis over time. This information has been reviewed and discussed by the countries in question and can therefore be considered accurate and authoritative. While various aspects of the reviews could be strengthened (Keesing, 1998), there is little dispute over the accuracy of the information they provide.

and Uruguay Round bound rates and the proportion of tariff lines unbound for the 50 developing countries in the sample, are presented in Table 4.1. The table also contains a column that shows the average applied rates for 40 countries for which TPRs were conducted in the 1990s.

The average applied rates in the 50 countries range from zero in Hong Kong and Singapore to 5–10 per cent in many countries in Latin America, to 10–20 per cent in most of the rest of the countries except Tunisia which has an average of over 20 per cent. Tariff rates vary substantially within each country with overall standard deviations in excess of ten for several countries such as Egypt, India, Korea and Tunisia, and similarly high coefficients of variation.

Perhaps the most interesting aspect of the table is the comparison of the applied rates over time. Only three countries (Benin, Brazil and Senegal) had a higher average applied rate in the 1990s than in the 2000s and that by a small margin. Hong Kong and Singapore, with zero rates, showed no change. The remaining 45 developing countries showed a decline in their average applied rates, frequently by more than half. The simple average applied tariff rate for the 50 countries in the sample was 17 per cent in the 1990s and 9.1 per cent in the 2000s.[5]

The table also shows significant variations in the proportion of total tariff lines that developing countries have bound in the Uruguay Round: while all WTO members have bound all their agricultural tariff lines, many developing-country members have bound only a small proportion of the lines in the rest of their tariff schedules.

There is an apparent regional pattern. In Latin America all the countries analysed have bound virtually all their tariff lines. But in Africa and Asia many countries have bound only a small proportion of tariffs outside agriculture. In Hong Kong and Singapore, which are committed to zero applied tariff rates, 54 and 30 per cent respectively of the tariff schedule is unbound. Their practice appears to be motivated primarily by a desire to use the portion of the unbound tariff as a bargaining chip in the multilateral trade negotiations. In other countries, for example India, Nigeria and Pakistan, where an equal or even higher proportion of the tariff schedules are unbound, there may be a mixture of motivations including the desire to maintain the freedom to increase protection as needed, for development or other objectives.

---

[5] The simple arithmetic average should be interpreted with care: the data refer to different years in each of the decades. Some rates may have also increased since the data were collected.

Table 4.1 also illustrates the large differences, on average, between Uruguay Round bound and applied rates in most developing countries. Developing countries have bound their tariffs at substantially higher rates than those they apply, if they have bound them at all. For example, Brazil has bound its whole tariff schedule but at ceiling rates of 31 per cent. Sometimes (for example, Nigeria) the differences are in excess of 100 per cent. For countries which have bound the whole tariff schedule (Latin America, and a few others, for example Morocco) the average difference between applied and bound rates is 30 percentage points. In some cases, such as India, Nigeria and Pakistan, countries have bound a small portion of their tariff schedule and have used ceiling bindings with high average rates for that part which has been bound. In a very few countries, for example Ghana and Zimbabwe, a number of applied tariffs were higher than the bindings (TPRs, Ghana 2008, Zimbabwe 2010).

Ceiling bindings, just like unbound rates, allow flexibility in developing-country policy, when governments feel the need to increase protection. Since 2008, a number of developing countries, notably Brazil and Indonesia but also Fiji and Sri Lanka, increased their MFN tariffs.

Ceiling bindings offer flexibility but also carry significant risks. First, domestically, they are an invitation to particular interest groups to exert pressure on governments to increase protection. Second, for foreign suppliers they reduce predictability and increase uncertainty in terms of the market access barriers they will be facing. This in turn impedes the activity of private agents, especially where investments are marked by a degree of irreversibility, and could result in reduced inflows of foreign financing. At the same time, their widespread existence undermines developing countries' arguments that their development requires intrinsically higher levels of protection than those agreed in the WTO.

The amount of actual policy flexibility that ceiling bindings offer is much less than the formal difference between the MFN and the bound rates: some of the bound rates are so high as to be redundant and economically meaningless, in the sense that no imports would occur, even if the rates were substantially lower. Similarly, some of the applied rates are based on preferential agreements and thus cannot be increased without retaliation or other adverse trade repercussions. About a third of the difference between bound and MFN rates is thus not available as policy space for low and middle income developing countries (Foletti et al., 2009). Perhaps the greatest usefulness of ceiling bindings is as part of developing-country bargaining in multilateral trade negotiations.

Table 4.2 provides the same information as Table 4.1, but distinguishes between 'Agriculture' (HS1–24) and 'Manufactures' (HS25–97).

Table 4.1 Bound and applied tariffs in developing countries

	Latest year	Bound rate (%)	Applied rate (%)		Standard deviation	Coeff. of variation	Tariff margin	% of unbound
			Mid-1990s	Latest year				
Argentina	2011	31.9	14.4	9.8	7.2	0.7	22.1	0.0
Bangladesh	2008	167.1	26.7	14.0	9.3	0.7	153.2	84.3
Benin	2011	28.3	12.3	13.3	7.1	0.5	15.0	60.9
Bolivia	2011	40.0	9.6	9.1	8.7	1.0	30.9	0.0
Brazil	2011	31.4	13.2	13.5	8.4	0.6	17.9	0.0
Cameroon	2011	79.9	21.0	18.9	9.9	0.5	60.9	86.7
Chile	2010	25.1	11.0	4.9	2.4	0.5	20.3	0.0
China	2011	9.9	22.0	7.8	6.9	0.9	2.1	0.0
Colombia	2011	42.8	12.2	6.8	5.4	0.8	36.0	0.0
Costa Rica	2009	43.0	9.7	4.7	6.9	1.5	38.3	0.0
Côte d'Ivoire	2011	11.1	21.0	12.9	6.9	0.5	–1.9	66.6
Dominican Republic	2010	34.9	20.0	8.3	9.0	1.1	26.6	0.0
Egypt, Arab Rep.	2009	36.8	24.3	12.3	130.0	10.5	24.4	0.7
El Salvador	2010	36.7	10.0	5.0	7.3	1.5	31.6	0.0
Fiji	2011	40.1	12.4	11.8	11.0	0.9	28.4	48.9
Ghana	2009	92.5	17.5	13.0	7.3	0.6	79.5	85.6
Honduras	2009	32.4	9.6	6.4	6.9	1.1	26.0	0.0
Hong Kong, China	2011	0.0	0.0	0.0	0.0	–	0.0	53.6
India	2009	49.4	37.0	10.1	14.5	1.4	39.3	25.6
Indonesia	2011	37.2	10.8	5.0	7.8	1.6	32.3	3.4
Jamaica	2011	49.6	21.1	8.4	11.2	1.3	41.3	0.0
Kenya	2011	95.1	32.1	12.3	11.2	0.9	82.8	85.2
Korea, Rep.	2010	15.8	15.0	10.1	43.4	4.3	5.7	5.4
Kuwait	2009	100.0	6.0	4.1	2.0	0.5	96.0	0.1
Malawi	2011	74.7	25.5	12.3	10.8	0.9	62.4	68.0
Malaysia	2009	14.6	8.9	5.3	9.8	1.9	9.3	15.9
Mauritius	2011	94.4	32.7	1.2	4.8	4.0	93.2	82.2
Mexico	2010	35.0	12.6	7.3	8.7	1.2	27.7	0.0

(*continued*)

Table 4.1 Continued

	Latest year	Bound rate (%)	Applied rate (%)		Standard deviation	Coeff. of variation	Tariff margin	% of unbound
			Mid-1990s	Latest year				
Morocco	2009	41.3	23.5	9.1	13.9	1.5	32.1	0.0
Mozambique	2010	97.5	15.6	7.7	7.5	1.0	89.8	86.4
Nepal	2011	26.0	14.8	12.3	9.1	0.7	13.7	0.6
Nigeria	2010	118.3	23.0	10.9	8.2	0.8	107.4	80.8
Pakistan	2009	60.0	50.1	14.7	12.3	0.8	45.3	1.3
Paraguay	2011	33.4	11.7	8.4	7.4	0.9	25.0	0.0
Peru	2011	30.1	16.2	3.1	4.1	1.3	27.0	0.0
Philippines	2010	25.6	19.8	5.3	7.1	1.3	20.4	33.2
Saudi Arabia	2009	10.7	13.0	4.0	2.1	0.5	6.7	0.0
Senegal	2011	30.0	12.3	13.3	6.9	0.5	16.7	0.0
Singapore	2010	7.0	0.0	0.0	0.0	–	7.0	30.0
South Africa	2011	19.2	15.0	7.0	10.7	1.5	12.3	4.0
Sri Lanka	2011	29.9	20.0	9.0	12.3	1.4	21.0	61.6
Taiwan, China	2011	6.0	7.8	4.2	7.2	1.7	1.8	0.0
Thailand	2009	25.7	21.0	10.5	12.2	1.2	15.3	24.6
Tunisia	2008	57.2	29.7	21.8	17.8	0.8	35.4	41.6
Uganda	2011	73.0	16.8	12.1	11.6	1.0	60.9	84.2
Uruguay	2011	31.5	12.7	9.5	7.9	0.8	22.0	0.0
Venezuela	2011	36.5	12.8	11.8	8.2	0.7	24.7	0.0
Vietnam	2010	11.5	13.0	7.1	11.0	1.5	4.4	0.0
Zambia	2011	106.0	14.7	10.6	10.3	1.0	95.4	83.2
Zimbabwe	2007	89.8	17.2	14.7	16.2	1.1	75.1	77.6
Average		46.3	17.0	9.1	11.6	1.3	37.2	27.7

Notes: Bound and applied tariffs are based on simple averages in the mid-1990s and the latest year for which data are available. For applied tariff rates in the mid-1990s, detailed data are available for each country in Michalopoulos (2001, Table 4.1). Coefficient of variation is calculated as the standard deviation divided by the applied rate. Tariff margin is computed as the difference between bound and the latest applied tariffs. '% of unbound' is the share of tariff lines unbound.

Sources: UNCTAD TRAINS (applied tariffs) and WTO IDB (bound tariffs) databases.

Table 4.2 Bound and applied tariffs by sector in developing countries

	Latest year	Sector (HS-2)	Bound rate (%)	Applied rate (%)		Standard deviation	Coeff. of variation	Tariff margin
				Mid-1990s	Latest year			
Argentina	2011	Agriculture	32.5	11.1	8.4	7.1	0.8	24.0
		Manufactures	31.8	14.7	9.9	7.3	0.7	22.0
Bangladesh	2008	Agriculture	192.3	30.0	18.5	8.9	0.5	173.8
		Manufactures	39.6	27.0	13.6	9.2	0.7	26.0
Benin	2011	Agriculture	61.8	17.0	15.9	7.1	0.4	45.9
		Manufactures	11.3	13.7	12.9	7.1	0.5	–1.6
Bolivia	2011	Agriculture	40.0	10.0	8.2	7.2	0.9	31.8
		Manufactures	40.0	9.6	9.2	8.8	1.0	30.8
Brazil	2011	Agriculture	35.6	11.7	9.9	7.0	0.7	25.7
		Manufactures	30.8	15.4	13.7	8.4	0.6	17.1
Cameroon	2011	Agriculture	80.0	23.9	24.4	9.9	0.4	55.6
		Manufactures	62.0	17.6	18.5	9.8	0.5	43.5
Chile	2010	Agriculture	26.1	11.0	4.4	2.7	0.6	21.7
		Manufactures	25.0	11.0	4.9	2.3	0.5	20.1
China	2011	Agriculture	15.8	34.9	13.4	10.9	0.8	2.4
		Manufactures	9.1	20.8	7.4	6.2	0.8	1.6
Colombia	2011	Agriculture	91.5	14.5	9.9	9.1	0.9	81.6
		Manufactures	35.4	12.1	6.6	5.0	0.8	28.8
Costa Rica	2009	Agriculture	43.2	15.6	7.8	13.6	1.7	35.4
		Manufactures	43.0	11.4	4.5	5.6	1.2	38.5
Côte d'Ivoire	2011	Agriculture	14.9	21.5	16.3	6.5	0.4	–1.3
		Manufactures	8.6	19.2	12.5	6.9	0.5	–4.0
Dominican Republic	2010	Agriculture	39.6	14.8	13.9	9.8	0.7	25.8
		Manufactures	34.2	8.9	7.8	8.8	1.1	26.4
Egypt, Arab Rep.	2009	Agriculture	98.9	35.9	57.1	428.0	7.5	41.7
		Manufactures	27.5	23.6	9.1	61.0	6.7	18.4
El Salvador	2010	Agriculture	42.8	14.5	10.7	13.8	1.3	32.0
		Manufactures	35.7	9.6	4.6	6.1	1.3	31.1

(continued)

Table 4.2 Continued

	Latest year	Sector (HS-2)	Bound rate (%)	Applied rate (%)		Standard deviation	Coeff. of variation	Tariff margin
				Mid-1990s	Latest year			
Fiji	2011	Agriculture	40.5	14.3	15.8	12.0	0.8	24.6
		Manufactures	40.0	12.4	11.3	10.7	0.9	28.7
Ghana	2009	Agriculture	97.2	20.6	18.1	4.9	0.3	79.1
		Manufactures	37.2	13.1	12.5	7.2	0.6	24.7
Honduras	2009	Agriculture	32.1	14.5	11.7	11.3	1.0	20.4
		Manufactures	32.5	9.1	5.9	6.1	1.0	26.5
Hong Kong, China	2011	Agriculture	0.0	0.0	0.0	0.0	–	0.0
		Manufactures	0.0	0.0	0.0	0.0	–	0.0
India	2009	Agriculture	113.6	34.7	34.6	38.8	1.1	79.0
		Manufactures	34.4	28.6	8.5	6.6	0.8	25.9
Indonesia	2011	Agriculture	47.4	15.4	4.2	20.5	4.9	43.2
		Manufactures	35.6	10.4	5.0	5.9	1.2	30.6
Jamaica	2011	Agriculture	97.3	24.5	16.1	14.7	0.9	81.2
		Manufactures	42.5	20.5	7.7	10.4	1.4	34.8
Kenya	2011	Agriculture	100.0	35.2	18.7	12.9	0.7	81.3
		Manufactures	56.5	31.0	11.8	11.0	0.9	44.6
Korea, Rep.	2010	Agriculture	51.9	49.0	44.9	124.4	2.8	7.0
		Manufactures	10.2	7.7	6.7	4.6	0.7	3.5
Kuwait	2009	Agriculture	100.0	–	2.9	2.4	0.8	97.1
		Manufactures	100.0	–	4.2	1.9	0.5	95.8
Malawi	2011	Agriculture	121.3	24.5	16.5	10.5	0.6	104.8
		Manufactures	42.2	25.6	11.9	10.7	0.9	30.3
Malaysia	2009	Agriculture	12.4	4.8	2.2	5.9	2.8	10.3
		Manufactures	14.9	8.7	5.6	10.1	1.8	9.3
Mauritius	2011	Agriculture	119.6	28.8	0.7	4.1	5.5	118.9
		Manufactures	23.3	35.2	1.2	4.9	3.9	22.0
Mexico	2010	Agriculture	35.9	12.2	14.0	18.8	1.3	22.0
		Manufactures	34.9	12.4	6.9	7.8	1.1	28.0

(*continued*)

Table 4.2 Continued

	Latest year	Sector (HS-2)	Bound rate (%)	Applied rate (%)		Standard deviation	Coeff. of variation	Tariff margin
				Mid-1990s	Latest year			
Morocco	2009	Agriculture	54.4	33.3	26.2	27.9	1.1	28.3
		Manufactures	39.2	19.7	8.1	11.2	1.4	31.1
Mozambique	2010	Agriculture	100.0	26.1	10.1	8.9	0.9	89.9
		Manufactures	15.5	15.9	7.4	7.2	1.0	8.1
Nepal	2011	Agriculture	41.5	21.1	14.6	8.6	0.6	26.9
		Manufactures	23.6	21.8	12.0	9.1	0.8	11.6
Nigeria	2010	Agriculture	150.0	32.8	14.0	7.7	0.5	136.0
		Manufactures	48.9	22.3	10.6	8.2	0.8	38.3
Pakistan	2009	Agriculture	95.6	43.3	19.1	16.6	0.9	76.5
		Manufactures	54.8	50.6	14.4	11.9	0.8	40.4
Paraguay	2011	Agriculture	33.1	13.1	7.7	7.9	1.0	25.5
		Manufactures	33.5	11.5	8.5	7.4	0.9	25.0
Peru	2011	Agriculture	30.8	16.8	2.6	3.1	1.2	28.2
		Manufactures	30.0	16.2	3.2	4.2	1.3	26.9
Philippines	2010	Agriculture	35.3	27.2	8.6	10.7	1.2	26.7
		Manufactures	23.3	19.1	5.0	6.6	1.3	18.3
Saudi Arabia	2009	Agriculture	12.3	11.8	3.0	2.6	0.9	9.3
		Manufactures	10.5	12.4	4.1	2.0	0.5	6.4
Senegal	2011	Agriculture	29.8	15.6	15.7	7.0	0.4	14.2
		Manufactures	30.0	13.7	13.1	6.9	0.5	16.9
Singapore	2010	Agriculture	9.5	0.0	0.0	0.0	–	9.5
		Manufactures	6.4	0.0	0.0	0.0	–	6.4
South Africa	2011	Agriculture	41.5	10.7	6.4	10.0	1.6	35.1
		Manufactures	15.7	15.4	7.0	10.8	1.5	8.7
Sri Lanka	2011	Agriculture	49.8	29.9	21.8	14.9	0.7	28.0
		Manufactures	19.8	18.9	8.2	11.4	1.4	11.6

(continued)

Table 4.2 Continued

	Latest year	Sector (HS-2)	Bound rate (%)	Applied rate (%)		Standard deviation	Coeff. of variation	Tariff margin
				Mid-1990s	Latest year			
Taiwan, China	2011	Agriculture	14.0	19.4	8.7	13.3	1.5	5.4
		Manufactures	4.8	6.9	3.9	6.2	1.6	0.9
Thailand	2009	Agriculture	35.9	33.9	23.0	18.9	0.8	12.9
		Manufactures	24.1	20.3	9.7	11.1	1.1	14.5
Tunisia	2008	Agriculture	116.0	33.4	38.6	19.9	0.5	77.4
		Manufactures	40.1	29.5	21.0	16.6	0.8	19.1
Uganda	2011	Agriculture	77.4	21.7	18.1	14.1	0.8	59.4
		Manufactures	50.9	16.2	11.6	11.2	1.0	39.4
Uruguay	2011	Agriculture	34.0	12.1	6.2	7.0	1.1	27.9
		Manufactures	31.2	13.1	9.7	7.9	0.8	21.5
Venezuela	2011	Agriculture	55.2	13.7	13.9	10.5	0.8	41.4
		Manufactures	33.6	12.7	11.7	8.0	0.7	21.9
Vietnam	2010	Agriculture	19.0	30.0	13.5	14.9	1.1	5.5
		Manufactures	10.3	13.3	6.6	10.4	1.6	3.8
Zambia	2011	Agriculture	123.3	18.7	9.4	11.1	1.2	113.9
		Manufactures	43.5	15.1	10.6	10.2	1.0	32.9
Zimbabwe	2007	Agriculture	144.5	38.5	23.3	28.5	1.2	121.2
		Manufactures	10.4	40.8	14.2	14.3	1.0	–3.8
Average: all above developing countries		Agriculture	61.1	21.3	14.4	21.5	1.3	46.7
		Manufactures	31.7	17.2	9.0	8.9	1.1	22.7
Average: developed countries		Agriculture	17.3	9.3	6.2	12.2	2.3	11.1
		Manufactures	6.6	5.5	3.2	4.5	1.9	3.4

Note: The classification of sector is defined as agricultural products HS 1–24 and manufacturing products HS 25–97.
Sources: UNCTAD TRAINS (applied tariffs) and WTO IDB (bound tariffs) databases.

The table shows that for most countries average applied tariffs on agricultural products are higher than tariffs for the rest of the product groups – which include raw materials, fuels and manufactures. But there are many exceptions, especially in Latin America (Argentina, Brazil, Chile) as well as in South Africa and Malaysia. The exceptions are even fewer in the case of bound tariffs, with only Malaysia and a number of countries which have chosen ceiling bindings at the same rates for both agricultural and other products.

Developing countries' average applied tariff rates are much higher than for developed countries both for agriculture and manufactures. Interestingly, however, the variation in the applied tariff rate structure of the developing countries is lower than that for developed countries. This is true both in manufactures where there are many tariff peaks (see p. 141) and in agriculture where the main reason was the developed countries' tariffication of non-tariff barriers in agriculture following the Uruguay Round. For both sets of countries the import weighted tariff rates tend to be lower, especially in manufactures, partly because of the predominance of zero rates for many products (in particular in developed countries), and partly because of the PTAs in these countries. And the bias against agriculture appears to have diminished over time.[6]

Finally, Table 4.3 shows simple averages for applied and bound tariffs as well as for differences between the two for different developing-country income groups and regions for agricultural and manufactured products and for total trade. The averages contained in this table should be used with caution for reasons discussed earlier (see note 5). It is interesting, nonetheless, to note the pattern that both average bound and applied tariffs tend to vary inversely with per capita income: the poorer the country, the higher the tariffs. This holds for all sectors and groups with the exception of applied tariffs in agriculture, where there is little difference between the average for the low and middle-income developing countries. Similarly, the average differences in the margins between applied and bound tariffs tend to be highest in the low-income countries and lowest in the highest income ones.

There are a few points to note in the regional breakdown as well. First, the few sub-Saharan African countries that have bound tariffs have done so at levels on average higher than in the other regions. But this is due primarily because of higher bindings on agricultural products. On manufactures the highest average rates are in Latin America. Also, the

[6] For import weighted tariff data by country grouping see Anderson et al. (2005).

Table 4.3 Average tariffs in sectoral product categories by income group and region

Country group (no. of countries)	Bound rate			Applied rate			Tariff margin		
	All goods	Agric. goods	Manuf. goods	All goods	Agric. goods	Manuf. goods	All goods	Agric. goods	Manuf. goods
By income level									
Developed economies (21)	8.5	17.3	6.6	3.4	6.2	3.2	5.1	11.1	3.4
Developing economies (135)	43.2	59.3	32.8	9.8	13.6	9.5	33.4	45.7	23.3
High income developing (18)	26.9	37.9	25.2	7.8	9.9	7.7	19.1	28.0	17.5
Upper middle income (39)	37.0	57.6	31.1	9.5	12.4	9.2	27.5	45.1	21.9
Lower middle income (46)	41.6	57.1	33.0	9.8	15.5	9.3	31.8	41.7	23.7
Low income (32)	62.1	76.2	38.6	11.5	14.5	11.3	50.5	61.7	27.3
Least developed countries (42)	61.2	76.2	41.8	12.0	15.3	11.7	49.1	60.9	30.0
World (156)	39.0	54.3	29.6	9.0	12.6	8.7	30.1	41.6	20.9
By region (developing countries)									
Asia (36)	32.4	44.0	23.2	8.1	13.3	7.7	24.3	30.7	15.5
Latin America and Caribbean (34)	42.0	61.1	38.7	9.7	12.3	9.4	32.3	48.8	29.3
Europe, Middle East and N. Africa (21)	28.9	43.8	26.1	8.2	13.6	7.8	20.7	30.2	18.3
Sub-Saharan Africa (44)	57.4	74.5	37.0	12.2	14.9	11.9	45.2	59.6	25.0
BRICS 5 countries	27.5	51.6	22.5	9.2	14.3	8.8	18.3	37.3	13.6
OPEC 12 countries	47.1	55.9	37.7	8.5	10.4	8.4	38.6	45.5	29.4
WTO 50 developing countries	46.3	61.7	30.8	9.1	14.5	8.7	37.2	47.3	22.1

Sources: UNCTAD TRAINS (applied tariffs) and WTO IDB (bound tariffs) databases.

simple average bound tariffs on agricultural products in Africa and Latin America tend to be much higher than in Asia.

For many developing countries tariff escalation is also an issue, as other developing countries are becoming more important as markets. Escalation is measured by calculating the average tariff rates applied to three groups of products: raw materials, intermediate products and final goods. Table 4.4 overleaf summarizes the information. The table shows that by and large, and for most sectors, escalation seems to be inversely related to per capita income. With few exceptions, low-income countries and sub-Saharan Africa tend to have the highest degree of escalation. In some cases, however, (LDCs' parts and accessories relative to capital goods) there is reverse escalation. Among sectors, automobiles and food processing have the highest escalation. By comparison, tariff escalation in developed countries, while still present in some sectors, is minimal compared to that of developing countries.

Non-tariff measures

The analysis of non-tariff measures (NTMs) has three main dimensions:

- The relative importance of the different policy measures employed by all developing countries in the sample, as measured by the frequency of their use;
- The main product categories whose importation is affected by NTMs across the countries in the sample;
- The overall use of NTMs by developing countries to control imports over the period 1990–2012, as measured by the overall frequency of application of such measures.

The analysis relies on frequency ratios as indicators of the existence and scope of protective measures on different products by various countries. The advantages and limitations of frequency ratios as indicators of protection are well understood (Nogues et al., 1986; OECD, 1997). These ratios are indicators of the extent to which countries resort to particular measures and the proportion of total products in terms of tariff lines or product groups that are affected by such measures, irrespective of the value of the products actually imported. They do not necessarily capture the protective effect of the measures taken. The protective effect of a prohibition of the importation of a product into, for example, Thailand is going to be completely different from the application of a variable levy in Uruguay or the use of a non-automatic licence by India. The frequency ratios are presented here in order to give overall impressions of the trade regimes in place in individual countries and the various measures used by different countries on different products – not to measure the actual protection provided to each product or product group. A detailed discussion of the estimating procedures and their limitations is presented in Appendix B. It is important to bear in mind these limitations and use the estimates of the prevalence of NTMs with caution. These indicators are more useful in tracing the evolution of trade regimes within each country over time, than for making intercountry comparisons, especially when the differences in indicator values are small.

The NTMs include non-automatic import licensing (and approvals), import prohibitions (partial or total), quotas, tariff quotas, variable levies and/or minimum pricing, and import monitoring. Frequency ratios were calculated for each measure as well as a total for each country.

The relative importance of different kinds of NTMs

The relative importance of different kinds of NTMs employed by developing countries over time is shown in Table 4.5. The table shows the product coverage of each NTM employed by each developing country relative to 97 product categories at the HS 2-digit level or for some countries and measures at the HS 6-digit level.[7] Thus, for example, the row for Argentina shows that non-automatic licensing affected products in 3 per cent of the 97 product categories during the GATT period (1992).

The data reveal several policy tendencies for the developing countries analysed. First, non-automatic import licensing (including various forms of administrative approvals) continues to be the measure that affects by far the greatest number of products imported into these countries, with prohibitions of various kinds ranking second. An effort was made to exclude from consideration in these calculations the large number of products which are subject to non-automatic licensing to ensure public health, safety, environmental and other standards. These are frequently justified by reference to GATT Article XX. Even so, during the early period considered (1990–94) non-automatic licensing affected large proportions of developing country imports: more than a quarter of the product categories. Several countries, such as Bangladesh, India, Nigeria and Pakistan, have indicated that the licensing and prohibition measures which they used were due to balance-of-payments difficulties.

No effort was made in this study to determine the consistency of these licensing arrangements or, for that matter, any other member

---

[7] These estimates have been obtained from the UNCTAD/World Bank NTM database.

Table 4.4 Tariff escalation in developed and developing countries in 2010 (unweighted average, %)

Country group	Food & bev products			Industrial products			Capital goods			Transport equipment					Consumer goods		
	Final goods	Food prim.	Food proc.	Final goods	Ind prim.	Ind proc.	All cap	Cap goods	Pts & acc.	All transp.	Auto	Others	Pts & acc.	All cons	Durable	Semi-dur.	Non-dur.
By income level																	
Developed economies	7.3	6.2	7.9	3.0	2.0	3.0	1.7	1.7	1.8	2.8	2.9	3.8	2.5	6.0	3.8	7.1	5.3
Developing economies	14.9	13.1	15.7	8.7	6.7	8.8	6.2	6.0	6.6	11.0	21.7	9.9	10.3	14.8	14.1	16.4	13.0
High income developing economies	10.6	11.6	10.4	7.4	6.4	7.5	7.4	7.4	7.5	8.5	13.0	6.6	8.5	9.2	9.1	9.6	8.5
Upper middle-income econ.	13.8	12.4	14.3	7.6	5.0	7.7	5.7	5.6	5.7	11.5	26.3	11.0	10.8	16.1	14.0	17.9	14.2
Lower middle-income econ.	17.1	14.0	18.5	8.7	7.4	8.8	5.5	5.2	6.0	10.9	22.2	9.9	10.0	14.9	14.2	16.7	13.0
Low income economies	15.5	13.4	16.3	10.8	8.1	10.9	7.3	6.9	8.0	11.6	20.1	10.1	11.0	16.2	16.8	17.9	13.9
Of which least developed	16.4	14.6	17.0	11.7	9.8	11.7	8.0	7.6	8.9	12.4	20.8	10.7	11.7	16.6	17.1	18.1	14.3
By region																	
World	13.9	12.2	14.6	7.9	6.1	8.0	5.6	5.4	5.9	9.9	19.1	9.0	9.2	13.6	12.7	15.1	11.9
Developing economies	14.9	13.1	15.7	8.7	6.7	8.8	6.2	6.0	6.6	11.0	21.7	9.9	10.3	14.8	14.1	16.4	13.0
Asia	14.5	13.9	14.9	7.4	6.7	7.4	5.4	5.1	5.8	11.1	28.0	10.3	10.1	11.4	10.3	12.6	10.2

(continued)

Table 4.4 Continued

Country group	Food & bev products			Industrial products			Capital goods			Transport equipment					Consumer goods		
	Final goods	Food prim.	Food proc.	Final goods	Ind prim.	Ind proc.	All cap	Cap goods	Pts & acc.	All transp.	Auto	Others	Pts & acc.	All cons	Durable	Semi-dur.	Non-dur.
Latin America and Caribbean	13.7	12.8	14.0	7.9	5.0	8.1	6.2	6.3	5.9	10.6	21.4	9.9	10.0	15.2	15.0	16.4	13.5
Europe, Middle East and N. Africa	15.4	10.2	17.8	6.9	5.7	7.0	5.6	5.4	5.9	8.7	12.9	8.1	8.4	12.8	11.6	14.5	11.2
Sub-Saharan Africa	15.9	14.1	16.5	11.2	8.6	11.3	7.2	6.7	8.1	12.2	21.8	10.4	11.5	18.2	17.4	20.3	15.6
BRICS-5	15.9	12.3	17.5	7.7	4.4	7.9	6.1	6.2	6.0	10.2	34.1	13.1	8.1	13.6	10.0	15.4	12.2
OPEC-12	12.1	9.8	13.1	7.7	5.4	7.8	5.8	5.8	5.7	8.2	19.0	8.7	7.5	15.0	13.0	17.2	13.3
WTO-50	16.4	13.5	17.7	8.2	5.4	8.3	5.2	4.9	5.6	10.7	23.7	10.4	9.8	14.7	13.1	16.4	12.9

Notes: The product categories are defined on the basis of the UN Broad Economic Categories (BEC) as follows: food & beverages include food primary (111) and food processed (112); industrial products include primary products include industrial primary (221) and, industrial processed (222); capital goods include capital goods (441) and parts & accessories (442); transport equipment include automobiles (551), other transport equipment (552), and parts & accessories (553); consumer goods include durable goods (661), semi-durable (662), and non-durable (663). Data are based on the latest year available in applied rates from each country.

Sources: UNCTAD TRAINS databases.

Table 4.5 Non-tariff measures in developing countries

	Year	Non-auto licensing	Prohibition	Quotas	Tariff quotas*	Other	Variable levies
Argentina	2008	85*	34*	3*			
	1999	1		1			1†
	1992	3		2			
Bangladesh	2012						17†
	1992	34	43				
Benin	2010		1				
	1997		1				
Bolivia	2008	12*	4*				
Brazil	2009				1		
	1996	11	11	1			1
	1993	10	7			100**	
Cameroon	2007	3			1		
	1995	8					
Chile	2009				1		3
	1997		1				4
	1991		1				5
China	2012	1			1		
Colombia	2012	19*	4*		3		6
	1996	6	1				6
	1990	55	7	3			
Costa Rica	1995	6			6		
Côte d'Ivoire	2012				1		
	1995	31		5			
Dominican Rep.	2008				0		
	1996	5	1			1**	
Egypt	2011						42*†
	1993	14	53				
El Salvador	1996	5	1	1			
Fiji	2009						4†
	1997	5					
Ghana	1992		3				
Hong Kong, China	1990					16**	
India	2011	4				4**	4
	1998	94	3				
	1993	99	1				

(*continued*)

Table 4.5 Continued

	Year	Non-auto licensing	Prohibition	Quotas	Tariff quotas*	Other	Variable levies
Indonesia	2011	26*					
	1998	31					
	1991	53	5	3			1†
Jamaica	2011	4					
Kenya	2011	37*					10*†
	1994	87					
Korea Rep.	2008			1	2		0.1
	1996			1	25		
	1992	32		3	26		
Kuwait	2012	1					
Malawi	2010	4					
Malaysia	2010	6			3		
	1997	20	14	2	7		
	1993	55	4	2			
Mauritius	2009	14*					
	1995	9	7				
Mexico	2008				2		
	1997	6	1		7		
	1993	28		2			2
Morocco	2011	2*		2*			
	1996	13			1		
	1990	51					24
Mozambique	2009						3
Nepal	2012	1					
Nigeria	2011	17					
	1998	2	9				
	1991		14				
Pakistan	1995		17	1			
Paraguay	2008	1*	1*				1
Peru	2008		1*				2
	1994						6
Philippines	2012	5		1			
	1993	7	4	1			
Senegal	2011	2*	1*				
	1994	10		5			
Singapore	1996	1					
	1992	1					

(*continued*)

Table 4.5 Continued

	Year	Non-auto licensing	Prohibition	Quotas	Tariff quotas*	Other	Variable levies
South Africa	2009			1	5		3
	1998	5		3			
	1993	36					
Sri Lanka	2010	4					
	1995	23					
Taiwan, China	2010				1		
Thailand	2007	3			8		
	1995	11	6	1	12		
	1991	36		2		2**	3
Tunisia	2011						22*†
	1994	54					2
Uganda	1995	3					
Uruguay	2012	3					
	1998					4**	
	1992			1	1		31
Venezuela	2008	24*	3*	1*			
	1996	2	3				13
Zambia	1996		1				
Zimbabwe	2011					100***	
	1995	23					

Notes: Frequency ratio in percentage of HS 2-digit products affected by each NTM. All countries report several product categories – usually 15–30 per cent of tariff lines as subject to licensing and/or prohibitions for health, sanitation, safety or defence reasons. Only licensing and/or prohibitions for economic reasons are reported here.
* in per cent at HS 6-digit level; ** import monitoring; *** exchange control; † surcharges.
Sources: GATT TPR (1989–1994); WTO TPR (1995–2012); UNCTAD/World Bank NTM database.

policies with GATT provisions. The limitations of the WTO's system of voluntary notifications are well understood (Bachetta et al., 2012). A significant part of the total membership has not provided information on the licensing procedures they use or notifications of quantitative restrictions they employ. Most of the members notifying the use of quantitative restrictions did so under GATT Article XX. Three members, India, Korea and the Philippines, also justified restrictions under the balance-of-payments provisions of Article XVIIIb.

While caution is needed when interpreting the findings on the evolution of policy over time – because the sample of countries is partly different in the three sub-periods examined – the data do strongly suggest that the utilization of all 'core' NTMs with clearly protective effect, such as licensing, prohibitions, quotas and variable levies/administrative pricing, has declined over time. This is shown by the decreasing frequency ratios over time for the large majority of countries for which data are available. The only measure clearly showing an increase is the use of tariff quotas, which is permitted under the Uruguay Round Agreement in agriculture.

The main products affected by NTMs

The TPRs show that agricultural products (Group I–IV or HS1–24) were the most subject to overall controls especially in the earlier period. The number of countries imposing these controls has substantially declined in the period 1995–98, following the tariffication in agriculture under the Uruguay Round Agreements (see Michalopoulos, 2001, Table 4.6). In addition to agriculture, mineral products, in particular fuels (HS-27), rubber products (HS-40), machinery, especially electrical machinery (HS-85) and precious stones and metals continued to be subject to controls, especially through licensing in a significant number of countries in all periods (see also Michalopoulos, 1999b, Table A3).[8]

The Uruguay Round Agreement subjected the agricultural sector for the first time to some of the same trade disciplines that apply to other sectors. However, it did not result in significant liberalization of developed-country policies. At the time the agreements were being negotiated, the main developing-country concerns focused on the market access issues and the benefits that some of the key agricultural exporters would obtain, as well on the possible adverse impact that reduced export subsidies in developed countries would have on developing countries that were net food importers.[9] Little attention was focused, until the decade of the 2000s, on the level of support and the kinds of measures appropriate for developing countries to implement in pursuit of their own agricultural development which is essential to the elimination of poverty, itself very often mainly a rural phenomenon.

The Uruguay Round Agreement on Agriculture contains provisions which permit developing countries to increase their support to

[8] Table 6.3 suggests that the product groups that are the focus of anti-dumping actions, both in developed and developing countries, tend to be somewhat similar and include especially basic metals and chemicals.

[9] It should be recalled, however, as part of the Uruguay Round agreements and previous negotiations, that there were significant reductions in tariffs on horticultural and floricultural products of interest to developing countries.

agriculture (and of poor consumers) through means not available to developed countries. For example, direct and indirect investment and input subsidies to poor farmers are excluded from the calculation of aggregate measures of support (AMS); reduction of the support commitments by developing countries may take ten years to implement, while LDCs are totally exempt; and food subsidies to the urban and rural poor are excluded from the calculation of AMS. However, a number of critics have pointed to the 'unfairness' of the agriculture agreement as it still permits greater support levels for developed countries (which in the past have given a great deal of assistance to their agricultural sector) than developing countries which penalized agriculture in the base period (Das, 1998). Also, the Special Safeguard Mechanism in the agreement was designed in such a way as to be of limited use to developing countries that had not tariffed their agricultural protection.

Following the launching of the Doha Round, developing countries focused without success on developing a viable Special Safeguard Mechanism that would cover all of their agricultural production, emphasizing the special concerns that arise in relation to the welfare of their poor farmers in the case of an import surge. In practice, the most common cause of import surges has been shortfalls in developing-country domestic production. Developing countries which are keen to reduce the variability of food prices both to their poor consumers as well as to their farmers have resorted to an extensive use of variable price supports and export taxes on agricultural commodities.

Trade remedies

Trade remedies include anti-dumping, countervailing and safeguard actions. In principle, such actions are consistent with GATT provisions. The legal basis and procedures for the imposition of trade remedies in each instance are as various as are remedies, which usually do not involve quantitative restrictions but changes in duties and charges to address the problem appropriately in each case. In the case of anti-dumping and countervailing duties, these remedies are intended to correct for distortions that occur when exporters are obtaining subsidies and engaging in discriminatory pricing practices which result in injury to domestic producers. In the case of safeguards, the issue is simply injury to domestic producers, even if no unfair trade practices are involved.

Evidence regarding the frequency with which developing countries have taken trade remedy actions is presented in Table 4.6. Since it

Table 4.6 Anti-dumping investigations in developed and developing countries, 1978–2011

	By reporting member (no. of cases)			By exporting member (no. of cases)		
	Developed members	Developing members	Developed as % of total	Developed members	Developing members	Developed as % of total
GATT						
1978	6	0	100	5	1	83
1979	58	0	100	54	4	93
1980	72	0	100	66	6	92
1981	94	0	100	77	17	82
1982	221	0	100	174	47	79
1983	178	0	100	130	48	73
1984	159	0	100	119	40	75
1985	206	0	100	131	75	64
1986	156	5	97	105	56	65
1987	101	19	84	86	34	72
1988	112	12	90	78	46	63
1989	87	9	91	55	41	57
1990	149	18	89	80	87	48
1991	209	19	92	139	89	61
1992	260	65	80	167	158	51
1993	149	157	49	140	166	46
1994	138	91	60	96	133	42
WTO						
1995	78	79	50	71	86	45
1996	79	147	35	95	131	42
1997	127	119	52	125	121	51
1998	90	176	34	135	131	51
1999	176	182	49	154	204	43
2000	138	160	46	130	168	44
2001	179	193	48	145	227	39
2002	109	206	35	127	188	40
2003	86	148	37	90	144	38
2004	113	107	51	61	159	28
2005	62	139	31	44	157	22
2006	71	133	35	49	155	24
2007	61	104	37	38	127	23
2008	75	138	35	48	165	23
2009	64	145	31	48	161	23
2010	38	133	22	66	105	39
2011	63	92	41	44	111	28

Sources: GATT and WTO anti-dumping database.

has been argued that the mere initiation of an investigation on anti-dumping action tends to have a restraining effect on imports, irrespective of the outcome of the case (Finger, 1993; OECD, 1997), the main indicator used in this table is the number of anti-dumping investigations that had been initiated each year going back to 1978. The table shows that the percentage of actions by the developing countries and against them changed spectacularly over the period of the last 30 plus years. Until 1986 no developing country had initiated an anti-dumping action, although they were subject to some anti-dumping actions by the developed countries. Over time the situation was totally reversed: developing countries initiated the majority of the actions and were the subject of most of the anti-dumping actions, both by other developing countries and the developed countries. The peak year for anti-dumping investigations (206) by developing countries was 2002, while 2001 was the peak year for investigations against them (227). Since that time anti-dumping investigations appear to have declined both by developed and developing countries.

Table 4.7 shows the number of anti-dumping, countervailing and safeguard measures taken by the 50 countries in our sample cumulatively over the period 1995–2011 as well as the number of products affected by these actions. The last four columns show the number of trade remedy measures in place in each country in mid-2011. The first thing to note about the table is that anti-dumping is by far the most popular instrument, dwarfing countervailing or safeguard actions. Indeed, out of 50 countries, 24 initiated anti-dumping measures, 15 safeguards and only nine took countervailing actions. As of mid-2011, 19 developing countries had trade remedy measures in place involving at least some anti-dumping, which accounted for over 90 per cent of the remedial actions they took.

Among developing countries, anti-dumping is, for the most part, a middle and higher income developing-country practice. Argentina, Brazil, China, India, Korea, Mexico and South Africa account for the bulk of developing-country actions. Pakistan is the country with the lowest per capita income ($1,190 in 2011) that has an anti-dumping action. India is the country that has taken the most measures over the period. It is also the country with the most measures in place in 2011. Mexico is the country that has used anti-dumping actions affecting by far the largest number of products over time (1,685), earlier estimated at 28 per cent of the tariff lines (Michalopoulos, 2001). The main reason for this is that it applied anti-dumping measures across broad categories of products, such as all the tariff lines in several whole HS2 product groups, for instance textiles against China.[10] However, a great number of these measures have at present expired.

The overall use of NTMs

The overall use of NTMs by developing countries during the GATT and WTO sub-periods is presented in Table 4.8. Column one shows country per capita income in 2011. Column two shows an openness index for each country calculated as the ratio of exports plus imports divided by GDP, also in 2011. Column three shows the presence of tariff peaks in the latest tariff schedule. Column four shows the total number of cases of NTMs in place as of June 2011. The other columns show total frequency ratios (*Tfm*) for 'core' NTMs (see Appendix B for a discussion of the meaning of total frequency ratios) for different periods. Core measures are defined as those that involve quantitative restrictions or price controls on imports, such as non-automatic licensing of any kind, prohibitions, quotas and tariff quotas as well as variable import levies and administrative/minimum pricing. As a particular product category may be affected by more than one NTM, duplicative measures have been excluded in this calculation.

The first point to note from the table is that in the GATT part of the period covered (1990–94) the values of the total frequency ratios for NTMs were extremely high for several countries – covering more than 50 per cent of products in such countries as Bangladesh, Colombia, Egypt, Kenya, India, Indonesia, Malaysia, Morocco and Tunisia. Without doubt NTMs at that time were an important feature of many developing countries in all regions. Subsequently, the data strongly suggest that the total frequency ratios have been substantially reduced. There are exceptions: for example both Argentina and Zimbabwe have introduced extensive foreign currency controls which de facto substantially limit trade. Tariff quotas have increased since the earlier period as a consequence of the implementation of the Uruguay Round provisions in agriculture.

Second, as with tariffs, there is a tendency for the total frequency ratios of NTMs to be greater in countries with lower levels of per capita income and lower degrees of openness. Third, the most important recent development is the very large increase during the period 1999–2011 in the use of trade remedies, especially anti-dumping, compared to the period 1990–98. While strictly comparable data are not available, the tariff line frequencies of anti-dumping measures in the earlier period rarely exceeded 1 per cent

[10] The anti-dumping measures taken by Mexico and several other countries had been increasingly directed against imports from non-WTO members (see also Chapter 6).

Table 4.7 Trade remedy measures 1995–2011 and in force in 2011, by developing country

Country	Antidumping (AD) 1995–2011		Countervailing (CV), 1995–2011		Safeguards (SG) 1995–2011	
	No. of measures	No. of products**	No. of measures	No. of products**	No. of measures	No. of products**
Argentina	206	1,075	4	32	4	82
Brazil	119	541	7	53	2	23
Chile	9	35	2	85	7	158
China	151	378	4	40	1	223
Colombia	24	196	–	–	1	7
Costa Rica	3	10	1	2	–	–
Dominican Republic	1	1	–	–	2	12
Egypt	53	69	–	–	4	25
India	478	1,465	–	–	13	108
Indonesia	42	288	–	–	10	60
Jamaica	4	15	–	–	–	–
Korea, Republic of	72	336	–	–	2	17
Malaysia	25	59	–	–	–	–
Mexico	85	1,685	8	65	–	–
Morocco	–	–	–	–	2	23
Pakistan	36	294	–	20	–	–
Paraguay	2	2	–	–	–	–
Peru	49	379	5	35	–	–
Philippines	11	51	–	–	7	18
Singapore	2	2	–	–	–	–
South Africa	128	460	5	20	1	2
Taipei, Chinese	15	172	–	–	–	–
Thailand	34	318	–	–	1	1
Uruguay	1	12	–	–	–	–
Venezuela	25	94	1	8	5	109
Memo items:						
Other Developing (3)	9	37	–	38	16	87
Developed (13)	1,017	20,963	133	11,460	44	1,728
All countries (41)	2,601	28,937	170	11,860	122	2,683

Notes: – data not available; * number of measures in force based on notifications to WTO as of 30 June 2011; ** total products affected by AD, CV and SG are based on number of products on raw data files at HS 6, 8, 9, 10-digit level or mixed together in reporting countries.

Sources: WTO Anti-dumping database and Trade Profiles data; Bown (2012).

Total AD+CV+SG, 1995–2011		Measures in force, 2011*			
No. of measures	No. of products**	Anti-dumping	Counter-vailing	Safeguards	Total AD+CV+SG
214	1,189	96	0	0	96
128	617	75	1	1	77
18	278	1	0	0	1
156	641	115	2	0	117
25	203	12	–	0	12
4	12	2	0	–	2
3	13	1	–	2	3
57	94	15	–	0	15
491	1,573	206	–	2	208
52	348	16	–	9	25
4	15	–	–	–	–
74	353	33	–	0	33
25	59	6	–	–	6
93	1,750	38	0	–	38
2	23	–	–	0	0
36	314	33	–	–	33
2	2	–	–	–	–
54	414	21	2	–	23
18	69	1	–	5	6
2	2	–	–	–	–
134	482	33	1	0	34
15	172	6	–	–	6
35	319	23	–	1	24
1	12	–	–	–	–
31	211	–	–	0	0
25	162	1	–	3	4
1,194	34,151	604	74	11	689
2,893	43,480	1,338	80	34	1,452

Table 4.8 Income level, openness and trade restrictions

Country	GDP per capita in 2011 (in US$)	Openness in 2011 (trade/ GDP)	Tariff peak /a (as % of total tariff lines)	No. of antidumping products /b	No. of cases & measures in AD, CV, SG /c	Ratio of core NTMs (in %) /d			
						Core NTMs 1990–95	Core NTMs 1995–98	Tariff quota /e 2001–2012	Core NTMs 2001–2012
Kuwait	62,664	86	0.0	0	0	..	..	0	1
Singapore	46,241	386	0.0	2	0	1	2	0	0
Hong Kong, China	34,457	440	0.0	0	0	15	0	0	0
Korea, Rep.	22,424	102	6.4	336	33	35	1	2	1
Saudi Arabia	20,540	97	0.0	..	0	..	..	..	..
Taiwan, China	20,139	140	0.0	172	6	..	..	1	0
Chile	14,394	70	0.0	35	1	6	5	1	3
Uruguay	13,866	53	29.0	12	0	32	0	0	3
Brazil	12,594	23	27.5	541	77	17	23	1	1
Argentina	10,941	40	21.6	1075	96	5	3	0	100
Venezuela	10,810	46	44.0	94	0	..	18	0	28
Mexico	10,064	62	5.8	1685	38	32	7	2	0
Malaysia	9,656	177	15.9	59	6	61	36	3	6
Mauritius	8,797	116	6.0	0	0	..	16	0	14
Costa Rica	8,676	78	0.6	10	2	..	6	1	..
South Africa	8,070	55	22.6	460	24	36	8	5	4
Colombia	7,067	34	17.3	196	12	65	13	3	29
Peru	6,009	48	0.0	379	23	6	1	0	3
Jamaica	5,562	71	42.9	15	0	..	..	0	4
Dominican Rep.	5,530	56	30.4	1	3	..	-	0	0
China	5,445	55	13.3	378	117	--	--	1	6
Thailand	4,972	135	18.9	318	24	41	18	8	3
Fiji	4,391	117	36.8	0	0	..	5	0	4
Tunisia	4,297	103	57.0	0	0	56	...	0	22
El Salvador	3,702	69	1.7	0	0	..	7	..	..
Paraguay	3,635	112	20.2	0	0	..	..	0	3
Indonesia	3,495	47	7.4	288	25	61	31	0	26
Morocco	3,054	76	23.6	1	0	75	13	0	4
Sri Lanka	2,835	52	42.6	0	0	..	23	0	4
Egypt, Arab Rep.	2,781	47	18.4	69	15	67	..	0	42

(*continued*)

Table 4.8 Continued

Country	GDP per capita in 2011 (in US$)	Openness in 2011 (trade/ GDP)	Tariff peak /a (as % of total tariff lines)	No. of antidumping products /b	No. of cases & measures in AD, CV, SG /c	Ratio of core NTMs (in %) /d			
						Core NTMs 1990–95	Core NTMs 1995–98	Tariff quota /e 2001–2012	Core NTMs 2001–2012
Bolivia	2,421	76	17.5	0	0	--	..	0	16
Philippines	2,370	71	5.0	51	6	12	..	0	6
Honduras	2,226	108	0.5	3	0	..	..	..	..
Ghana	1,570	71	40.5	0	0	3	..	..	..
India	1,489	50	6.3	1465	208	100	97	0	8
Nigeria	1,452	69	35.0	0	0	14	11	0	17
Zambia	1,425	79	48.6	0	0	..	1	..	..
Vietnam	1,411	165	23.1	0	0	..	..	..	..
Cameroon	1,271	61	54.1	0	0	8	..	1	3
Cote d'Ivoire	1,195	77	46.8	0	0	36	..	1	0
Pakistan	1,194	32	44.5	294	33	18	..	..	..
Senegal	1,119	68	50.1	0	0	10	..	0	3
Kenya	808	65	37.7	0	0	87	..	0	47
Benin	802	42	50.3	0	0	..	1	0	1
Zimbabwe	776	126	32.9	0	0	23	..	0	100
Bangladesh	735	43	38.0	0	0	77		0	17
Nepal	619	46	45.3	0	0	..	..	0	1
Mozambique	535	71	23.8	0	0	..	..	0	3
Uganda	487	58	37.7	0	0	..	3	..	..
Malawi	371	78	33.9	0	0	..	..	0	4

Notes:
a Number of tariff lines in percentage at HS 6-digit level with applied rate at 15% or above in 2011 or latest data available.
b Number of antidumping products at HS 6-, 8-, 10- or mixed digit level under investigation as of 2011.
c Number of cases or measures in notifications to WTO in antidumping, countervailing duties, and safeguards as of 2011.
d Frequency ratio in percentage of core non-tariff measures (NTMs) in HS 2-digit product categories.
e Tariff quota data are computed in HS 6-digit products due to data available in WTO TPR reports.
.. data not available.

Sources: World Bank WDI database (GDPPC, GDP and trade data), UNCTAD TRAINS database (tariff data), World Bank TTB database (Antidumping products), and WTO Trade Profiles and TPR reports (various years).

(with Mexico being the exception), while in the later period the number of products affected by trade remedies in countries like Argentina, India, China, Korea and Chinese Taipei are likely to be much higher. In some cases (e.g. India) liberalization of the trade regime has taken the form of reducing licensing and increasing the use of trade remedies.

Overall, Table 4.8 suggests that high income developing countries tend to have less overall tariff and non-tariff restrictions to trade; low income countries have higher tariff barriers but limited use of trade remedies; while middle income countries have high use of trade remedies while their tariff structure is somewhat in-between that of the low and high income developing countries.

Finally in some lower income economies the greatest NTMs have little to do with formal barriers. The latest TPR (2012) of the East African Community (EAC) is instructive in this regard. The EAC has no formal NTMs either with respect to the rest of the world or for internal trade. Yet in December 2008 the EAC Secretariat identified 35 NTMs that impeded trade, of which 12 involved customs and administrative procedures, 11 business licensing and roadblocks, and nine TBT and SPS (WTO, 2012h, p. 8).

SPS and TBT

The establishment of the SPS and TBT agreements has had a variety of implications for developing countries. Practically all developing-country members of the WTO have institutions that deal with the maintenance of technical standards and enforce the health, sanitary and phyto-sanitary regulations, as agreed. However, there is serious doubt about the capacity of many of these institutions to implement regulations. For example, most developing countries have legislation on national standards that are based on those of the International Standards Organization (ISO), of which many are also members. But in some cases, for example Zambia, there appear to be no government testing facilities. Most countries report that they have concluded numerous formal bilateral mutual recognition agreements on technical standards. But it is not clear whether these agreements provide adequate information to producers on the standards applicable in countries where they may consider marketing their products.

The situation regarding sanitary and phyto-sanitary measures appears to be quite similar. Countries have established regulations requiring sanitary or phyto-sanitary certificates for imported food, drugs and agricultural and veterinary products. Again, the standards used are supposed to be based on those laid down in international agreements such as the Codex Alimentarius. But it is difficult to judge the adequacy of the regulations or the effectiveness of the institutions entrusted with their implementation. The TPRs suggest that the situation in many low-income countries is far from satisfactory. For example, in Malawi the SPS legislation is reportedly outdated and the country also lacks adequate facilities to test products for import or for export. Similarly, in Tanzania 'the Plant Health Service (PHS) has 165 inspectors based at 28 entry points (out of 51). However, most entry posts are poorly equipped for pest inspection, staff often do not have specific training in phytosanitary matters and have little or no direct communication with PHS headquarters. Hence pest surveillance capacity is severely constrained. Due to these shortcomings, Tanzania has suffered some outbreaks of plant pests and diseases (including cassava green mite, large grain borer in maize, banana wilt disease and a variety of fruit fly that infests citrus and mango-growing areas' (WTO, 2012h, p. A4–416).

In recent periods, concern has been expressed by many that the TBT and SPS provisions are used by countries to camouflage protection (Gourdon and Nicita, 2012). This may well be the case in some situations. But it is difficult to discover protective intent when there are legitimate reasons to introduce more effective TBT and SPS controls. And the problem in some developing countries may be not that there are too many controls but not enough.

Measures that affect exports

There are clear links between a country's trade policies that affect its exports and those that affect its imports: for example, measures to control exports of raw materials that are used as inputs by domestic industries distort resource allocation in much the same way as import protection measures for that industry. Similarly, the imposition of measures that restrict the quantity and increase the domestic price of imports may adversely affect the profitability of exports and a country to take offsetting measures in favour of exporters.[11] Thus, it is not surprising to find that, over the period reviewed, developing countries liberalized their policies affecting exports in much the same direction as they liberalized policies affecting imports.

Developing countries' policies towards exports are characterized by the following broad tendency: to impose controls and taxes on their exports

---

[11] The broad theoretical point is covered in the so-called Lerner symmetry theorem on the equivalence of import and export taxes (Lerner, 1936).

of primary products and foodstuffs while providing incentives and subsidies to their exports of manufactures. The control and taxation of exports of primary products have had two purposes: to capture some of the rents from the production and sale of raw materials; and to provide incentives for industrialization by taxing exports of raw material and other inputs, thereby making them available to domestic industries at lower than world prices. For foodstuffs, the main justification is the promotion of food security. Manufacturing or non-traditional exports (some of which may involve processed agricultural or agriculture-related products) are being backed by incentives because they are believed to contribute to long-term growth and development, and because it is felt that, without government assistance, exporters will have difficulty breaking into foreign markets due to externalities of various kinds. Also, some of the so-called incentives amount to no more than a government effort to offset the disincentives to non-traditional exports created by the import regime.

Measures which tend to tax or regulate exports

Table 4.9 shows the frequency of developing-country use of various kinds of policy measures to tax or regulate their exports. The table is constructed much like those on imports and shows snapshots of the frequency of use of different measures by various countries in different time periods. The frequencies are defined in terms of the proportion of total product groups at the HS2 level which may contain products that are taxed or regulated by different measures in different countries. The measures include export taxes or similar levies, minimum export prices, non-automatic export licensing (or approval), export prohibitions (total or partial) and export quotas. The last column shows whether the country also uses export subsidies.

Just as with imports, export taxes are the most commonly used measure, although licensing used to be very important in earlier periods. The variation among countries, especially during the earlier periods, is rather large, with some countries, such as Brazil, Indonesia and Malaysia, controlling more than 20 per cent of export product groups through licensing or other approval procedures, while many others limited such licensing to the implementation of health and safety standards and environmental obligations.[12] There is no obvious pattern with

---

[12] Just like the estimates of non-automatic licensing affecting imports, the analysis has attempted to exclude licensing which the authorities state they undertake in order to meet health, environmental and safety standards or for national security reasons.

Table 4.9 Developing-country policies on exports

	Year	Export taxes and levies	Minimum export prices	Export licensing	Export prohibi-tions	Export quotas	Export subsidies
Argentina	2008		1		1		
	1999	2					x
	1992	1					x
Bangladesh	2012				3		x
	1992	3	1	20	9		
Benin	2010				4		
	1997	3		1	2		
Bolivia	2005	3					
	1999			1			
Brazil	2009	5					
	1996	3		1	1	3	x
	1993	1	1	29		3	x
Cameroon	2007	2			3		
	1995	6		3	1	2	
Chile	1997						x
	1991						x
China	2012	4*					xx
Colombia	2012	3					
	1996	3	3	2	1	1	x
	1990	1	2		1		x
Costa Rica	2007	2					
	1995	4	1			1	x
Côte d'Ivoire	2012	5		5			
	1995	5	9	2		3	
Dominican Rep.	2008	2					
	1996					1	
Egypt	2011	2*	2*	2*			
	1993	1		1	4	3	x
El Salvador	2010						x
	1996				1	1	x
Fiji	2009	3		3			
	1997	2		7			
Ghana	2008	2					
	1992	1	24	3	1		
Honduras	2010	1		1			x
Hong Kong, China	1990			1			
India	2011	9	3	3*	4	4	x
	1998	13	1	9	3	5	x
	1993	1	4	10	2	4	x

(*continued*)

Table 4.9 Continued

	Year	Export taxes and levies	Minimum export prices	Export licensing	Export prohibitions	Export quotas	Export subsidies
Indonesia	2007	5		4			
	1998	5		19			x
	1991	6		33	6	3	x
Jamaica	2011			4			x
Kenya	2011	4*		18*			
	1992	10		16			
Korea Rep.	2008					2	x
	1996					4	x
	1992			42			
Kuwait	2012			1	7		
Malaysia	2010	5*		1			
	1997	10		35			
	1993	9		15			
Malawi	2010	3		10	2		
Mauritius	2008				1		x
	1995	1		4	3		x
Mexico	2008	9					
	1997	14		7			x
	1993	3		24	9		x
Morocco	2011			2*			
	1996	2		2		2	x
	1990	2		5			x
Mozambique	2009	5					
Nepal	2012			1			
Nigeria	2011	1			6		
	1998	1		2	5	1	
	1991			2	5		
Pakistan	2008	10		4			x
	1995	21	3	20	13		x
Paraguay	2005	2		1	1		
	1997			6	1	1	
Peru	2007			3			
	1994				1		
Philippines	2012	1	2	3	1		
	1993			26		15	
Senegal	2009	1		3			
	1994	1	3	4			x
Singapore	1995			2			
	1992	1		6			
South Africa	2009			1			
	1998	1		8	1		x
	1993	1		9	2		x

(*continued*)

Table 4.9 Continued

	Year	Export taxes and levies	Minimum export prices	Export licensing	Export prohibitions	Export quotas	Export subsidies
Sri Lanka	2010	14		3			
	1995	6	1	7	1		
Thailand	2007	2		7			
	1995	4		8	4	1	
	1991	3	2	11			x
Tunisia	2011	2*					
	1994		1		1	1	
Taiwan, China	2010			1			
Uganda	2012	3					
	1995	1	1	4			x
Uruguay	2012	3					x
	1995	4					
	1992	3					
Venezuela	2002	10					x
	1996	1					x
Zambia	2009			3			
	1996			1			
Zimbabwe	2011	12		8	8		
	1995			9			

Notes: Frequency ratio of percentage in HS 2-digit products affected by each measure; xx no export subsidies but extensive domestic supports; * computed at the HS 6 or 8-digit level.
Sources: GATT TPRs 1990–1995; WTO TPRs, 1995–2012; UNCTAD/World Bank NTM database.

respect to export taxes: their use has increased in some cases (Brazil, Sri Lanka) but decreased in others (India, Kenya).

The TPRs suggest that often a combination of measures – sometimes a quantitative measure, such as a licence in combination with a price linked measure, such as an export levy – would be used. A rather crude adding up of the number of countries and measures that are important by product group showed that the most frequently regulated/taxed product groups of exports by developing countries in 1990–98, at the HS 2-digit level, were live animals, coffee, cocoa and tea, fuels, hides and skins, wood products, and cotton (Michalopoulos, 2001, p. 70). Much the same products appeared to be regulated in the later period, except that controls on foodstuffs became more common as a measure aimed to deal with rising international prices of these products.

Export Incentives

Practically all the countries reviewed have a variety of policies and institutional support measures for non-traditional exports, including export promotion agencies. In some cases explicit export subsidies have been introduced, though their use is declining. Table 4.9 shows that about one-sixth of the 49 countries for which there are data provided export subsidies in the period 2005–11 while 40 per cent of the total gave subsidies in the 1990s. The experience in a number of countries with export subsidies suggests that they are frequently needed to offset incentives to sell to the domestic market that is created by protection. But when protection is relatively low and the exchange rate not overvalued, subsidies tend to be an expensive way of promoting exports whose main impact is to provide additional profits to established exporters.

More frequently the measures involve policies aimed at off-setting the impact of import controls as well as institutional support through the provision of export financing – sometimes on concessional terms – and insurance, marketing and the establishment of export processing zones (EPZs) or similar arrangements of temporary admission aimed at export promotion. In most cases the measures are not product specific but apply to broad categories of products, usually defined as non-traditional or manufacturing exports. Sometimes, the incentives are available only to certain groups of producing/exporting units, such as small and medium sized enterprises. For these reasons it is not possible to undertake an analysis at the tariff line or product group level as has been done for other policies affecting imports or exports; rather, it is only possible to note the presence or absence of a particular kind of programme and its main characteristics. Nor is it possible to evaluate in detail the effectiveness of any of the programmes or institutions reported. While some TPRs have identified problems or constraints affecting the effectiveness of programmes this has not been the general rule. Indeed a recent study (Cadot et al., 2012) reported findings suggesting that these agencies were on the whole successful in stimulating exports. However, the evidence from Africa (Farole, 2011, p. 3) suggests that 'most African programs are not fulfilling their potential and are underperforming compared with the Asian and Latin American products'.

Practically all countries have introduced some type of duty drawback system.[13] In many of the countries the system is intended to cover

[13] The only economies in which such a programme was not reported to exist were Hong Kong (which has no import duties), three African countries (Benin, Cameroon, Ivory Coast) and the Dominican Republic, where the export incentives focus on the EPZ.

duties and other border taxes as well as domestic taxes such as VAT. In an increasing number of cases it also covers taxes on domestically produced inputs. Frequently, in order to facilitate administration, the actual tax rebate mechanism involves the reimbursement or credit for a certain percentage of the firm's overall tax liability, rather than a rebate of specific duties or taxes. As a consequence, some of these programmes may contain an element of implicit export subsidy. On the other hand, this is one area where several of the TPRs reported problems and difficulties with delays in payment and rebates which result de facto in penalizing exporters relative to their overseas competitors (World Bank, 2000).

With few exceptions countries reported the existence of one or more EPZs or temporary admission schemes. The importance of these zones varies tremendously: in Korea they amounted to $4.6 billion of exports in 2008 compared to $11 million in Nigeria in 2011. While EPZs are still large in countries like Costa Rica and India, they are declining in importance in a number of countries, for example Mauritius and the Dominican Republic where they had played an important role in earlier periods. In Mauritius the government announced in 2008 that it was going to create an island-wide EPZ, at the same time unilaterally eliminating tariffs on more than 1,200 lines (WTO, 2008).

Preferential arrangements

In tandem with global integration, many developing countries have made intensive integration efforts at a regional level. Two types of measure can be distinguished in this regard: regional preferential trade agreements (PTAs) with other developing countries, and similar PTAs with developed countries. Examples of the former include the MERCOSUR customs union which involves several countries in South America, and the Southern African Development Community (SADC), a free trade area among 14 developing countries in South and East Africa. Examples of North–South regional integration include the North America Free Trade Area (NAFTA) as well as the various regional agreements between the EU and the different groups of ACP countries (WTO, 2011c).

In the last decade there has been a large increase of both North–South and South–South PTAs. The total number of PTAs in place is estimated at 360 with over two-thirds of the agreements being among developing countries. Mongolia is the only WTO member which has not declared that it participates in a PTA. Chile is the developing country with the largest number of PTAs with 26. It is estimated that, as a result, 95 per cent of Chilean trade is with PTA partners. But not all trade between

PTA partners involves preferences. While more than 50 per cent of world trade is among PTA partners only 16 per cent of world trade involves PTA preferences. This is because for a lot of world trade the MFN tariffs are zero.

Although developing countries are involved in a lot of PTAs the total trade involved is relatively small: almost 50 per cent of all trade among PTA partners involves the EU and another 13 per cent involves NAFTA. The bulk of the PTAs involve preferential tariffs on merchandise trade; but there are also a few involving only services; and a growing number involve both goods and services as well as other aspects of 'deeper integration' such as cooperation in competition policy, investment and protection of intellectual property rights.

The preferential margins on tariffs on average are small, only about two per cent, as MFN tariffs have come down in many countries; and developing countries enjoy other unilateral preferences in developed-country markets. Few tariff lines have preferential margins of more than five percentage points. However, for some countries, for example Mauritius, preferential margins in EU markets are high as a number of its products (e.g. textiles and sugar) are subject to substantial barriers. There are reports that in a number of preferential arrangements in sub-Saharan Africa (WTO, 2011c) non-tariff barriers in intra-regional trade may de facto negate the preferences accorded to regional partners.

The 2000s saw a veritable explosion of PTAs: in the 1990s on average WTO members were parties to two PTAs. In 2011 the average number of PTAs per WTO member rose to 13. Developing countries, especially in Africa, have committed to participate in a number of overlapping PTAs giving rise to the familiar 'spaghetti bowl' image. A huge literature has emerged to analyse the causes of this phenomenon and its implications for developing countries and the trading system. Some of the reasons for the increase, especially of PTAs with deeper integration commitments in Asia, had little to do with the traditional preference motive and more to do with off-shoring and the establishment or safeguarding production networks. In other cases it may be economically advantageous to join a PTA or become part of a new one to offset the disadvantages of being excluded. In some other cases, such as PTAs involving developed and developing countries, the motivation for deeper integration may have been the desire to liberalize beyond what was possible to agree in the context of the WTO negotiations – with the anticipation of multilateralizing agreements at a later date, as the political economy of liberalization makes it easier to move forward through a PTA rather than through multilateral negotiation. In still other situations, the main motivation for increasing regional integration may stem from political/security considerations.

The trend towards more PTAs by developing countries raises questions about the effects on the participants as well as third countries. There are also issues as to consistency with broader multilateral efforts to liberalize trade under the WTO.

First, regarding the effects on non-participants, there is some evidence that trade diversion effects in some cases, for example MERCOSUR, can be adverse and substantial (Chang and Winters, 2002). But as more and more PTAs involve commitments toward greater integration, the traditional trade creation/trade diversion analysis appears to be less relevant and more attention needs to be devoted to determining the impact of other PTA provisions. In this area, one of the important developing-country issues has to do with commitments they have undertaken in PTAs with developed countries to impose less flexible intellectual property rights regimes than required under the TRIPS agreement (Nkomo, 2011). Also, a number of ACP countries have failed to implement PTAs concluded with the EU in part because of concerns about the 'deeper integration' provisions of these agreements.

The question of consistency with the multilateral trading system has two aspects: a narrow (and less interesting) one which has to do with the consistency of the multitude of PTAs with Article 24 of GATT and the Enabling Clause Provisions; and the broader one of whether the spread of PTAs benefits or hurts global welfare and whether it undermines future efforts to liberalize trade on a multilateral basis.

The WTO had established a committee to review the very large number of PTAs which had been notified to it in order to determine their consistency with WTO provisions. After several years of reviewing dozens of the more than 400 PTAs that had been notified, the WTO gave up. In 2006 the General Council decided that it would no longer attempt to determine consistency – rather it would opt for transparency, i.e. information on what is happening. Any member who wished to challenge consistency would have to use the dispute settlement mechanism. Few of them have taken that route.

The problem derives from the fact that existing WTO provisions are broad enough to give considerable latitude of interpretation. The lack of consensus results primarily from the desire of many members, including developing countries, to have as much flexibility as possible in the conclusion of such agreements. One can take a relaxed attitude about the current situation. There has been a lot of MFN liberalization under the previous Rounds, thus reducing the chance of trade diversion. And many of these agreements contain provisions which have little to do with preferences. Still, there is a danger that the multiplicity of agreements will yield welfare-reducing results both for the participants and for the rest of the world (Panagaryia, 2000). Some of the non-trade-related provisions pose dangers for developing countries. And, there is also the danger that the existing preferential arrangements will result in a reluctance to engage in multilateral MFN reductions on account of many countries losing preferences.

This concern has been voiced by a number of mostly low-income developing countries in the context of the Doha Round. But it is doubtful that this concern has been decisive in the failure to reach agreement on MFN tariff reduction. Indeed, it could be argued that some of the PTAs were put in place precisely because of the lack of progress in the Doha Round negotiations. Moreover, it could be argued that PTAs among developing countries are useful training grounds for those among them wishing to 'deepen' their integration in other spheres of economic cooperation beyond trade and thereby may strengthen their future participation in global cooperative efforts.

Services

There are no comparable international data that permit a systematic examination of the state of policies regarding restrictions on trade in services in developing or developed countries. The reasons are well known: because many of the modes of delivery of services are intangible, there are no barriers that take the form of tariffs. Barriers take the form of quantitative restrictions – sometimes involving complete bans, and often government regulation.

Some of the latter may be explicitly discriminatory against imports of services or foreign providers; others may be of a general regulatory nature that apply equally to national and foreign service providers. And to date no general description of the barriers to trade in services that cuts across all four modes of delivery (cross-border supply, consumption abroad, commercial presence, temporary entry) and all sectors has been attempted – and may not be feasible with the present state of data collection.

Some general impressions can be obtained as to what the actual policy situation tends to be by using a recently developed World Bank database whose results are summarized in Table 4.10. The first impression from the existing data is that developed countries have liberalized far more than developing countries, especially in the financial,

Table 4.10 Sectoral trade restrictiveness indices in developing countries

	Overall	Financial	Telecom	Retail	Transport	Professional
Argentina	17	10	0	0	22	49
Bangladesh	44	46	63	25	63	35
Benin	—	—	—	—	—	—
Bolivia	14	19	25	0	10	21
Brazil	23	36	0	0	10	58
Cameroon	26	21	0	25	30	43
Chile	23	22	25	25	19	27
China	37	35	50	25	19	66
Colombia	18	25	50	0	4	34
Costa Rica	29	29	38	0	30	60
Côte d'Ivoire	26	14	25	0	31	68
Dominican Rep.	12	3	0	0	22	33
Egypt	52	43	25	50	50	82
El Salvador	—	—	—	—	—	—
Fiji	—	—	—	—	—	—
Ghana	18	25	25	0	6	44
Honduras	21	7	50	0	35	34
Hong Kong, China	—	—	—	—	—	—
India	66	48	50	75	62	88
Indonesia	50	23	25	50	66	76
Jamaica	—	—	—	—	—	—
Kenya	30	23	25	0	31	73
Korea, Rep.	23	2	50	0	21	66
Kuwait	52	42	75	50	50	57
Malawi	34	35	50	25	32	38
Malaysia	46	45	25	25	55	73
Mauritius	17	9	0	0	31	42
Mexico	30	15	38	0	62	43
Morocco	21	14	25	0	28	46
Mozambique	19	17	75	0	6	30
Nepal	43	23	50	25	56	76
Nigeria	27	26	25	25	24	36
Pakistan	28	49	13	0	25	48
Paraguay	16	22	38	0	5	25
Peru	16	42	0	0	3	28
Philippines	54	45	50	50	44	80
Saudi Arabia	43	46	25	25	39	72
Senegal	19	16	25	0	25	37
Singapore	—	—	—	—	—	—
South Africa	35	20	25	25	41	62
Sri Lanka	38	24	50	25	46	57
Taiwan, China	—	—	—	—	—	—
Thailand	48	49	50	25	47	74
Tunisia	45	33	25	25	55	79
Uganda	35	28	25	50	21	38
Uruguay	28	45	63	0	41	11
Venezuela	35	23	25	25	32	69

(*continued*)

Table 4.10 Continued

	Overall	Financial	Telecom	Retail	Transport	Professional
Vietnam	42	41	50	50	39	32
Zambia	21	8	75	0	10	44
Zimbabwe	64	56	63	75	68	60
Average	32	28	35	19	33	51
Memo Items:						
EU	26	4	0	25	37	54
United States	18	21	0	0	8	54

Notes: indices: 0 = open; 100 = closed; data are based on the latest year available from 106 countries in the database; – data not available.

Source: World Bank, DECTI Service Trade Restrictions database.

telecommunication and retail service sectors. The differences are smaller in the transport sector and even less in professional services, which frequently requires the movement of natural persons.

Service protection in developing countries can have serious implications on efficiency and growth: protection causes high cost expensive service inputs which results both in waste of resources and in adverse effects on export performance of both goods and other services. A protected and inefficient banking sector can be as damaging to profitability of exportables as the imposition of high tariffs on imported components used in the production of these same exportables.

In telecommunications, most countries have introduced some competition by private providers in both mobile and fixed services, although foreign providers are often limited in Asia. State ownership of banking is being reduced, but the allocation of licences 'remains opaque and highly discretionary' (Borchert et al., 2011, p. 12).

Among developing countries, there is strong evidence that countries in Latin America and the Caribbean have liberalized far more than developing-country regions in all sectors. In retail and transport their liberalization is at least as great as that of developed countries. There are few differences in the degree of service liberalization by sector in other groups of developing countries classified by region or income level. Some low income developing countries, such as Ghana and Nigeria, have relatively liberal regimes while several economies in Asia with fast growing export sectors, such as China, India, Indonesia, Malaysia and the Philippines, have restrictive service sectors (see Table 4.10).

As to the trend over time, it is clear that developing countries are moving, in general, towards more liberal regimes in services. A large number of developing countries made forward liberalization commitments in the Uruguay Round Agreements on Financial Services and Telecommunications with many of the commitments to start in 2000. TPRs made in subsequent years confirm this trend for most countries.

Following the Uruguay Round agreements, the situation regarding the formal commitments of developing countries to maintain a liberal services trade regime parallels the situation with respect to tariffs: in both cases the actual policies are far short of the commitments. Except in the case of services the difference is often greater. Table 4.11 shows that actual policies in developing countries in all major regional groupings, restrictive as they may be, are still far more liberal than their commitments – just like applied tariffs are far lower than bindings. As with tariffs, developing countries argue that this is needed to maintain policy flexibility – and the possibility of pursuing other social objectives. But the cost, as with tariffs, is the increased risk of policy change which often inhibits foreign investment.

Looking at the pattern of commitments in the Uruguay Round by the range of commitment and degree of development, a similar pattern develops to that observed in trade policy on goods: the degree of liberalization appears to increase with the level of income. Lower income countries appear to have committed to much less liberalization than higher income ones. The same conclusion can be drawn by looking at the commitments of the 50 developing countries whose trade regimes were analysed more systematically. Indeed, the pattern in Table 4.11 has a striking parallel to the pattern in Table 4.3, with the lower the developing country income, the lower the number of commitments and hence the highest the remaining protection (see also Borchert et al., 2011, p. 123). The basic justification that low income countries make for not liberalizing their service sector is the same infant industry argument used for so very long in the areas of merchandise trade. There are obvious dangers and limits to such a strategy as many developing countries have realized in the areas of goods. These dangers have to be seriously evaluated by low income developing countries which continue to protect their service sectors.

On the other hand Table 4.11 shows that this relationship between the extent of liberalization and the level of development does not hold true for the financial services sector which includes banking and insurance. In this case there is basically no pattern discernible, with most groups of countries liberalizing about a quarter of the maximum possible – if one weighs partial restrictions in each of the modes of supply. Again the LDCs made the fewest commitments. Only nine of the

Table 4.11 Services trade liberalization by country income group

Region (no. of countries)	Actual policies	Overall offer improvement (UR commitment-Doha offer)	As % of UR commitments	Overall binding gap (UR commitment actual policies)	As % of actual policies	Total services liberalization commitments at UR (%)	Financial services (no. of commitments as % of max.)
Developed countries (27)	18.0	6.6	18	18.9	105	57.8	—
Developing countries (65)	29.5	5.5	8	42.6	144	16.5	24.0
High income developing (7)	38.7	3.7	5	30.1	78	18.9	23.4
Upper middle income (21)	29.2	8.7	12	40.5	139	25.5	26.4
Lower middle income (18)	27.8	–2.5	–4	43.4	156	14.4	27.8
Low income (19)	28.2	—	—	48.8	173	14.7	27.6
Of which LDCs (13)	27.8	—	—	57.1	206	3.0	15.0
World (92)	26.2	6.4	16	35.6	136	21.7	—

Note: — data not available; UR = Uruguay Round.

Sources: World Bank Services Trade Restrictions database and Borchert et al. (2011).

twenty-nine LDCs made any commitments. But those which did, on average made greater liberalizing commitments than other developing countries.

Earlier analysis (Mattoo, 1998) suggests that in the area of commitments on commercial presence for financial services, Latin American countries tend to limit the number of suppliers, while Asian economies limit either solely the percentage of equity or both equity and the number of suppliers; and they are both more restrictive than African countries in this respect. This is actually an encouraging sign for African countries, especially if the pattern is repeated for other sectors, because of the implications it has for attracting FDI more generally.

The main conclusion to be drawn from this analysis is that the service sector continues to offer opportunities for further liberalization as well as for action by developing countries to create more secure access to their markets which in turn could have beneficial effects on their long-term development. As we will discuss in Chapter 6 similar opportunities exist in developed countries.

The continuing debate on trade policy

The integration of the developing countries into the multilateral trading system was substantially advanced by the Uruguay Round, which contributed to the liberalization of developing countries' own trade regimes and improvements in the conditions affecting access to the major markets for their export products. The integration process has been especially impressive for a group of perhaps 20–30 middle and higher income countries in Latin America and Asia. For many others, progress has been slower.

Following the Uruguay Round Agreements, protection both through tariff and non-tariff measures appears to be greater in low income than in middle and higher income developing countries. While this conclusion is subject to a number of methodological caveats it is suggestive of the many challenges and opportunities low income developing countries face in their efforts to achieve fuller integration into the multilateral trading system.

There is continuing debate over whether lower protection promotes faster development especially regarding the direction of causality. A number of studies (Dollar, 1992; Edwards, 1993; Frankel and Romer, 1999; Sachs and Warner, 1995) have found that trade openness is associated with more rapid economic growth. On the other hand, Rodrik has argued that these studies have not adequately controlled for other economic policies; that there is a strong association between exports and growth, but that we are unable to be sure whether this association is a consequence of exports causing output growth, or of the two being jointly determined by the strength of countries' institutions which are the main determinants of overall growth performance (Rodrik, 1992; Rodriguez and Rodrik, 1999).[14]

At the same time, although there are strong links between export growth and GDP growth as well as between overall openness to trade and GDP growth, there appears to be a less robust (though still positive) cross-country relationship between indicators of trade policy (such as average tariff levels, coverage ratios of NTM) and GDP growth. The reason is that there are several different groups of countries with different trade policy regimes that have experienced large changes in their trade to GDP ratios:

1. Countries like Hong Kong, Singapore and Chile that have very liberal trade regimes, whose integration in the international economy needs little further discussion.
2. Some of the very successful exporters which experienced rapid growth in trade and GDP did so in the context of trade regimes characterized by significant import controls on the domestic market: Korea is a classic example; India and China are more recent 'integration' success stories with a very strongly protective regime.
3. In the absence of generally effective trade institutions, the benefits of free trade regimes can be partially obtained through export processing zones (EPZs). As shown above, while very many countries have introduced EPZs, few have actually succeeded in stimulating exports substantially and on a sustainable basis through this mechanism. There are examples also of countries like the Dominican Republic and Mauritius, where EPZs have been successful but which are moving away from these towards more broadly liberal trade regimes.
4. There are several major oil exporters such as Saudi Arabia and Kuwait whose trade/GDP ratio varies substantially over time depending primarily on the price of oil and without much link to their trade regime.[15]

---

[14] Even if we were to accept this agnostic view, the resulting policy prescription is a relatively comprehensive approach to development that includes improvement of a range of institutions, including trade liberalization.

[15] This should not be interpreted to imply that trade policy is not relevant for oil exporters: Nigeria is now almost wholly dependent on oil exports, with most other exports reduced by earlier weaknesses in its trade-related policies and institutions.

The key to understanding experiences of countries which have integrated their economies in international trade while retaining substantial protection has to do with the variety of factors that affect competitiveness and the incentives to produce and sell to the domestic versus the export market. Protection strengthens the incentives to sell domestically and creates a serious handicap in selling abroad, especially when it includes intermediate products and services – which raises the costs of potential exporters to levels higher than those of their competitors in international markets. But these increased costs can be offset through export subsidies and effective drawback systems – or avoided through an EPZ.

The problem is that low incoming developing countries have weak institutions and the implementation of drawback systems has been ineffective, resulting in additional costs to exporters. Nor do they have the budgetary resources to subsidize exports – even assuming such subsidization was appropriate.

The main conclusion from this discussion is that for many low income countries, which have currently high protection and weaknesses in trade-related institutions, the most practical way of stimulating trade and opening up to the international economy is through liberal trade regimes, rather than through a complex structure of protection and export incentives.

This debate about the appropriate trade policy, especially for low income countries, appears to have become increasingly academic. While the importance of institutions and capacity building is receiving increasing recognition, regarding the specifics of trade policy, developing countries are revealing their preferences through their practices: very few countries have actually increased protection in recent periods; and the ones that did (Argentina) appear to have done so on a temporary basis for balance of payments reasons. Bhagwati and Srinivasan (1999, p. 6) point out that the many in-depth country analyses that were undertaken from the 1960s through to the 1980s 'have shown plausibly, and taking into account numerous country-specific factors, that trade does seem to create, even sustain, higher (economic)' growth. Similar conclusions were reached by Panagariya (2004) and a more recent CUTS research project on the linkages between trade, development and poverty reduction in 13 developing countries stated that 'an open economic regime is a necessary, but not sufficient, factor for sustained and high economic growth' (CUTS, 2008). A review of the Sachs and Warner versus the Rodrik and Rodriguez analysis (Wacziarg and Welch, 2008) concluded that trade liberalization was associated with more investment and more growth; and similar views were expressed in an even more recent review of the trade and development literature (Hallaert et al., 2013). Moreover, even sceptics do not seem to recommend high protective barriers as a policy to promote growth and poverty reduction.

Poverty reduction has properly been the focus of more recent debate. Supporters of liberal trade regimes have pointed out that, to the extent that a more liberal trade regime impacts positively on economic growth and the latter is an essential ingredient for poverty alleviation, there is a presumption that more liberal trade policies would have a beneficial impact on poverty. Indeed, there is evidence that growth is good for alleviating poverty and there appears to be no systematic evidence (based on regression analyses) that trade openness (defined as a ratio of total trade to GDP) is correlated to income inequality (Dollar and Kraay, 2000). But the link between trade policy and poverty is very complex (Winters et al., 2004).

There are clear concerns that trade liberalization needs to be accompanied by efforts to strengthen domestic factor markets as well as the establishment of appropriate safety nets to mitigate its short-term adjustment costs (Stiglitz, 2000). Yet, the evidence from the review of developing country institutions (see Chapter 5) suggests that very few such safety nets exist. Moreover, where markets are not functioning properly – for example in rural areas of low income countries – appropriate government interventions and supports may be needed to stimulate agricultural production and rural incomes, which would have implications for example for the maintenance of appropriate provisions dealing with the issue in the Agreement on Agriculture.

There is considerable evidence that income inequality has increased within many developing countries in the last two decades. A substantial reduction of developing-country applied tariffs would have had a positive effect on reducing poverty, although the total effects of potential outcomes of the Round on the poor were quite complex and depended very much both on the assumptions about specific agreements and particular countries (Hertel and Winters, 2006). Regrettably, as will be discussed in Chapter 9, few concerns about either poverty or inequality entered the debate between developed and developing countries in the Doha Round negotiations.

5
Developing-Country Trade-Related Institutions and Aid for Trade

Introduction

As progress is being made by many developing countries to introduce more liberal trade policies, increasing attention is being paid to the capacity of their institutions to implement policies that support their fuller integration in world trade and help them transform their economies. The increased emphasis on institutions partly reflects a more general shift in priorities in development thinking and practice. It also reflects specific concerns about the increased burdens placed on developing-country institutions by their commitments under the Uruguay Round Agreements.

There are several kinds of institution whose operations affect developing countries' participation in world trade and the WTO. First, there are various institutions that are generally linked to the operation of a market economy – such as the banking system, accounting services and contract enforcement – but which also have a bearing on trade. Second, there are institutions that focus more narrowly on international trade, some of which may be related to exports and others to imports, for example export/import finance and insurance, and marketing. Third, there are governmental institutions that are specifically chartered with the design and implementation of trade policy, including the ministry of trade and the customs administration body, and some, such as those dealing with standards or intellectual property rights, that were previously perceived as domestic in nature, but have become 'internationalized' by the Uruguay Round Agreements. In addition, of course, developing-country participation in international trade depends on the supply and quality of key inputs, such as those of power, transport and telecommunication, as well as the availability of a broad range of specialized human skills.

Weaknesses in the very wide range of institutions, infrastructure and skills that are needed for effective integration in international trade define the very essence of underdevelopment and exist to some or other degree in practically all developing countries. They are obviously most pronounced in LDCs. This very wide definition of institutions that are important for foreign trade is not helpful, however, in defining priorities for governments or the international community, because it suggests that anything that is done to help strengthen skills, power generation, the transport infrastructure or development in general would benefit developing-country integration into international trade. Thus, a somewhat more narrow definition of 'trade-related' institutions is the focus of this analysis. Even this more narrow definition covers many institutions, especially since the broadening of the mandate under the WTO of what is deemed 'trade-related'.

It was because of the recognition of widespread weaknesses in a number of these new areas that the WTO agreements included extensive transition periods and developed-country commitments to provide technical assistance to developing country members, as noted in Chapter 2. The purpose of this chapter is twofold: to review the challenges developing countries face in transforming their economies because of weaknesses in their trade-related institutions generally, as well as those linked to specific requirements imposed by the Uruguay Round Agreements; and to review the international community's efforts to provide technical and financial assistance, especially to LDCs.

Institutional development and capacity constraints

There is a growing amount of information regarding the effectiveness of the operations of trade-related institutions in developing countries. Most of the available information pertains to LDCs and suggests that strengthening these countries' integration into international trade means addressing a great variety of supply side constraints including those deriving from trade-related institutions.

An early WTO report based on the needs assessments of LDCs concluded that their trade is constrained by the following:

- infrastructural deficiencies such as erratic power supplies, underdeveloped telecommunication networks and poor terrestrial, sea and air transport links;

- weaknesses in technological capacity;[1]
- underdeveloped financial and banking systems;
- shortfalls in a broad range of skills and the institutional capacity needed to participate in international trade and implement effective trade policies;
- deficient regulatory regimes that are unable to cope with weakness in the operations of markets.[2]

The focus of this discussion is primarily on the fourth of the above constraints, but it is important to keep in mind that these are not the only and nor perhaps the most important constraints in many of the LDCs and other lower-income developing countries.

There are various trade-related institutions, usually in the public sector, on which some relatively comprehensive information is available: (1) government institutions charged with designing or implementing trade-related policies, including those for the so-called 'new areas'; (2) activities – usually with some public sector involvement – aimed explicitly at promoting exports; and (3) public institutions and policies needed to cope with the potential costs of closer integration into the international economy.

The increasing range and complexity of issues handled by the WTO, some of which are very technical, implies that the capacity of developing countries to participate effectively in the work of the WTO depends very heavily on the analytical capacity and strength of the developing-country institutions charged with handling WTO issues. This is all the more so because the WTO is a member-driven organization, with a very small secretariat, so a great deal of the analysis of issues and development of positions is done by members.

Developing countries face a variety of challenging tasks in this regard: the drafting of appropriate legislation and regulation; the meeting of procedural notification requirements; the staffing of government institutions with technical personnel able to implement the policies and commitments undertaken; and the monitoring of trading partners'

[1] The General Agreement on Trade in Services (GATS) attempted to address the question of deficiencies in technology by providing, through Article IV:1, for the strengthening of the domestic service capacity efficiency and competitiveness by amongst other things the provision of access to technology on a commercial basis and the improvement of access to distribution channels and networks. LDC members maintain that this provision has not been sufficiently implemented.

[2] Based on responses to a needs assessment questionnaire, as recorded in WTO (1999b).

implementation of WTO obligations to assess whether market access has been unfairly denied or trade rights infringed, and to prepare an appropriate response (UNCTAD and WTO, 1996).

Weaknesses in these areas have been clear for some time, especially in the case of Africa (Oyejide, 1990). But they have become an even greater constraint in the light of the heavy burden of reporting and implementation entailed by the Uruguay Round Agreements. They are amply documented in the assessments of technical assistance needs prepared by LDCs in the context of the Integrated Framework. Practically, all of the more than 40 needs assessments completed by LDCs in 1997–99 requested assistance in strengthening domestic institutions connected with international trade, including the training of staff at trade ministries and customs offices, the preparation of legislation and regulations, and the development of a local capacity to enable countries to participate more effectively in future discussions and negotiations especially in respect of the new issues handled by the WTO. The same priorities were emphasized in the 30 odd Diagnostic Trade Integration Studies of LDCs undertaken in the early 2000s.

Institutions related to 'new areas'

These include a variety of institutions whose task is to ensure proper classification and valuation of products entering trade, as well to ensure that such products meet technical and sanitary and phyto-sanitary standards, and institutions that deal with the implementation of the TRIPS agreement.

The importance of customs institutions in developing countries cannot be overstated – they are critical to the implementation of trade policy. Proper valuation and classification of products is also important in these countries because they rely to a much greater extent than industrial countries on tariffs as a source of budgetary revenue.[3] At the same time the existence of regulations on technical and other standards and the effectiveness of domestic institutions entrusted with the implementation of these regulations is of importance not only to the health of the population and the performance of firms but also to their capacity to export abroad. Weak domestic institutions and non-adherence to international standards can result in developing-country exports being denied access to foreign markets.

---

[3] Developing countries have faced problems in under-valuation of products more broadly which give rise to requirements for pre-shipment inspection.

While the developing countries made an effort to bring their customs valuation procedures into conformity with the WTO valuation system by the year 2000, as required in the WTO Agreement on Customs Valuation, many were not able to do so. In the meantime the designated transition period has expired, and while a number of countries have notified the WTO to request an extension, others have not, even though they have not made the necessary changes (WTO, 2012g).

In many countries the changes required are significant because the valuation of goods for customs purposes is frequently based on the Brussels definition of value. It involves the enactment of new legislation, changes to the relevant rules and procedures, the issuance of new documentation, the adoption of new software and the training of officials in the new procedures and documentation requirements. Many LDCs have requested technical assistance for this purpose in the context of the needs assessments they have prepared. While it is clear that LDCs have significant needs in this area, it is also likely that other developing countries have needs that have not been assessed and will have difficulty meeting their commitments without technical assistance.

The cost of making these customs-valuation changes may well be substantial (Finger and Schuler, 2000) and hence in all these countries, where budget and aid resources are scarce, the question of the priority to be attached is of importance. In places where customs administration is generally weak, should the highest priority be given to changing the customs valuation system, or should it be given to strengthening the customs administration more generally? Recent estimates of the upfront costs of introducing trade facilitation measures in four developing countries (Burkina Faso, Dominican Republic, Kenya and Mongolia) that included the establishment of a 'single window' for customs clearance, enquiry points and the like ranged from $4 to $20 million, depending on the quality of IT used and the annual recurrent costs (only salaries) of about $3 million (OECD, 2012).

Practically all developing-country members of the WTO have institutions that deal with the maintenance of technical standards and enforce the health, sanitary and phyto-sanitary regulations, as reported in the TPR. However, there is serious doubt about the capacity of many of these institutions to implement regulations. For example, most developing countries have legislation on national standards that are based on those of the International Standards Organization (ISO), of which many are also members. But as noted in Chapter 4 in some countries there are significant weaknesses in government testing facilities. Most countries report that they have concluded numerous formal bilateral mutual recognition agreements on technical standards. But it is not clear whether these agreements provide adequate information to producers on the standards applicable in countries where they may consider marketing their products.

The situation regarding sanitary and phyto-sanitary measures appears to be quite similar. Countries have established regulations requiring sanitary or phyto-sanitary certificates for imported food, drugs, agricultural and veterinary products. Again, the standards used are supposed to be based on those laid down in international agreements such as the Codex Alimentarius. But it is difficult to judge the adequacy of the regulations or the effectiveness of the institutions entrusted with their implementation. In addition certification costs can be particularly taxing for small firms. For example ISO 9000 certification for a small company plant can cost up to $250,000, with additional auditing costs being incurred after initial approval (World Bank, 2000, ch. 3).

The existing standards have been designed by industrial countries to reflect their technology mix and preferences which may or may not be appropriate for developing countries. While a country may apply other standards at the border, it has the burden to prove their scientific merit. Upgrading existing standards or developing new ones and performing risk assessments is also a costly and difficult procedure and is neither technically feasible nor affordable for most developing countries.

Thus, it is not surprising that the needs assessments for technical assistance of LDCs have revealed many weaknesses in the institutions entrusted with the enforcement of technical or sanitary and phyto-sanitary standards. The areas in which assistance has been sought range from the preparation of appropriate TBT and SPS legislation and regulations, to the setting up of standards institutions, to testing facilities and inspection services, to staff training in all aspects of standards monitoring and implementation. Most of the assessments revealed an urgent need to increase the general dissemination of information on (1) bringing standards into line with WTO regulations and (2) setting up of 'enquiry points' in respect of the standards used by major importers to enhance access to their markets.

Actual project costs of typical SPS-related World Bank livestock projects ranged from $11.8 million in Madagascar to $108 million in Brazil. A project to modernize laboratories for residue control in Turkey cost $3.3 million (Finger and Schuler, 2000).

There is little to suggest that lower-income countries do not suffer from similar institutional weaknesses in these areas. Again, the cost for establishing an appropriate set of institutions can be quite substantial for these countries; and the question of the priority that a developing country should attach to the establishment of such institutions has to be raised. Yet, in the absence of suitable institutions, a country's exports may be penalized. Reportedly $1.75 billion of exports from developing countries were disrupted by SPS standards in 2002.

Perhaps in no other area are the institutional weaknesses so glaring as in international legal matters that involve the use of the Dispute Settlement Mechanism (DSM). The legal aspects underlying the WTO agreements are very complex and require specialist expertise in international law, which in most developing countries is absent from both the private sector and the government. Governments often also lack the necessary expertise to make the initial case assessment and direct the case during its preparation, whether in defence or as a complainant.

Engaging international law firms with the necessary knowledge and expertise is an extremely expensive proposition with costs ranging from $250 to $1,000 an hour, raising the total cost of prosecuting a case to a level that cannot be supported by a developing country's budget. Trying to pass on these costs to the industries affected is also a problem. A legal system that relies totally or predominantly on the participants' capacity to pay for the legal costs involved introduces inequities and distortions, and may result in situations where the DSM is primarily seen as the locus of adjudication of the interests of large and/or wealthy companies and countries.

Export support institutions

As discussed in Chapter 4, many countries have introduced programmes or institutions aimed at ensuring the availability of trade finance (as well as insurance) for both imports and exports. Roughly half of the countries, on which there are reports of such programmes, indicate that they offer concessional credit terms. In some countries, for example Bolivia, concessional terms are reserved for small and medium-sized enterprises, in others, for example Fiji, they are not. In some cases (Costa Rica) concessional export financing has been considered an export subsidy. Finally, practically all countries have established some kind of an export promotion agency to help market their exports abroad. And recent evidence is reported to suggest that these institutions have been effective in achieving their objective of stimulating exports (Cadot et al., 2012).

Adjustment assistance

The trade liberalizing policies pursued by developing countries since the early 1990s undoubtedly generated significant benefits, but they also imposed costs on firms and individuals that are adversely affected by import competition. The private costs of trade liberalization take the form of reduced employment and income in industries affected by increased competition from imports. They are not the same as social costs which are likely to be lower than private costs because of the benefits – in the form of employment and income – that accrue to workers in export industries, whose output is likely to increase after import liberalization (Matusz and Tarr, 1999). But whatever their size, private costs are likely to exist and influence the political economy of trade reform. It could be argued that the prospect of further liberalization could be influenced by whether or not developing countries have institutions that can effectively mitigate the costs to firms or individuals of increased competition resulting from trade liberalization.

The TPRs showed that only a few of the 49 developing countries had trade-related adjustment assistance programmes. In some countries, for example Mexico, the programmes focus on providing assistance to firms facing increased competition from imports. In others, for example Egypt, they have focused on providing a safety net for affected workers. In still others, trade-related adjustment assistance has been offered in the context of programmes with the wider objective of raising productivity or strengthening the profitability of small and medium-sized enterprises. In none of the cases is it possible to estimate the private costs associated with trade reform. The experience with aid for trade programmes discussed below suggests that very little attention has been paid to adjustment assistance programs (OECD/WTO, 2011a). There is little information to suggest that developing countries more broadly have the institutional capacity to cope with the adjustment costs associated with trade reform, especially the private costs incurred by displaced workers.

It may not be necessary or even optimal to design adjustment assistance programmes that focus narrowly on adjustment linked to increased competition from imports. More broadly based programmes and/or a broad and effective social safety net may be a better way of dealing with adjustment costs. The point is that whatever the optimal instrument may be, few countries appear to have the institutional capacity to deal with the problem of adjustment to increased competition from abroad.

International assistance efforts

The main burden for strengthening institutional capacity has to be borne by the developing countries themselves. However, as noted in Chapter 2, the WTO agreements refer extensively to technical assistance to be provided by the developed-country members to all developing countries that need it, and especially to LDCs. The latter have been a focus of the international community's efforts in recent years.

The Integrated Framework for assistance to LDCs

Based on the conclusions reached at the first WTO ministerial meeting in Singapore, the High Level Meeting on Trade-Related Technical Assistance to the LDCs was held in Geneva under the WTO's auspices in October 1997 to develop an assistance programme (as well as to discuss improved market access) for LDCs. An important conclusion of the meeting was that it was not the lack of assistance per se that was the problem, but that it had been supply driven, not effectively coordinated, and that the reforms supported were not 'owned' by the recipient countries.

The meeting adopted an Integrated Framework for trade-related technical assistance to LDCs. The framework envisaged that LDCs would conduct their own needs assessments, which would then be discussed at roundtables with the six agencies involved in the effort (the IMF, the ITC, the UN Development Program, UNCTAD, the World Bank and the WTO) plus other interested donors in order to develop an integrated programme of technical assistance activities aimed primarily at institution building.

Reference has been made to the information contained in the more than 40 needs assessments which were prepared following this first initiative. Progress in meeting these needs by means of coordinated assistance programmes was slow, for a variety of reasons. According to one report (WTO, 2000a), developing countries expected the process to result both in improved delivery of assistance and in increased amounts of funding, while the donors originally focused on the efficiency gains and synergies resulting from better coordination. Difficulties with coordination by the recipients and among the agencies emerged; and the very problems of institutional weaknesses in LDCs that the initiative was designed to address appear to have contributed to implementation delays.

A review of the Integrated Framework by the six international agencies concerned under the leadership of the World Bank was undertaken by independent consultants in mid-2000. The review recognized many of the difficulties noted above and made the following recommendations:

- The Integrated Framework should focus solely on technical assistance activities, and not on overall policy and the development of human resources and infrastructure.
- Trade-related technical assistance in the World Bank's operations should be 'mainstreamed' (that is, it should actively incorporate trade concerns in the project and programme design at the country

level) and coordinated through the Poverty Reduction Strategy Papers (PRSPs) prepared by low income countries for consideration by the IMF and the World Bank.
- LDCs should have greater ownership and more oversight of the framework activities.
- The procedures and coordination mechanisms of the six agencies should be simplified and strengthened.

Following the issuance of the report, in a joint statement the six agencies announced a number of steps to implement some of its recommendations. In particular the agencies accepted the recommendations regarding 'mainstreaming' as well as strengthening LDCs' ownership of the activities. In this connection they proposed the establishment of a Steering Committee representing LDCs and the six agencies, and a trust fund for feasibility analyses.

In late 2001, the Doha Declaration endorsed the Integrated Framework 'as a viable model for LDCs' trade development' and urged the six agencies to explore its enhancement. However, experience in the implementation of the Integrated Framework identified a number of problems highlighted in various evaluations (Liebrechts and Wimenga, 2004; USAID, 2005; World Bank, 2004; WTO, 2003a). While there were some success stories (e.g. Cambodia), in many others the Integrated Framework had not been effective:

- There were weaknesses in developing-country ownership, partly as a result of the absence of national leadership that can promote the importance of trade.
- Trade-related activities require the coordination among many agencies; trade ministries, usually the focal points for assistance under the Integrated Framework, were found to be weak in the councils of government and key government ministries, in particular the Ministry of Finance, had not been involved early in the process.
- There was a lack of synchronization between the diagnostic studies and the PRS process.
- The PRS process was dominated by the social ministries and the Ministry of Finance which see it as a means of obtaining significant aid financing; Integrated Framework funding has been far more modest than LDC expectations.
- The diagnostic studies were far too broad and did not yield directly fundable projects.

The three years following the Doha Declaration saw little progress in the trade negotiations and a great number of international meetings inside the WTO and in other forums – for example the World Bank/ IMF Development Committee – to discuss ways in which to enhance the Integrated Framework. These meetings were helpful in clarifying two issues: first, institutional weaknesses constrained the capacity to trade, not only of LDCs but of many other lower income developing countries as well; and second, that feasibility studies and technical assistance alone were not sufficient to address supply side constraints in developing countries.

Partly in recognition of these realities and partly as an inducement to continued developing-country participation in the Doha Round negotiations, in 2005 the WTO Ministerial in Hong Kong agreed to establish two task forces: one to develop proposals for the establishment of an Enhanced Integrated Framework (EIF) for helping LDCs; and another to develop proposals for increased Aid for Trade (AFT) more generally. Consistent with the lack of policy coherence between trade and aid institutions that has characterized international cooperation (see pp. 240–1), governments pursued these proposals outside the actual WTO trade negotiations. This may have been a good thing, as the WTO trade negotiations stalled and the aid related initiatives may be the only major tangible and lasting result of the Doha Round.

The enhanced integrated framework for LDCs

The task force on LDCs produced a set of proposals which were approved by the WTO in 2007. It took another two years for the EIF to become fully operational in mid-2009: more than a decade after the WTO first focused on LDC aid needs.

The EIF's management structure is complex: there is an executive secretary and a small secretariat (seven professionals) located in the WTO, in Geneva. There is an EIF Focal Point, a Donor facilitator and a National Implementation Unit in each LDC. There is a trust fund managed by the UN. There is a Board consisting of three LDC representatives from capitals and three from bilateral donors with the participation of the six implementing agencies, the executive secretary and the trust fund manager. And there is a steering committee composed of all the LDCs with the participation of donors and the six agencies.

This complex structure implements activities using a trust fund whose total receipts in late 2012 amounted to $165 million, contributed to primarily by 23 donors, mostly European Union countries, Norway and Canada. As of the end of 2012 the EIF still had about $100 million available for projects.

The projects funded by the EIF fall into two categories, so-called 'Tiers'. Tier 1 projects help mainstream trade into national development plans such as the Poverty Reduction Strategy Papers that countries which obtain assistance from the IMF and the World Bank have to prepare. These projects include diagnostic studies which help identify priorities for trade-related assistance and capacity building as well as interfacing with donors for accessing funding beyond that available through the EIF trust fund. As of late 2012, Diagnostic Trade Integration Studies had been validated for 42 countries and a number of them had been updated. Tier 2 projects involve project preparation, feasibility studies and the funding of smaller projects. Proposals for these projects have been approved for seven countries.[4] Interviews with World Bank staff suggest that a number of the EIF identified projects are being considered for implementation by the Bank and other institutions.

The effectiveness of these activities has to be evaluated in the context of the overall assistance efforts to mainstream trade in development (see pp. 134–5). Discussions with practitioners, donors and staff of international organizations suggest that a lot depends on the effectiveness of the local 'Focal Points' and, not surprisingly, on partner country ownership. Problems also arise in countries where there is no PRSP. Putting the EIF in the context of an agreed poverty strategy with the World Bank and other international finance institutions is a good thing in so far as it would provide better assurances that it receives the proper priority and adequate resources. But it would seem that certain aspects of trade-related institutional capacity can be strengthened and receive international support – if they are priorities for a particular country, even if the country does not have a World Bank/IMF programme. For example, many LDCs are not even members of the WTO. EIF assistance to such countries may well need to focus on helping them become WTO members – not a simple task as we have seen in Chapter 3.

The most recent review of the EIF by independent consultants gave a mixed report. Some old problems continue to exist, namely that the EIF suffers from unrealistic expectations as it is widely misunderstood by both donors and recipients as another programme as opposed to being a framework for coordination and integration. At the same time it has been used by a number of LDCs to reinforce and catalyse positive trends in supporting the use of trade for development, country ownership and

[4] See EIF website: www.enhancedif.org.

capacity building. It has done less well in helping spur donors and agencies to coordinate their responses.

Aid for trade

The institutional weaknesses and problems of LDCs are common to many other lower income developing countries, and the differences are primarily a matter of degree. There is a more general question therefore as to what the international community does to assist them as it has promised it would do in the context of the WTO agreements.

The WTO

WTO Director General Pascal Lamy had repeatedly stated that the WTO is not a 'development institution'. The WTO provides a very small amount of assistance for training (about 2 per cent of its 190 million Swiss francs regular budget for 2012). However, it spends about 25 million Swiss francs in development-related activities financed by trust funds provided by bilateral donors. Despite the fact that the WTO is not a development assistance institution, it still appears desirable for it to increase the resources it allocates from its own budget to the provision of (1) staff to analyse issues of interest to developing-country members, and (2) technical assistance to developing countries to enable them to discharge the obligations entailed in WTO membership. Dealing with issues of interest to developing countries and strengthening their institutional capacity involve many parts of the WTO and its secretariat. It is important that the secretariat be adequately staffed to handle these matters, while preserving the neutrality of its staff and the character of the WTO as a member-driven institution (see pp. 197–8).

The EIF secretariat has been housed in the WTO at the insistence of LDCs. However, it has been institutionally insulated from the rest of the WTO, presumably so as not to be 'contaminated' by the vagaries of the political negotiations going on in the rest of the institution. While this structure may have been helpful in setting up the operations of the EIF during the stalemated Doha Round negotiations, it raises serious questions about coherence between trade and aid policies, which will be discussed in detail in Chapter 10.

UNCTAD

UNCTAD has a programme of technical cooperation focusing primarily on capacity building in trade-related institutions, including on such issues as helping developing countries with WTO accession. The programme has an annual budget of about $35 million and is funded primarily by trust funds of bilateral donors, some of the same that contribute to similar activities in the WTO and the World Bank. It is difficult to distinguish this programme from other similar ones carried out by other international organizations.

The International Trade Center (ITC)

The Center is jointly sponsored by WTO and UNCTAD and is the main international institution that over the years has provided technical assistance to developing countries aimed at expanding their exports. ITC, with an annual budget of around $20 million, works with both governments and the private sector in developing countries to strengthen their institutional capacity to trade as well as to market their products abroad. Most recently the Center has collaborated actively with the World Bank and the WTO in increasing transparency in trade and developing a data base that identifies non-tariff measures that adversely affect developing country exports worldwide.

The Advisory Centre

The providing of assistance in the legal area raises complex issues. Many governments dislike the idea of providing bilateral aid to developing countries that could be used to do legal battle with their own commercial interests or Trade Ministry. The WTO is required by Article 27.2 of the Dispute Settlement Mechanism to provide legal advice and assistance to developing countries. Accordingly, the WTO Secretariat has engaged the services of two legal experts to assist developing countries in their cases. But the support they can offer is extremely limited: their services are available for a total of four working days a month, or roughly 400 hours a year – which is usually not enough to deal with one case. Although the Secretariat could use additional resources to provide basic technical assistance, such as training courses on dispute settlement procedures and general advice on the meaning of legal provisions, its staff or consultants cannot by their very nature as neutral civil servants provide much-needed case-by-case assistance.

For this reason, in 2001 the Advisory Centre on WTO Law (ACWL) was established to provide assistance to developing countries in matters related to specific cases involving the WTO DSM, either as complaints or plaintiffs. The Centre, which is located in Geneva but is legally separate from the WTO itself, is funded partly by 11 developed-country donors and partly by developing-country users. There are currently 41 members of which 30 are developing countries. LDCs are entitled to ACWL services at no cost, even though they are not formally members.

In the ten years of its existence, the ACWL has proven to be a valuable resource for developing countries. It engages in three main activities: (1) provision of legal opinions; (2) support to developing countries in ongoing dispute settlement proceedings; and (3) training. Of the 99 legal opinions provided in 2011, roughly half concerned issues that arose in WTO negotiations. The remaining were divided between opinions responding to countries requesting advice on the consistency of their own policies with WTO provisions and others requesting advice on third country measures affecting their exports. In the decade 2001–11, the ACWL also assisted developing countries in 38 dispute settlement proceedings. This represents 21 per cent of all disputes over this period and about 40 per cent of disputes involving developing countries. At the end of each year the ACWL conducts a satisfaction survey of users. The latest survey showed that 90 per cent of developing countries found the Centre's legal advice 'highly or 'very' satisfactory. None were dissatisfied (ACWL, 2011).

Agency for International Trade Information and Cooperation (AITIC)

This small agency, established in 1998 and originally sponsored by the Swiss government, focused on strengthening the capacity of low income developing countries to participate effectively in WTO operations – by increasing the information flows to their Geneva delegations and in particular to members that did not have resident missions. In 2004 AITIC was transformed into a multilateral organization with a combined membership of a dozen developed and about 30 developing countries and an annual budget of about $1million. Its main functions were to organize training seminars and disseminate analyses and other information on matters related to the Doha Round of negotiations and other aspects of WTO operations. Although its work was well received by developing-country members, donor funding terminated in 2009 and the organization ceased operations, leaving a gap that has not been filled to this date.

NGOs

In addition to the official donors and agencies, a number of NGOs have emerged that provide technical assistance and advice on trade policy issues of importance to developing countries. Probably the most important and influential is the International Center for Trade and Sustainable Development (ICTSD). Founded in Geneva in 1996, ICTSD aims to influence the international trade system in ways that advance the goal of sustainable development using an annual budget of 7–8 million Swiss francs, contributed by a variety of official and private donors. It carries out policy-based research and analyses on a wide range of trade and sustainable development issues using a global network of institutional partnerships. One of its most useful innovations is the convening of 'dialogues' on various topics that bring together groups and individuals from developed and developing countries with differing points of view. It disseminates the results of its work through a large number of publications as well as seminars and other vehicles of policy dialogue with stakeholders in both developed and developing countries. Its advice is well received as it is perceived to be independent and objective.[5]

The Standards and Trade Development Facility

The purpose of this facility set up in 2004 is to improve developing countries' capacity to implement international sanitary and phytosanitary standards. The Facility, with an annual budget of about $5 million, represents a joint effort by five institutions (the Food and Agriculture Organization (FAO), the WHO, the World Bank, the WTO and the World Organization for Animal Health) using partly trust funds donated by bilateral donors and partly their own funding to provide technical assistance on SPS.

The main multilateral and bilateral donors

The resources needed for trade-related capacity building are so large that none of the above efforts will go very far without the support of the World Bank and other regional development banks and the main bilateral donors. The commitments in the WTO agreements made by the trade negotiators, mostly at the last moment in order to obtain developing-country consent, were not coordinated with the rest of their governments, either in developed or developing countries. Thus, there was no serious link between the commitments made and the agenda of the national or international institutions which would be implementing them.

In the aftermath of the Hong Kong meeting, there was a lot of international soul searching as to how to mobilize additional resources for aid for trade. A number of proposals were made for setting up special Funds for this purpose (Stiglitz and Charlton, 2006), including one by me (Michalopoulos, 2005).

In the end, the WTO Aid for Trade Task Force did not set up a new fund except for LDCs, but concluded that 'additional, predictable,

[5] A number of other notable NGOs dealing with trade issues are CUTS International based in India with an office in Geneva, and the South Center, also based in Geneva.

sustainable and effective financing is fundamental to fulfilling the Aid-for-Trade mandate' (WTO, 2006, p. 1) and recommended 'additional targeted resources for trade-related programs' as well as a series of procedural steps for donor coordination, country-level implementation, reporting and evaluation. The IMF/World Bank staff study in 2007 concluded that 'non-LDC low income countries have been overlooked in the effort by the trade community to mobilize aid for trade ... The countries could use aid for trade for technical assistance projects, funding preparation of projects and funding legal and other reforms in implementing WTO obligations, notably for an agreement on trade facilitation' (IMF/World Bank, 2007, p. 17). However, it did not recommend a new fund for this purpose.

One of the fundamental questions that had to be decided early on was what constituted 'Aid for Trade'. This was especially important because the major donors engaged in a beauty contest in Hong Kong promised vast amounts of assistance: Japan talked about $10 billion over three years, the US and the EU $2.7 and $2.0 billion respectively by 2010.

As the main source of information for aid flows has been the OECD, the WTO agreed to partner with the OECD in developing information on AFT flows. This resulted in the development of a joint WTO/OECD database, whose main source, however, was the OECD database on resource flows by the major bilateral and multilateral donors, a database that had been in existence for several decades and was adapted to address the information requirements on AFT. Since the main donors in OECD had a strong interest in showing that they were doing a lot to help developing countries strengthen their capacity to trade, the OECD/WTO secretariats were under strong pressure by the developed countries to adopt a very wide definition of AFT which included not only aid activities that were directly linked to strengthening trade-related institutions, but also all aid to economic infrastructure (except water and sanitation) and building productive capacity.

The resulting totals showed that very large amounts of aid are 'trade-related' and rising. According to OECD estimates (OECD, 2013), total AFT commitments in 2010 amounted to $45 billion or 35 per cent of total Official Development Assistance (ODA) commitments, compared to $25 billion or 22 per cent of the total in 2002–05. Total AFT disbursements were $29 billion in 2009, or 21 per cent of total ODA, compared to $21 billion or 12 per cent in 2006 (OECD/WTO, 2011b).

The problems with this very wide definition of AFT flows are obvious: while it is clear that productive supply constraints inhibit developing country exports, not all assistance which aims at helping developing countries increase their productive capacity is 'trade-related'. To address this issue, the OECD at the beginning in 2007 started including a slightly narrower concept of aid whose 'principal' or 'significant' objective was trade-related. The resulting estimates show that only 15–20 per cent of AFT that builds productive capacity is trade-related.

Similarly, energy supply, transport and communications constraints limit the capacity to trade of developing countries. There is considerable evidence that reliable energy supplies in particular and transport infrastructure especially affect export performance (Hallaert et al., 2013). But it is absurd to include all infrastructure aid as trade-related as the WTO/OECD database does. To give an idea of how little meaning the OECD definition of AFT has, consider the following: in 2009, using this definition, more than 60 per cent of all 'other official flows' – primarily loans from the World Bank and other regional development banks which do a lot of infrastructure financing – were trade-related. Using a more realistic definition of Aid for Trade, the World Bank estimates that it provided $1.8 billion in trade-related activities in 2010, compared to $27 billion according to the OECD/WTO definition (Hoekman, 2011). A recent country-level evaluation of AFT in Nepal concluded that 'the definition of AFT is too broad, encompassing even aid flows remotely related to trade' (Adhikari et al., 2011, p. 69; see also Adhikari, 2011).

Despite the overall increases in the volume of aid for trade it is hard to say whether the original commitments made by the major donors in 2006 have been fulfilled as the base line from which the increases were supposed to occur is unclear. A number of observers (Ismail, 2007; Stiglitz and Charlton, 2012) doubt their additionality. Others have noted that the big increases have come from the multilateral agencies rather than bilateral donors (Cadot et al., 2012, p. 15). And declines in the volume of ODA and in AFT likely to be registered starting with 2011 will not mean much either, given the very wide definition used.

Clearly AFT has been increasing in many specific areas for many countries and for some institutions. In the case of the World Bank, AFT activities tripled between FY 2003 and FY 2010, whether using its own definition or that of the OECD/WTO (Hoekman, 2011, p. 247). The Bank has initiated a broad range of programmes in support of trade facilitation. Strengthening developing-country institutions in customs clearance and broader border management is both costly and of critical importance to their trade (McLinden et al., 2011). 'On average it takes three times as many days, nearly twice as many documents and six times as many signatures to trade in a poor country as it does in rich countries' (Hoekman, 2009, p. 35).

Trade facilitation is also one of the few areas in which the moribund Doha negotiations have made some progress. World Bank programmes include loans for trade and trade facilitation and the worldwide Trade Facilitation Facility – a multi-donor trust fund aimed at enhancing developing countries' competitiveness by strengthening the quality of trade facilitation systems and reducing trade costs. According to one study (Portugal-Perez and Wilson, 2008) feasible improvements in trade facilitation will result in benefits equivalent to an 8 per cent reduction in tariffs for African countries.

The World Bank has also developed the Logistics Performance Index which measures logistics performance in 155 countries worldwide. The Index is developed with the collaboration of the private sector, based on a survey of freight forwarders, and can be helpful to individual countries in identifying problems in logistics encompassing all kinds of issues that affect the cost of international commerce: freight transport, warehousing, border clearance, payment systems and many other functions (Arvis et al., 2012). The main regional development banks have also developed a varied set of initiatives on aid for trade (see Hynes and Holden, 2012).

It is difficult to say much about the allocation of these funds among developing countries. The latest OECD estimates suggest that almost 50 per cent of AFT commitments in 2010 went to low income countries, and 30 per cent of that to LDCs, boosted by very large amounts going to one country, Afghanistan, whose official exports are miniscule. Undoubtedly, there are many lower income countries and LDCs that are benefitting from the increased emphasis on AFT since 2005. However, OECD/WTO data show that the largest recipient of AFT in both 2009 and 2010 based on disbursements was India; others among the top ten recipients in 2009 included Indonesia (fifth largest), Turkey (sixth) and China! (seventh) – hardly countries whose trade performance would suggest much need for AFT.

Country evaluations

The increased international attention paid to AFT has also resulted in greater focus on evaluating the results of AFT activities. Some of the earlier evaluations of the Integrated Framework were highly critical (IOB, 2005). The OECD has undertaken a very large effort to monitor progress, collect information and develop up to date a variety of analyses of AFT activities based on specific cases in a large number of developing countries, including a major review of a large number of country and econometric studies of AFT effectiveness (OECD/WTO, 2011a). A seminar in early 2013 also generated a wealth of information on approaches to making AFT more effective (OECD, 2013). The International Centre for Trade and Sustainable Development (ICTSD), an independent NGO based in Geneva, recently undertook evaluations of AFT initiatives in six countries (Cambodia, Caribbean Regional, Malawi, Mauritius, Nepal, Peru). And a number of other studies have addressed various aspects of AFT effectiveness (Cadot et al., 2012; Hynes and Holden, 2012).

The results of these evaluations provide insights about what has worked well and what has not, as well as ways to increase future AFT effectiveness. Regarding, first, the results of econometric studies, there is little evidence of a direct link between AFT and an increase in exports (Cadot et al., 2012). This is actually quite surprising given the extraordinary export growth characterizing many developing countries in the 2000s, as shown in Chapter 1, and the claims of large increases in AFT. It is probably due to the weaknesses in the overall statistical definitions of AFT and the fact that the allocation of the bilateral portion of ODA and AFT resources is often guided by political/strategic factors and bears little relation to recipient country needs or effectiveness of aid use. There is some evidence that aid to infrastructure can have the strongest positive effect on exports compared to other forms of AFT. But according to an OECD report (OECD/WTO, 2011a), citing a Commonwealth Secretariat study, a doubling of aid to infrastructure (i.e. a 100 per cent increase) would increase exports by 3.5 per cent. This pales to insignificance compared with the *annual* increase of 12 per cent in developing-country exports achieved in the decade 2000–10.

The results of the country-based studies are far more interesting:. 'the diversity of the case stories reveals many activities that do not routinely show up in the OECD aid for trade data. Virtually none of the stories from middle-income countries in Latin America are financed by ODA. Projects undertaken by the private sector arms of the multilateral and bilateral agencies are for the most part not included, yet figure prominently in the cases'. The evaluation goes on to conclude that the community of trade negotiators and arguably OECD donors should focus less on the dollar amounts transferred and more on capacity building, policy studies, technical assistance and knowledge transfer (ibid., p. 35).

The OECD report notes the rising importance of South–South aid for trade and the need for even greater increases of such aid in the future, and the apparent effectiveness of proactive industry-specific projects that translated into benefits for low-income participants including women. On the other hand, the report concluded that the paucity of case study examples related to infrastructure activities, services trade as well as programmes involving adjustment assistance tended to reflect the unfortunately low relative priority assigned to these areas by developing-country governments.

Evidence from the ICTSD evaluations of Cambodia, Malawi, Mauritius and Nepal also provide interesting conclusions about the effectiveness of AFT activities in these countries. In many respects the conclusions are not different from those about the effectiveness of overall aid programmes. Ownership by governments, such as that which occurred in Cambodia and Mauritius, was critical to the success of the programme. Both countries used aid to diversify their exports. Cambodia's success was entirely predictable, as the government incorporated trade as a priority in its development plan from the late 1990s (Sok et al., 2011).

On the other hand in Malawi the government focused on maize production as opposed to export diversification as the main instrument for poverty reduction. As a result, little has been achieved to strengthen the country's trade performance – nor for that matter to decrease poverty. Typical of Malawi's lack of government commitment to sustainable trade development was the lack of provision of funds for computer maintenance in reference centres established by the WTO. Once WTO funding ended the reference centres closed (Said et al., 2011).[6]

While the overview paper suggests that there has been an increase in AFT funding in most of the countries evaluated, the individual studies available tell a somewhat more sombre story: in Nepal, there has been an increase in commitments but not in disbursements; but the categories are so broad that it is difficult to say for sure what has happened. Donor performance also needs to improve: 'while AFT has received attention at the global level, there is a lack of knowledge/awareness of AFT and/or lack of commensurate attention to it in country offices' (Adhikari et al., 2011, p. 69). In Cambodia, 'while coordination among donors is better today than a decade ago ... stakeholders identified the prevalence of multiple uncoordinated donor-driven projects' (Sok et al., 2011, p. xi).

Conclusions

The international community has shown increased awareness of the significant constraints developing countries face in implementing their

[6] Sadly this is a predictable result: in early 2002, I was approached by the World Bank to lead the initial Diagnostic Trade Integration Study for Malawi. After initially accepting the assignment, I resigned in part because it was clear from the beginning that the government was not committed to trade reform.

WTO commitments because of serious institutional weaknesses. A number of initiatives have been undertaken to address these constraints, especially in LDCs, such as the EIF and the ACWL, and through broader increases in aid for trade.

There is a need to improve the reporting system on AFT as the current definition is not useful in assessing progress in raising the volume of resources devoted to these activities in countries that need assistance. There is also a tendency of creating a variety of specific funds to address specific problems. This adds to the problem of donor coordination. And it makes it very difficult for the EIF to play a coordinating role. In aid, as in any other programme, having the weakest agency with the least amount of funds and staff trying to coordinate the World Bank, UK Department for International Development (DFID) and the United States Agency for International Development (USAID) is like having the tail wag the dog.

More efforts are also needed to link assistance to specific developing-country commitments undertaken in the WTO. Developing countries have correctly argued that they would be prepared to accept only new commitments that they can implement and would only accept such commitments if they are assured of assistance that would help them put in place the implementing capacity that they need, for example in areas such as trade facilitation. Developed countries are not willing to accept legally binding aid commitments while they are seeking legally binding developing-country commitments in the WTO.

In the absence of a link between increased commitments and increased assistance, there is little scope for obtaining developing-country participation in agreements such as trade facilitation which requires them to make WTO commitments in areas where they face institutional constraints. The ways that a link might be forged between WTO commitments and the provision of assistance is a broad issue which would need to be addressed in the context of the future role of the WTO (discussed in more detail in Chapter 10). While the WTO is not a 'development institution' at present it may have to become more development oriented than it is now. There is nothing wrong with that: after all the bulk of its membership consists of developing countries, whose main interest is development.

6
Developed-Country Trade Policies

Introduction

Since the 1980s the role of developed-country markets in determining demand for developing countries exports has shrunk as the role of the emerging economies increased, especially in the decade of the 2000s. However, developments in developed-country markets continued to be an important factor that shaped developing-country trade performance. On the demand side, developed countries' GDP increased at a rate slightly lower than the long-term growth trends in these countries – just under 2.5 per cent for 1990–99 and 1.7 per cent for 2000–10 compared to 3.1 per cent in the 1980s and 3.6 per cent in the 1970s (OECD, 2000; World Bank, 2012). On the other hand, the market access conditions for developing countries improved, partly as a result of standstills and subsequent liberalization linked to the Uruguay Round Agreements and reductions in tariffs following the Information Technology Agreement, the termination of the Agreement on Textiles and Clothing and as a result of numerous preferential arrangements concluded between developed and developing countries.

The implementation of the Uruguay Round Agreements took a number of years to complete[1] and there was some retrogression following the severe economic crisis of 2008. But there is little doubt that access to developed-country markets was much better at the end of the period than at the beginning. Access continued to be impeded by high trade barriers in certain sectors, such as agriculture; and while progress was made on tariff escalation, the problem persisted in textiles and leather

[1] Reportedly Japan did not finish implementing its commitments until 2009 (WTO, 2011d).

products. More barriers are also appearing connected to the implementation of the TBT and SPS agreements. Finally, as part of the Uruguay Round Agreements, WTO members committed themselves to take several explicit additional steps in favour of developing countries in anti-dumping, whose implementation is important to review.[2]

Tariffs

Overall averages

The effects of the Uruguay Round Agreements on the MFN tariffs of the developed countries have been extensively considered in other studies whose main findings will be summarized here (Martin and Winters, 1996; OECD, 1997; UNCTAD/WTO, 1997). Broadly speaking, MFN tariffs on imports of manufactures into the major industrial countries' markets were reduced by an average of 40 per cent from a trade weighted average of 6.3 to 3.8 per cent with the reductions to be phased in over five years and the first instalment to be put in place on 1 January 1995.[3] Countries have reduced their tariff rates accordingly since then. Moreover, in 1997, following the Information Technology Agreement, the duty on a number of products in this sector was reduced to zero on an MFN basis (Finger and Schuknecht, 1999). Canada undertook a further unilateral liberalization of about 1,800 lines of MFN tariffs in 2008–09 (WTO, 2011e). Applied rates are even lower, averaging 3.2 per cent, reflecting various preferential arrangements (See Table 4.3).

MFN tariffs on products other than agriculture range, for example, from an average of 0.8 per cent in Japan to 3.7 per cent in the US and 4.0 per cent in the EU (UNCTAD/WTO, 1997, Annex Table 1). But the rates are higher on products of interest to developing countries (Hertel and Martin, 1999). At the same time, for the Quad countries (Canada, the EU, Japan, the US), one-third of all MFN tariff lines are duty free, involving a large range of products of export interest to the developing countries.

The tariffication of various measures of support and protection in the agricultural sector resulted in substantial increases in the initial tariffs on a wide range of agricultural products in some major markets. Thus,

[2] See Article 15 of the Uruguay Round Agreement on the Procedures for Implementation of GATT Article VI.

[3] The EU advanced from 1 January 1997 to 1 January 1996 its schedule of implementation of the third stage of tariff reductions for most non-agricultural products as part of its compensation for the EU enlargement through the accession of Austria, Finland and Sweden (WTO, 1997c, p. 15).

the average applied MFN rate for agricultural commodities (production weighted) in 1996 ranged from 7.9 per cent in the US to 10.7 per cent in the EU (OECD, 1997, Table 3.1). Subsequently, developed countries were to reduce agricultural tariffs by 36 per cent across the board, at the same time as access for agricultural products would be enhanced by reductions in domestic support measures.

The problem was that developed (and developing) countries chose to bind their tariffs at higher rates than the actual tariff equivalents during the years just before the conclusion of the Uruguay Round Agreements (1989–93). For example the final bindings for the EU were almost two-thirds higher than the tariff equivalents for 1989–93 (Binswager and Lutz, 2000, p. 9) and for the US, they were more than three-quarters higher. Binding the tariffs at such high levels allowed countries to vary actual tariff rates according to the results they wished to achieve in protecting their domestic markets – much as the EU used to do with the variable levies, which have been prohibited since the Uruguay Round. The result of this so-called 'dirty tariffication' has not been improved market access, merely that protection has become more transparent. Similarly, commitments to reduce export subsidies were made relative to a base period in the early 1990s when these subsidies were at very high levels.

During the 2000s aggregate measures of support (AMS) to agriculture as well as export subsidies by the two major developed WTO members, the EU and the US, fell significantly from 1990 levels both because of budgetary constraints and because of rising prices for many agricultural commodities (Blandford and Josling, 2011; Gorter et al., 2003). But the overall structure of protection negotiated in the Uruguay Round Agreements has remained intact, despite strong efforts by developing countries during the Doha Round discussions to obtain better treatment in agricultural products, such as cotton, which are of critical importance to some of the poorest countries and LDCs.[4]

Preferences

The actual tariff rates applied to imports from individual developing countries tend to be even lower than the above MFN rates, however. There are two main reasons for this: (1) the generalized system of

---

[4] With the exception of the 'Peace Clause', under Article 13, a provision which expired in 2003 and which had constrained members from taking action under the DSM in connection with their commitments on domestic support, market access and export subsidies in agriculture.

preferences (GSP) which further reduced tariffs on selected commodities and countries; (2) the existence of preferential arrangements for particular countries in specific developed-country markets, for example, the preferences afforded to the ACP countries in the EU market, the ones enjoyed by Mexico as part of NAFTA, and the Caribbean and Central American countries' preferential treatment in the US market as a consequence of the Caribbean Basin Initiative and the African Growth and Opportunity Act (AGOA) initiative affecting low income countries in Africa. In addition, individual developed countries have granted even more preferential treatment to LDC imports following the WTO High Level Meeting on Trade-Related Measures for LDCs in 1997.

The overall margin of unilateral non-reciprocal preferences for developing countries as a group is of the order of 3.5 percentage points (Hoekman et al., 2009) though it varies significantly for different groups and in different markets from 6.6 points for LDCs in the EU to 0.5 for low income countries in the US. The various GSP programmes have narrower coverage and lower margins of preferences than regional non-reciprocal programmes. Among the regional *preferential* programmes the ones in Latin America and the Caribbean contain larger preference margins than the ones in sub-Saharan Africa.

Given the complexity of the various preferential systems in place, it is difficult to assess their overall effect on the average tariffs applied and most importantly on the exports of eligible developing countries. An earlier study suggested that the GSP remains a valuable tool for promoting developing-country exports' (UNCTAD/WTO, 1997, p. 9). More recent estimates suggest that the regional non-reciprocal programmes are much more important than the GSP for individual countries.

A number of these programmes had been especially beneficial for particular countries and products because of quotas in various export markets, for example bananas and sugar in the EU and textiles in the US. The reduction of MFN rates, the spread of reciprocal preferential arrangements, the liberalization of the EU banana and sugar regimes in 2009, the termination of the Agreement on Textiles and Clothing in 2005 and the increasing limitations on product and country eligibility imposed by the 'graduation' features of various programmes, have all resulted in reducing the value of the non-reciprocal preferential programmes offered by developed countries.

Still, the programmes can be useful to individual developing countries and individual products. It is estimated (Hoekman et al., 2009, p. 20) that 'US preferences are equal to 5 percent or more of dutiable exports for 27 countries, while in the EU case the value of non-reciprocal preferences exceeds 6 per cent of dutiable exports for 16 countries'. Countries benefiting in particular include Malawi (tobacco) and Lesotho (textiles). Notwithstanding such benefits, some have argued that the GSP as well as other unilateral preferential schemes may offer the wrong types of 'dependency' incentives to developing countries and retard rather than promote their integration into the international trading system (Finger and Winters, 1998; Srinivasan, 1998).

Peaks

Despite the overall decline in the average applied MFN tariffs since the Uruguay Round, there are a number of sectors and product groups in various developed countries where tariffs are substantially higher, thus limiting market access. The Uruguay Round Agreements increased the tariff dispersion in some developed-country markets and decreased it in others (Daly and Kuwahara, 1998, p. 223; OECD, 1997, p. 18). But in all countries there are many products and product groups in which the average MFN applied tariff level exceeds 12 per cent, or roughly three times the overall average MFN applied tariff level of developed countries. These products and groups can be defined as having tariff 'peaks'. They exist in both agriculture and manufactures in a number of developed-country markets. But the very high rates typically have been the consequence of tariffication in agriculture.[5] The main products in which such tariff peaks can be observed in various markets are the following:

- Major staples, such as meat, sugar, milk and dairy products and cereals, where the tariffication of quantitative restrictions has resulted in tariff rates frequently exceeding 100 per cent and ranging, for example, up to 550 per cent for rice in Japan.[6]
- Cotton and tobacco: for similar reasons similarly high rates are applied to these products, with the rate on tobacco reaching 350 per cent in the US.
- Fruit and vegetables, including 180 per cent for above-quota bananas in the EU, and 550 per cent and 132 per cent for shelled groundnuts in Japan and the US respectively.

---

5 Some writers speak of 'mega-tariffs' for tariff lines in excess of 100 per cent. According to one report, in agriculture alone the US has 24 mega-tariffs, the EU 141 and Japan 142.

6 These are estimates reported in UNCTAD/WTO (1997). It is difficult to estimate accurately the *ad valorem* tariff equivalents for many agricultural commodities where tariffication involves the adoption of specific duties often combined with quotas.

- Processed food products, including fruit juice, canned meat, peanut butter and confectionery with rates exceeding 30 per cent in several markets and rising to 230 per cent for grape juice in the EU.
- Textiles and clothing: tariff rates are in the 12–30 per cent range for a large number of products in Canada, the EU and the US.
- Footwear and leather products, with tariff peaks in excess of 35 per cent for 10 per cent of products in Japan (rising to 160 per cent for shoes) and 17 per cent of products of Australia (Smeets and Fournier, 1998).
- Selected automotive and transport sector products (trucks in the US and the EU, ships and boats in Canada) with rates exceeding 20 per cent.

The GSP and other preferential schemes operated by the various developed countries tend to reduce, in some cases significantly, the tariff rates applicable to imports of these products from developing countries. However, in almost all cases where tariff peaks are present, the sensitivity of the domestic industry to imports has resulted in the exclusion of various products from the schemes or in some type of limitation being imposed either on the amount that can be imported under the preferential rates or the countries that are eligible. For example, the US excludes most textile products from its GSP scheme, the EU limits preferential margins and imposes country/sector quotas. Quota limitations also exist for non-traditional suppliers of various fruits and vegetables to the EU market and in Japan's market for leather goods and footwear. Some of the schemes favouring LDCs, however, do provide virtually total duty free and quota free (DFQF) access to a number of developed-country markets.

LDCs

The international community has made special efforts to address the market access problems faced by LDCs. Following the 1997 WTO high level meeting on the LDCs developed countries (and some developing ones) have made additional preferential market-access commitments to LDCs. The developed-country commitments were legally permissible under the GATT Enabling Clause of 1979. Those of the developing countries were formalized through a ten-year waiver under the WTO decision of 15 June 1999 and extended for another ten years in 2009.

At present, LDCs enjoy essentially DFQF market access to Australia, the EU, New Zealand, Switzerland and Turkey. Canada offers a DFQF scheme that covers 99 per cent of tariff lines, Japan 98 per cent and the US somewhat less, with 34 sub-Saharan African LDCs having a duty free but quota limited access to 96 per cent of tariff lines, while Asian LDCs much less – as the programme excludes textiles. Brazil, China, India and Korea also operate LDC preference schemes, which are considerably more restrictive than those offered by developed economies (Laird, 2012).

The average tariff rates that LDCs face in developed-country markets generally average about 2 per cent, about half those facing other developing countries. Tariffs in other developing-country markets against LDC products are much higher at 14.5 per cent (WTO, 1997b).

The low average tariff rates in developed-country markets reflect primarily the fact that the bulk of LDC exports are primary commodities where tariffs are low or non-existent and less the extensive preferences they obtain in these markets – which on average offer no more than a few percentage points of advantage.

On the other hand, the dutiable products in which LDCs tend to have comparative advantage, namely agriculture, textiles and footwear, are subject to tariff peaks and tariff escalation. For a number of products (beef, asparagus, cigarettes, processed wood, clothing and footwear) amounting to about 10 per cent of their total exports, tariffs in the Quad, Australia, Norway and Switzerland ranged between 5 and 15 per cent (ibid.).

In these cases DFQF can be meaningful as preference margins may be substantial. But for LDCs to exploit these they need to have relatively simple qualification requirements regarding rules of origin. The requirements for such rules can be prohibitive if they require substantial value added in the country benefiting from the preferences. LDCs typically do not have enough industrial capacity or the investment climate to attract the upstream suppliers needed to produce sufficient domestic value added or to transform inputs into a processed product (Francois et al., 2011, p. 7). The evidence from DFQF programmes which offer both a significant margin of preference and relatively liberal rules of origin (Canada, Australia and US – AGOA) show that eligible LDCs have expanded their exports significantly following the establishment of the programmes (ibid., p. 9).

In summary, market access problems for LDCs are concentrated in a few products and tend to be greater in developing than in developed-country markets. In the course of the Doha Round negotiations a variety of proposals have been aimed at enhancing the existing preferential arrangements benefiting LDCs. Some focus on expanding the coverage in the US and major developing-country markets. Others emphasize the importance of simplifying rules of origin. In all cases a key prerequisite is the need to address LDCs supply-side constraints that limit their capacity for using fully existing preferential arrangements.

Escalation

Tariff escalation is a matter of concern for developing countries in the context of market access because it tends to increase the rate of effective protection at higher stages of processing, thereby making market access more difficult for finished manufactured products, which in turn can adversely affect developing countries' industrialization efforts. As a consequence of the Uruguay Round Agreements the degree of overall escalation has decreased. Also, escalation is more pervasive in developing countries than in developed ones (see Table 4.4). But it continues to be a matter of concern for many developing countries and their exports of specific products, such as processed foods (wheat flour, orange juice, vegetable oils, dairy products), clothing, leather and wood products (Lindbland, 1997; UNCTAD/WTO 1997; WTO, 1998b). These results should be interpreted with caution because data limitations as well as the continued existence of quantitative restrictions in some of these product chains make it difficult to calculate the effective rates of protection. But they do suggest that tariff escalation – as with tariff peaks – in certain products, though reduced by the Uruguay Round Agreements, continues to be an area of concern in respect to market access for developing-country exports.

Non-tariff measures

Core measures

Since the Uruguay Round and until about 2009 it is probably fair to say that the pervasiveness of core non-tariff measures in developed-country trade regimes had fallen to its lowest point in more than 50 years. By core non-tariff barriers, I mean the use of non-automatic licensing, quotas and tariff quotas and voluntary export restraints as well as price control measures such as variable charges, minimum prices or voluntary export price restraints. Since 2009 there has been some resurgence of protectionism, but much less than had been feared, given the depth of the economic recession in developed countries. The key issues for the future relate to the use of trade remedies, i.e. anti-dumping, countervailing and safeguards, all of which are permitted under the WTO agreements, as well as the expanding use of SPS and TBT measures which have an impact on trade.

There is no reliable database that can be used for assessing coverage and frequency ratios of the incidence of non-tariff barriers in developed or developing countries over time.[7] But the available data suggest that these barriers have declined over time. Voluntary export restraints were phased out by the end of 1998 – although there have been some reports of their 'informal' re-emergence in recent periods. Some remaining export restraints in developed countries appear to be directed in significant measure against non-WTO members. The termination of the Agreement on Textiles and Clothing in 2005 as well as the end in 2008 of the special quantitative restrictions applied to imports from China as part of its WTO accession ended the last vestiges of formal 'legal' quantitative restraints in manufactures.

Non-tariff measures have been drastically reduced in agriculture, where only tariff quotas exist in a number of products in some of the major developed markets. These range from a few tariff lines in the US and Australia up to 1.5 per cent in Japan and 4.9 per cent in the EU (see Table 6.1; WTO, 2004a, 2004b, 2004c). At the same time, the use of non-automatic licensing has been reduced in all major developed-country markets and is now focusing primarily on restraints linked to the maintenance of sanitary, phyto-sanitary and technical standards or protection for the environment. Concerns, however, have been raised as to whether the implementation of WTO agreements in these areas has been motivated by protection of domestic industries, and a number of disputes have arisen regarding the compatibility of certain measures implemented by some countries with these agreements.

The reduction of NTMs in agriculture after the conclusion of the Uruguay Round does not seem to have resulted in significant improvements in market access for developing countries for a variety of reasons. First, there were problems with the way tariffication was implemented, as discussed earlier. Second, the reductions of AMS have not affected the significant supports to products of interest to developing countries such as cotton, sugar and dairy products. Third, despite the commitments to reduce export subsidies, these have been maintained at such high levels as to continue to undermine incentives provided to developing-country producers. Examples of the adverse effects of export subsidies on developing-country producers abound: subsidies in dairy products have hurt production in a large range of countries, including Brazil, Jamaica and Tanzania; subsidies on tomato concentrate impact especially on West African countries like Burkina Faso, Mali and Senegal;

---

[7] There is a major effort currently being undertaken by the World Bank in cooperation with UNCTAD/ITC and WTO. The UNCTAD TRAINS database has been in place for some time but it is not considered reliable and complete.

Table 6.1 Non-tariff measures and trade remedies in developed countries

Trade measure	Australia		Canada		EU		Japan		Norway		Switzerland		United States	
	1996	2011	1996	2011	1996	2011	1996	2011	1996	2011	1996	2011	1996	2011
NTMs (% of total tariff lines)														
Licensing, non-Automatic	0	X	0	X	0.8	X	1.3	X	2.6	X	0	X	0	X
Tariff quota	0	*	0	2.2	0	4.9	0.6	1.8	0	0.4	0.2	3.5	0	*
AD/CV and VERs	0.4	—	0.7	—	0.2	—	0	—	0	0	0	0	5	1.1
Trade remedies (no. of measures in force)														
Anti-dumping (AD)**	—	22	—	33	143	140	0	6	0	0	0	0	—	253
Countervailing (CV)	—	3	—	9	2	11	0	0	0	0	0	0	—	50
Safeguards (SG)	—	0	—	0	0	0	0	0	0	0	0	0	—	0
Total AD/CV/SG	—	25	—	42	145	151	0	6	0	0	0	0	—	303

Notes: X = licensing for health, sanitary, safety, environmental and/or defence; VERs: Voluntary Export Restraints; * = less than 1%; ** anti-dumping measures in effect in 2003: Canada 91, EU 156, US 279; — = data not available.

Sources: WTO Trade Profiles database, WTO TPRs and OECD (1997, Table 5.1).

support for beef has undermined efforts to raise livestock production in some of the same countries; and EU beef has come to dominate the markets of Benin and Ivory Coast for which Burkina Faso and Mali were once important suppliers. In effect, there was far less 'real' improvement in the agricultural sector than was anticipated.

Trade remedies

Over the last 30 years, as the incidence of quotas and other explicitly protective quantitative controls has diminished, the importance of trade remedies – anti-dumping, countervailing and safeguards – has risen in both developed and developing countries. However, there is no evidence that their use has increased in absolute terms during the most recent financial crisis relative to what happened in 1992–93: during those two years there were 326 and 299 total anti-dumping investigations respectively, while the peak number of investigations during the most recent crisis was 215 in 2008. In the US, which over the years has instigated the largest number of total anti-dumping investigations and still has some measures in place which were instituted more than 40 years ago, only 1.1 per cent of total imports are affected by trade remedies (see Table 6.1). At the same time, as discussed earlier, the evidence is extremely clear that the share of developing countries in the total remedies has increased dramatically.

Table 6.1 also contains some scattered information that permits us to gauge the evolution of trade remedies in major developed countries over time. In the US, the tariff line frequencies of anti-dumping, countervailing and safeguards have declined from 5 percent in 1996 to 1.1 per cent in 2011. For the EU over a comparable period, but measured in total number of cases, it appears that there has been little change in the totals. It is also interesting to look at the situation in 2003. At this intermediate point, the number of anti-dumping measures in place for both the US and the EU as well as Canada was higher than in 2011. Japan is the only country which unambiguously increased its use of trade remedies over the period. But its total use of these instruments is minimal.

The overall conclusion from this analysis of the frequency of use of trade remedies by developed countries is that, while still substantial, it is certainly not more extensive than in the 1990s. Combined with the earlier discussion of the declining trends in the use of other core non-tariff measures, it would appear that developed-country markets in 2011 were definitely no less and probably more open than they were in the mid-1990s.

The major product groups which are the object of anti-dumping investigations are much the same for developed as for developing countries: Table 6.2 shows that basic metals and chemicals are the two sectors which account for the bulk of anti-dumping investigations, between 40 and 50 per cent, in both developed and developing countries. Over the last 30 years, little has changed in this respect.

It is important to recall that during the Uruguay Round and in the context of the Agreement on the Implementation of GATT Article VI on anti-dumping, the developed countries committed themselves to give special regard to the special situation of developing-country members when considering anti-dumping measures under the Agreement. Article 15 urges the use of the constructive remedies provided for in the agreement before applying anti-dumping duties that would affect the essential interests of developing-country members.

There is no guidance regarding how this article is to be implemented, particularly in respect of the way in which 'the special situation of developing country members is to be taken into account'. The article does not appear to commit developed countries to do anything more than make use of the 'constructive remedies' mentioned in the agreement before applying anti-dumping duties. But presumably, they would have to do this in all cases, not only those involving developing countries.

In practice the results have been mixed. Most of the developed-country anti-dumping investigations and definitive measures against developing countries have been directed at higher and middle income developing countries (often the same countries that have themselves made increasing use of anti-dumping measures) and non-WTO members (see Chapter 4). China and Chinese Taipei in particular have been a target both before and after their accession to the WTO, both by developed and other developing countries. Bangladesh is the only LDC to have been subjected to anti-dumping investigations and definitive measures on three occasions, in 1992 (see Miranda et al., 1998).

Table 6.3 shows that developing countries are more frequently the target of anti-dumping actions by both developed and other developing countries. Developed countries, on the other hand, are the least targeted group both by other developed countries and developing countries. In particular, the share of overall investigations in which developing countries are affected is much higher than the share of developing countries in world exports.

The ratio of the two shares, *Rad,* should be interpreted with care because the proportion of investigations may not accurately reflect the actual amounts of exports affected. Nevertheless, it would be difficult

Table 6.2 Sectoral distribution of anti-dumping investigations by developed and developing countries, 1987–2011

	1987–94				1995–2001				2002–11			
	Developed countries		Developing countries		Developed countries		Developing countries		Developed countries		Developing countries	
HS Section	No. of cases	% share	No. of cases	% share	No. of cases	% share	No. of cases	% share	No. of cases	% share	No. of cases	% share
I Animals and products	8	0.6	17	2.2	11	1.3	13	1.2	10	1.6	20	1.4
II Vegetable products	11	0.8	18	2.3	12	1.4	16	1.5	8	1.2	20	1.4
III Fats, oils and waxes	4	0.3	13	1.7	2	0.2	2	0.2	3	0.5	7	0.5
IV Prepared foodstuff and tobacco	52	3.7	9	1.2	17	2.0	20	1.9	5	0.8	13	0.9
V Mineral products	41	2.9	11	1.4	20	2.3	26	2.5	9	1.5	18	1.2
VI Chemical products	210	15.0	157	20.2	140	16.4	183	17.1	154	25.0	348	23.6
VII Plastics and rubber articles	147	10.5	102	13.1	105	12.2	130	12.2	81	13.2	197	13.4
VIII Hides, skins and leather products	8	0.6	1	0.1	1	0.1	2	0.2	0	0.1	2	0.1
IX Wood and pulp	16	1.1	8	1.0	13	1.5	15	1.4	18	3.0	45	3.0
X Paper, paperboard and articles	65	4.6	47	6.0	42	4.9	48	4.5	36	5.8	82	5.6
XI Textiles and articles	95	6.8	55	7.1	61	7.1	77	7.2	43	7.0	122	8.3
XII Footwear and headgear	24	1.7	9	1.2	8	0.9	10	0.9	4	0.6	10	0.7

(*continued*)

Table 6.2 Continued

HS Section	1987–94				1995–2001				2002–11			
	Developed countries		Developing countries		Developed countries		Developing countries		Developed countries		Developing countries	
	No. of cases	% share	No. of cases	% share	No. of cases	% share	No. of cases	% share	No. of cases	% share	No. of cases	% share
XIII Glass, stone and ceramic	59	4.2	15	1.9	26	3.0	31	2.9	29	4.7	67	4.6
XIV Pearls and precious stones	0	0.0	0	0.0	0	0.0	1	0.1	0	0.0	0	0.0
XV Base metals and articles	374	26.7	178	22.9	274	32.1	342	32.0	148	24.1	339	23.0
XVI Machinery and electrical equipment	212	15.2	83	10.7	82	9.6	103	9.6	44	7.1	120	8.2
XVII Vehicles, aircraft and vessels	27	1.9	7	0.9	9	1.0	11	1.0	6	0.9	15	1.0
XVIII Instruments, clocks and recorders	19	1.4	21	2.7	12	1.4	13	1.2	6	1.0	17	1.1
XX Other miscellaneous manufactures	27	1.9	27	3.5	20	2.3	25	2.3	12	1.9	29	2.0
Total (all sectors)	1,399	100.0	778	100.0	855	100.0	1,068	100.0	615	100.0	1,472	100.0

Note: Excludes arms sector XIX.
Source: WTO antidumping database.

Table 6.3 Anti-dumping measures by affected country, 1987–2011

Affected country/group	1987–94			1995–2001			2002–11		
	AD Msre (%)	World exports share (%)	Ratio of Msre/exports	AD Msre (%)	World exports share (%)	Ratio of Msre/exports	AD Msre (%)	World exports share (%)	Ratio of Msre/exports
WTO members	74	88	0.8	63	89	0.7	93	98	0.9
Developed countries	41	66	0.6	33	68	0.5	23	62	0.4
Developing countries	33	22	1.5	30	21	1.4	70	36	1.9
Developing countries excluding China	—	—	—	13	18	0.7	39	27	1.5
Non-WTO members	26	12	2.2	37	11	3.4	7	2	3.5
China	—	—	—	17	3	5.7	31	9	3.4
Chinese Taipei	—	—	—	5	2	2.5	6	1	6.0
Former FSU	—	—	—	10	2	5.0	5	3	1.7
TOTAL: all countries	100	100		100	100		100		

Note: — data not available. AD: Antidumping.
Sources: WTO antidumping database and World Bank WDI database (trade data).

to conclude from the data in Table 6.3 anything other than that the developing countries have sustained a disproportionate amount of anti-dumping investigations over the last 20 years. *Rad* investigations for developing countries had a value of 1.5 compared to an *Rad* of 0.6 for the developed countries for the period 1987–94. The value of the ratio progressively increased for developing countries in the period 1995–2001 and 2002–11, while it decreased for developed countries. This means that developing countries, over the last 25 years, were more than twice as likely to have their imports affected by an anti-dumping investigation (relative to their share in international trade) than developed countries.

Table 6.3 also shows the very large incidence of anti-dumping actions taken against China, Chinese Taipei and non-WTO members, especially so-called 'non-market economies', which consist mostly of countries other than the Baltics that emerged from the former Soviet Union, in particular Russia, Ukraine, Belarus and Kazakhstan, which have seen their exports being targeted for anti-dumping measures at a far greater rate than their share in world trade. Indeed, controlling for the value of total exports over the last three decades anti-dumping measures were at least four times more likely to be directed against a product from a non-market economy which is not a WTO member than a product from a developed market economy.

China's and Chinese Taipei's situation is even more pronounced as they have been targeted for anti-dumping measures much more often than other countries or their share in world trade would justify. The situation did not change after they became WTO members, unlike a country like Ukraine which had been targeted a great deal before its accession and much less afterward.

Table 6.3 suggests that countries taking anti-dumping action may feel less constrained when taking action against non-WTO member countries. And with respect to so called non-market economies, there is evidence indicating that the procedures used tend to be more opaque and may well lead to a greater incidence of definitive findings than those against other economies (Michalopoulos and Winters, 1997).

What can be concluded from this analysis of the prevalence of anti-dumping actions against developing countries as an indicator of market access to developed-country markets? There appears to have been an improvement in recent years, because in general fewer anti-dumping actions have been taken by developed countries; but the developing countries' share of these actions, taking account of the value of their exports, has not changed and tends to be disproportionately high. This reflects an insufficient response by the developed countries to their commitment 'to give special regard' to the special situation of developing countries. Similarly, there is no evidence that Article 15 on using constructive remedies before applying anti-dumping duties on imports from developing countries has been employed.

SPS and TBT

The implementation of the SPS and TBT agreements has raised two sets of issues for developing countries. First, standards along with testing and certification represent between 2 and 10 per cent of overall product costs. Thus, they impose a burden on developing country exports – even when the standards are used for legitimate reasons and the countries are able to meet them. Second, while the two agreements may make developed-countries actions more transparent and force a degree of accountability, they may also serve to legitimize developed-country NTMs that unnecessarily restrain developing countries' trade.

The pioneering work of Otsuki et al. (2001), estimated that a 1998 EC regulation that imposed more stringent controls on the maximum level for certain types of aflatoxin (a toxic substance) found in foodstuffs and animal feed, than those required by the Codex Alimentarius, would cost close to $700 million in lost revenue to African exporters of groundnuts. Wilson et al. (2003) found that the stringency of antibiotics regulation in developed countries significantly reduced bovine meat exports for Argentina, Brazil and South Africa. And several studies have concluded that SPS regulations inhibit developing-country agriculture and food exports (Cadot and Malouche, 2012, p. 6).

Early complaints by developing countries that developed countries may be using the SPS agreement as disguised protection had focused on meat (Burkina Faso), fresh fruits and vegetables (Kenya), canned tuna (Papua New Guinea) and fish (Uganda). In 2001–12 more than one thousand notifications of new SPS measures and a slightly larger number of TBT notifications were submitted to the WTO. About 60 per cent of the SPS notifications and the bulk of the TBT notifications came from developing countries. As the overall developing-country share of world trade as well of SPS and TBT notifications is increasing, it is clear that this may not be a North–South problem but a general NTM issue.

WTO members have an opportunity to complain about the introduction of new SPS and TBT measures in the respective WTO committees by raising specific trade concerns (STCs). The STCs submitted to the TBT Committee per annum more than quadrupled (from 17 to 76) in the period 2000–11. Fourteen new STCs were raised in the SPS Committee in 2011, about half by developing countries. Some of these concerns were left unresolved and have led to cases going to the WTO's dispute settlement, although the number of cases that specifically refer to SPS and TBT is relatively small (WTO, 2012c, p. 111).

In light of the increased use of SPS and TBT measures, some writers have considered all of the measures imposed on these grounds to be NTMs, similar to quantitative restrictions and trade remedies (Gourdon and Nicita, 2012). If such a definition were used, then SPS and TBT measures would constitute the bulk of developed (and developing country) NTMs. On average countries apply TBT measures on approximately 30 per cent and SPS on 15 per cent of products and trade. Taken together these measures would cover almost half of a typical country's trade. And they are likely to be much more extensive than core non-tariff barriers such as quotas, trade remedies and non-automatic licences.

But it would be a mistake to lump together TBT and SPS measures together with other non-tariff barriers for two reasons. First, it is quite clear that there are very legitimate reasons for introducing such measures for health and safety reasons; and when they are abused there is a process for seeking redress – even though this process poses some constraints for developing countries. Second, it is possible that the establishment of standards can actually benefit developing-country exporters. A study of Chinese exports of agricultural products showed that the adoption of more stringent standards had a positive effect as the signalling of enhanced food safety and quality in foreign markets apparently surpassed compliance costs (Mangellsdorf et al., 2012). Similarly a recent study by Xiong and Beghin (2011) found that the predictions by Otsuki et al. of a dire effect of the introduction of EU regulations on aflatoxin content on West African groundnut exports did not materialize. Instead, they posit that the main constraints on these exports came from the supply side and that in the case of edible groundnuts the regulations may have actually stimulated trade by enhancing the safety of the products in the eyes of EU consumers.

Thus, while the impact of SPS and TBT regulations on developing-country exports is quite complex and they cannot all be considered as NTMs used for protection of domestic industry, these regulations certainly have the potential to do so. The problem is that in defining these as NTMs it is necessary to identify intent – which is inherently difficult to demonstrate as well as resolve for a variety of complex scientific issues.

The WTO undertook an exhaustive analysis of NTMs and especially SPS and TBT measures in its 2012 annual trade report. Its conclusions are important. It states that 'the existing empirical literature finds that at the aggregate level TBT/SPS measures may not be associated with lower trade'; and that 'TBT/SPS measures do not unambiguously increase or decrease trade. In general TBT/SPS measures have positive effects for more technologically advanced sectors, but negative effects on trade in fresh and processed goods' (WTO, 2012c, pp. 143, 153). Given these difficulties, it is important not to lump TBT and SPS measures with other non-trade barriers which quite unambiguously restrict trade such as quotas or trade remedies. To do so will result in 'crying wolf' too often and missing true increases in protection. The only recommendation is for continued vigilance, monitoring and transparency through timely reporting and discussion in the WTO and other relevant international bodies entrusted with the setting of these standards.

Services

There are no systematic investigations of developed-country policy regarding trade in services and the implications of restrictions they impose on potential exports from developing countries. Existing data suggest that their overall policies on service imports are more liberal than those of the developing countries and that the gap between actual policies and Uruguay Round commitments is smaller. But, there is one mode of delivery, the movement on natural persons, in which they tend to be more restrictive than developing countries, regardless of the sector. Liberalization in this area would be of considerable benefit to developing countries because of their comparative advantage of providing labour intensive services across all modes of supply. In addition, there is one sector, maritime services, where international competition is extremely limited and there are serious constraints deriving from national legislation that actively discriminates against foreign suppliers.

While some progress has been made regarding the movement of qualified professionals to work abroad, developed-country restrictions inhibit increased service earnings for developing countries through this mode of supply. The commitments on trade in services have tended to emphasize measures regulating commercial presence – which is important for foreign direct investment, rather than 'mode four' involving movement of natural persons.

There are various kinds of quantitative restrictions on the number of persons that are provided with visas annually. There are also restrictions deriving from the existence of qualification and licensing requirements of professional organizations that formally discriminate against foreign qualified professionals. Still other barriers involve wage matching requirements such as those demanding wages paid to foreigners be the same as those to nationals or those demanding the provision of local training.

Also, the commitments made regarding the movement of natural persons have primarily involved intra-corporate transferees and business visitors and, to a lesser extent, independent professionals, including those providing services within a service contract. One of the limitations imposed by a large number of countries is an economic needs test (ENT). This typically involves judgements by government agencies based on non-transparent criteria regarding market conditions, availability of local service providers and which foreign service providers to permit and which not. Indeed of the 54 countries which have made commitments subject to a needs test, only three have stated criteria for the ENT. Frequently, the result is to nullify access commitments involving 'mode four' supply of services.

There are many sectors in which developing countries have a comparative advantage, usually based on labour costs, and which can benefit from developed-country liberalization, in particular software development and construction services. The former is an area where developing-country exports, for example from India, have been expanding very rapidly in recent periods. A lot of these exports involve onshore delivery because of the importance of the need for continuous contact between client and programmer. While technological and managerial innovations may result in a decline of the share of on-shore delivery, and an increase to come mainly through cross-border trade, the increase in software demand from developing countries may be so high as to require continued liberalization of existing limitations in 'mode four' restrictions. Similarly, several developing countries, especially in Asia, have the capacity of exporting construction services based on their comparative advantage in labour intensive activities which are constrained by developed-country restrictions on 'movement of natural persons'.

In maritime services there are extensive government restrictions in cabotage and cargo handling. At the same time oceans continue to be populated by cartels known as shipping conferences. These cartels set prices and pursue other collusive activities in the substantial portion of maritime services they control and are often exempted from anti-trust law in developed countries (Francois and Wooton, 1999). Their impact in raising transport costs to poorer developing countries, especially to low volume, high distance destinations such as in Africa and poorer island economies can be even more important than further tariff liberalization: shipping margins on merchandise trade in sub-Saharan Africa exceed 6 per cent compared with OECD tariffs (after preferences are taken into account) of less than 2 per cent (ibid.). Liberalization in this sector, which would lead to increased competition and reduced margins, may be of great importance to many of the small economy members of the WTO.

The world since 2008

In October 2008, with the world gripped by financial panic, WTO Director General Lamy decided that the WTO Secretariat would monitor trade restrictive measures taken in response to the crisis using the WTO Trade Policy Review Mechanism. In November 2008, just after the US presidential election, leaders of the then new G-20, fearing a repetition of the experience of the great depression and its transmission across frontiers by trade-restricting beggar-thy-neighbour policies, promised to refrain from imposing new import barriers, export restrictions and WTO-inconsistent measures. Subsequently the G-20 also promised to minimize the negative impact of stimulus measures on trade and asked the WTO to monitor and publicize the extent to which they adhered to their promises.

In this manner a new reporting system of trade measures taken by both developed and developing countries has emerged. The WTO has produced a number of reports on the restrictive and trade liberalizing measures undertaken by WTO members worldwide. Initially, quarterly reports were prepared. In more recent periods they have been produced on a semi-annual basis. The sources for the reports are official notifications as well as press stories and third-party complaints. The Secretariat attempts to verify each measure and reports, both those that it has been able to verify – which are the vast majority – and those it has not (WTO, 2009, 2012b).

In parallel with the WTO a private database has been developed by Global Trade Alert (GTA), an independent group of experienced analysts who have published regular reports on trade measures. They classify them in three groups: 'green alerts' are measures that increase liberalization or improve transparency; 'amber alerts' are measures which have the potential of being discriminatory against trade; and 'red alerts' which involve measures that discriminate against or restrict trade (Evenett, 2009, 2012).

The novel feature of both sets of reports is that they extend the definition of trade measures far beyond the traditional border actions involving tariffs or other restraints. Both include for example measures that aim to provide general economic stimulus or strengthen the financial system, especially as such measures may discriminate against foreign suppliers or banks.

GTA also includes on occasion, but not always, TBT or SPS measures as well as migration measures. In both cases the result may be restrictive – but it is unclear whether the action was justified by a health or other hazard or in the case of migration whether they should be included at all. Similarly giving the same weight to a German 'Rescue aid scheme for the manufacturing industry' (amounting to a grand total of €5 million for six months) and to the US Trade Adjustment Assistance Act (which affects tens of millions of workers for years) makes a mockery of any quantitative analysis of this information. At the same time there are very few reports on actions that inhibit trade in services.

Both sets of reports suffer from a shortcoming which is also part of their strength: in an effort to be all inclusive they contain a number of notifications which are temporary in nature – for example, as part of the WTO agreement on agriculture, many countries impose seasonal or temporary tariffs on imports of various fruits and vegetables as well as other foodstuffs, which they subsequently reduce. All these show up as trade restrictive or liberalizing measures, although in fact nothing has changed in the underlying policy or regime. The other shortcoming is that they both focus on *changes in policy*, not on the overall policy set – which can be obtained, albeit with some delay, only through each country's TPRs.

The number of measures counted by the two sets of reports, as well as their conclusions tend to be similar, though their tone is very different: GTA reports tend to be far more alarmist while those of the WTO are much more measured (Wolfe, 2011). Since the actual situation has evolved much more in keeping with the WTO reports, and because they contain an effort to verify report measures, they are to be preferred; and their findings will be used as a basis for the remaining discussion. Over the whole period 2008–12, more than 1,000 verified trade measures were reported by the WTO and GTA. Of these more than 60 per cent were trade-restrictive. When these measures are cumulated over time they are estimated to impact on about 4 per cent of world trade. It is impossible to say how *much* of an impact. Also, note that this 4 per cent has not been offset by the amounts of trade that has benefited from liberalizing measures. For example, a number of the reported 'measures' took the form of termination of anti-dumping measures previously in place.

The actual measures taken in the early part of the period did not appear to have a major impact on trade: 'to date we have not observed large scale increases in the level of discrimination by major trading states' (Evenett et al., 2009, p. 5). Similarly Messerlin writing in late 2009 cautioned that 'evoking a rise in protectionism in April 2009 was premature – still is' (2009, p. 25). He goes on to argue that raising the fear of protectionism when few protectionist measures have been taken makes it harder to resist true protectionist measures when they actually materialize. Another writer concluded that the great collapse of trade in 2008 was not due to any failings in the trading system and that 'the amount of trade affected in relation to actual trade flows was trivial' (Wolfe, 2011, p. 13).

Finally, it appears that the trend, at least until the end of 2012, was towards greater rather than less liberalization: in the period mid-May 2012 to mid-October 2012, there were more liberalizing measures reported than restrictive ones. This does not mean that all is well in the trading system: a number of countries continued to take additional trade restrictive steps: Argentina has been the chief offender in recent periods resulting in a number of new complaints in the DSM. And in the United States there is an anti-dumping measure – which was supposed to be 'temporary' – which has been in place for over 40 years.

As in previous years trade remedies are the main restrictive measures reported. In the period between 2007 and 2009, there was an increase of about 25 per cent in remedies, though the amount of trade affected was only 0.3 per cent of total world trade. The remedies were directed at developing countries by developing countries; and the focus was on China (Bown and Kee, 2011; Bown, 2013). Even here the news was not all bad. In the last two years, anti-dumping investigations have fallen back to levels much lower than before. There were a total of 155 investigations reported in 2011, which was the lowest number since 1989. And in the period May–October 2012 there were 46 new investigations and other trade restrictive actions but an almost equal number (44) of liberalizing ones (WTO, 2012b). Similarly, there were export restraining actions and a significant number of tariff reductions, especially of capital goods and intermediates by Brazil. But there was no evidence that developed countries were more responsible for trade restrictive measures than developing ones.

In summary, the increasing attention devoted to trade policy is likely to increase awareness and transparency, which is a good thing not only in developed but increasingly in developing economies. But care should be taken to focus more explicit attention to specific obviously restrictive measures. Enlarging the scope of the definition of NTMs is not likely to be helpful unless detailed information about the motivation for the measures and the manner in which they are implemented is available. There is no way to inoculate the population against the protectionist virus which infects many with the notion that a specific measure would help 'us' against 'them' while undermining the health of the whole economy. And in keeping with the theme of the whole of this study, it is important to look with care at explicit practices in the service sector. This is the most important sector in developed economies and the most rapidly expanding sector of developing ones. Yet the information about recent measures taken by governments that limit competition with foreign providers is very limited.

As this is being written, the future trade environment is clouded by the obvious slowdown in trade during 2012 and the weak economic prospects of the major economies, including especially the EU but also China and India. So far the experience with increased protection has not been too bad. Whether it will continue in the future remains to be seen.

One of the most interesting developments involving the OECD countries and some of the emerging economies are the efforts to conclude preferential trade agreements. There are several major negotiations: (1) an agreement in services is being negotiated among 46 countries which includes the US, the EU, Canada and many developing countries in the WTO; (2) the proposed Trans-Pacific Partnership, a free trade agreement involving the US, Australia, Mexico, Canada but also Malaysia and Japan; (3) a US/EU trade and investment agreement; and (4) an EU/Japan free trade agreement. The participation of Japan in these agreements is especially significant as it had been the one major trading nation that in the past had avoided participating in preferential arrangements.

Clearly, these agreements are moving forward in large part because the Doha Round negotiations have stalled. If they are successful, they will result in a very significant fragmentation of world trade with a large number of important developing-country trading nations such as India and China being left out; and they will provide an alternative to moving forward in the WTO negotiations to the detriment of the WTO and of the large developing nations being left out of the agreements. On the other hand, it is possible that they will also galvanize future WTO negotiations. That also remains to be seen.

7
The TRIPS Agreement and Developing Countries

Introduction

Developed-country concerns about protection of the intellectual property rights (IPRs) owned by their firms have been the subject of major controversies with developing countries ever since the inclusion of rule making on IPRs in the WTO – a policy area not covered by GATT. The Uruguay Round negotiations on this issue had a clear North–South dimension. Developed countries wanted to raise the standards and strengthen enforcement of IPRs worldwide. Most developing countries saw little benefit in committing themselves to basic global standards for increased IPR protection, which was suited better to developed countries' interests, though it might be inappropriate for their own socio-economic and technological needs. They only agreed to participate in the WTO agreement on trade-related aspects of intellectual property rights (TRIPS) as part of a 'grant bargain' that involved the developed countries phasing out controls on textile and clothing and inclusion of agriculture into the GATT disciplines.[1]

From early on there were many concerns that the TRIPS agreement would actually result in net losses for many, if not most, developing countries (Deardorff, 1990; South Center, 1997; Third World Network, 1998). Developing countries raised many issues during the review of the implementation of the Agreement initiated by the TRIPS Council in 2000. With one important exception involving compulsory licensing for pharmaceuticals, the same issues have been the subject of inconclusive discussions during the Doha Round.

[1] The first part of this chapter, including the theoretical materials and the discussion of developments up until 1998, is based on Duran and Michalopoulos (1999).

The developing countries' trade interests do not always coincide with each other, either in the TRIPS or in other agreements. Still, within TRIPS most developing countries coalesce on the issue of patents, possibly the most contentious topic of discussion in the Uruguay Round of negotiations, and on the issue of compulsory licensing for pharmaceuticals, which ultimately led to the first and, so far, only amendment to the WTO texts of agreements.

In this chapter I examine developing-country concerns regarding the TRIPS Agreement as well as the possible strategies for addressing them. In the next section I examine the nature of IPRs and their significance for developing countries, before I consider the economic dimensions of IPR protection in developing countries, focusing especially on the question of patents. Finally I will examine various aspects of the implementation of the agreement that will be beneficial to developing countries.

The nature of IPRs: does one size fit all?

IPRs have three major components: patents, copyrights and trademarks, and geographic indications. The TRIPS agreement contains detailed provisions and rules on all three.[2] Its purpose is to standardize minimum IPR protection worldwide, and thereby extend it to sectors not previously covered in developing (and some industrial) countries. The agreement seeks to extend and standardize the period during which IPR protection is afforded. It lays down rules and procedures on the acquisition, maintenance and enforcement of IPRs, as well as providing a dispute settlement mechanism. The basic rules are the same for developing and developed countries alike. The only important difference is that developing countries were given longer periods to implement the provisions. The main Special and Differential provisions are as follows:

- Technical and financial assistance to facilitate implementation of the Agreement should be provided by developed countries to all developing ones and LDCs on mutually agreed terms and conditions (Article 67).
- Technology transfer should be encouraged to LDCs (not to all the developing countries) through developed-country provision of incentives to enterprises and institutions in their territories for this purpose (Article 66.2).

---

[2] The Agreement covers copyright and related rights, trade marks, geographical indications, industrial designs, patents (including IPRs regarding microorganisms and plant varieties), integrated circuits and trade secrets.

- Under the agreement a one-year period of grace was allowed to developed members of the WTO to implement its provisions (1 January 1996). Developing and transition countries were given four extra years from entry into force of the WTO agreements (1 January 1995) to begin to apply its provisions. LDCs were initially given an additional six years, or eleven years in total.[3] This was subsequently extended to 2013 and most recently to 2021. Under a separate provision, an additional five years were given to countries that would have to introduce product patent protection in areas of technology that lacked such protection at the time of general application of the agreement.[4]

One of the fundamental questions regarding the agreement is whether the rules that pertain to IPRs should be the same for developing and developed countries alike (Michalopoulos, 2003). Does one size fit all in TRIPS?

IPRs are not fundamental rights, such as the freedom of speech, applicable universally. They are rights which are conveyed by governments to individuals or groups for the pursuit of certain social objectives, such as the promotion of inventions and technological improvements. In the case of patents, societies consider the development of inventions as a worthwhile objective which they pursue through the provision of a monetary incentive (reward) in the form of the monopoly rents that result from the exclusive use of the patent for the production of a particular product. If a new product requires considerable ingenuity as well as investment in time and effort to produce, but can be copied easily, then there may be little incentive to invent and too few inventions from the viewpoint of the public interest. Patents (and copyrights) confer market exclusivity (and hence monopoly rents) for a period of time to permit inventors to recoup their costs and reap a profit in exchange for making the new product and the knowledge embodied in it available to consumers. The length of the patent (how many years the inventor has the exclusive rights) determines in part the size of the reward. But there is no reason to believe that all societies value inventions the same. Hence, there is no a priori reason why the reward or the length of time during which the inventor has exclusive rights should be the same (Deardorff, 1990).

---

[3] Except for obligations pertaining to MFN and national treatment.

[4] But WTO members agreed to accept patent applications and exclusive marketing rights for pharmaceutical and agricultural chemical products as from the date the Agreement entered into force.

Also, the patent system may provide an incentive, but in many developing countries there may be very limited local capacity to exploit it: 'even when technologies are developed, firms in developing countries can seldom bear the costs of acquisition and maintenance of rights and above all, of litigation if disputes arise' (CIPR, 2002, p. 14). Thus, the rewards are obtained primarily by multinationals that take out the patents, whereas the costs, in the form of higher prices due to market exclusivity, are born by the developing-country consumers. How costly patent protection is will also depend on market structure as well government policy to promote competition. Quite clearly the net benefit from protection of intellectual property will be uncertain, and is likely to vary from country to country and from sector to sector, depending on each country's value of invention and capacity to take advantage of the patent system, a country's capacity to implement competition policies, and so forth.

The fundamental problem arises with the minimum requirements under TRIPS, which are by definition the same for all, as are the rules – although there is some flexibility in their application at the national level. The minimum for patents under TRIPS is 20 years, which is even longer than the 17 years prevailing at the time of the agreement in the USA, the strongest supporter of the patent system.[5] Also, it does not permit a government to exclude an industrial sector from patents – although for plant varieties there is some flexibility regarding the nature of the IPR system that can be used.

An early analysis of this issue, even before an agreement had been reached on TRIPS, concluded that 'to standardize protection at advanced levels is to presume that each economy has in place a technological or creative infrastructure for which high protection is suitably stimulative over some reasonable time frame. This presumption is clearly false and the existence of various levels of economic and technological development points to the desirability of differing national protection schemes, if not outright discrimination' (Maskus, 1990, p. 6). Unfortunately none was provided under the original TRIPS agreement.

The agreement, however, does allow for flexibility in the implementation of its terms: implicitly, by establishing minimum standards but leaving their enforcement to the discretion of national legal bodies and by ambiguous provisions that permit alternative interpretations; and explicitly, by sanctioning, in certain circumstances, compulsory

---

[5] The earlier patent term in the US is from the date of the grant of the patent, not from the date of application; thus the increase in the patent term was in practice probably less than three years.

licensing and permitting the use of a *sui generis* regime of protection for plant varieties.[6]

Costs and benefits

Patents

History is full of examples of countries that developed well without patents: Switzerland and the Netherlands did well without them for over half a century between the 1850s and the 1900s (Schiff, 1971). China, Taiwan (China) and Korea all developed very rapidly in the last half of the twentieth century without strong IPR protection by emphasizing the importance of imitation and reverse engineering. In India, the relative weakening of IPR protection for pharmaceuticals (by allowing patents on process and not products) is widely considered to have been a contributing factor to the subsequent growth of that country's sector and its emergence as a low cost supplier of pharmaceuticals worldwide.

At present, industrial countries account for the vast majority of patents worldwide (about 95 per cent). Similarly they account for the lion's share of worldwide expenditure on R&D (Braga et al., 1999). In theory, better IPR protection should encourage more R&D and hence innovation. But even in the case of industrial countries with a long history of strong IPRs, there is limited empirical evidence of a positive link between IPR protection and R&D (World Bank, 1998, p. 34).

On the other hand, innovation in most developing countries is concentrated on minor adaptive changes that are not likely to be captured by the patent system (Correa, 1998). Other innovations and forms in which knowledge is held and utilized, for example indigenous communities' knowledge and utilization of plants and herbs for medicinal and other purposes, are not protected under the TRIPS agreement. And the less developed the country, the more likely that such innovations will be the dominant form of invention. Thus, most developing countries, with limited inventive and innovative capabilities, will be net importers and users of technology generated by foreign inventions. And the more stringent the IPR protection, the more it will deter imitation and adaptation of foreign inventions to domestic needs.

---

[6] Under Article 27 countries may exclude essentially biological processes, as well as plant and animals other than micro-organisms and micro-biological processes with the proviso that 'members shall provide for the protection of plant varieties either by patents or by an effective *sui generis* system, or any combination thereof' (Article 27.3(b)).

In agriculture, a sector of great importance to developing countries and especially LDCs, IPRs have traditionally played a limited role as most agricultural research has been conducted by public sector institutions in developed and developing countries alike. Over time, public sector R&D has declined in comparison with R&D conducted by private firms in developed countries. Consequently, an increasing share of new seeds and farming technology of importance to poor countries is owned by developed-country firms, sometimes based on biological and genetic material that originated in the developing world (Braga et al., 1999; World Bank, 1998).

A recent review of the literature on the link between IPRs and innovation (Correa, 2013) summarized that 'there is no conclusive evidence on IPR and innovation. IPR may promote innovation but it is not a magic tool. It may also deter it. A large number of factors (such as the R&D infrastructure, the availability of risk capital, the qualification of personnel) can influence the nature and rate of innovation in developing countries'.

While the developing-country WTO members did provide patent and copyright protection prior to the TRIPS Agreement, many (25) did not provide patent protection for pharmaceuticals,[7] and a somewhat smaller number (13) did not provide it for chemicals, while more than 50 per cent provided general patent protection for shorter periods (Braga, 1996). The underlying rationale for not extending protection in these areas was to promote the establishment of competitive markets with lower prices, so as to enhance the availability of drugs and health care to the poor, vulnerable and less-advantaged sections of the population, and to reduce the cost of fertilizers and other chemical inputs for low-income farmers. The shorter periods of protection were designed to make the technology generally available sooner, thereby reducing the rents accruing to producers and patent holders.

The main potential costs of TRIPS to developing countries are the economic losses that might be suffered by their consumers and producers, and the so-called 'deadweight' efficiency losses from reduced competition. These result from the introduction of patents held by producers in industrialized countries and the consequent monopolization of the sectors and industries in question by these patent holders, or by increasing the time frame over which the patents are valid in all sectors (Deardorff, 1992).

As the overwhelming proportion of all patents is likely to continue to be owned by producers in developed countries, developing countries'

[7] Four developed countries also did not.

losses will only be slightly offset by the gains obtained from their own inventions, stimulated by the introduction of more secure property rights in the context of TRIPS. In short, developing-country losses will be transferred as gains in rents by patent holders in developed countries. These gains, however, will be less than the developing countries' losses because of overall deadweight efficiency loss resulting from the creation of monopolies based on patent rights. One estimate put the rent transfer from developing to developed countries at $8.3 billion (Maskus, 2000). To place this estimate in perspective, it is equivalent to about 40 per cent of the total developing-country gains from the Uruguay Round Agreements (Harrison et al., 1996) and about as much as the annual aid for trade given to low income and LDCs from bilateral donors on average in 2002–06 (OECD/WTO, 2011b).

The actual costs incurred by developing countries will depend on market structures that prevail in the absence of the patent protection (Braga, 1996; Subramanian, 1995): the more competitive the market structure adopted as an alternative to patent protection, the larger the costs. An extreme case is where a previously competitive industry is substituted by a foreign monopoly. At the other extreme, if a foreign monopoly exists before patent protection, economic welfare will not be affected by the introduction of the patents.[8] But many in-between situations are likely to arise in which developing countries incur losses (Nogues, 1993).

Because the pharmaceutical industry had not previously enjoyed patent protection in many developing countries, it is the main sector for which the potential losses as a result of TRIPS have been estimated. The estimates vary widely between countries and depend on the assumptions made about market conditions as well as the share of patentable drugs in each market (Subramanian, 1995). In some other sectors, for example computer software or integrated circuits, better protection of intellectual property may result in gains to individual developing countries that are at the forefront of research and development.

There is a presumption that the costs of extending the patent periods may well be substantial, as they are likely to include pure rents to industrial-country patent holders. This is because developing-country markets account for only a small proportion of the world market for most products, and inventions usually occur in industrial countries, irrespective of whether protection is provided in a developing country for 10 years or 20.

---

[8] The duration of the patent will also affect welfare over time.

In summary, developing countries as a group are certain to suffer increased costs with the introduction of patents involving stronger IPR protection for both their and developed-country producers. The total magnitude of these costs is uncertain, but would vary substantially from country to country depending on market structures, the effectiveness of competition policies and the fundamental link between stronger IPRs and the creation of new technology. Against these costs, stronger IPR protection for developing countries was expected to lead to increased technology transfers and technological diffusion from developed countries, which would result in increasing developing-country productivity and reduced costs. It was thought that the publication of patents would make information available for use in adaptations and inventions; that the owners of technology in industrial countries would be more willing to transfer proprietary knowledge to developing countries through licensing or foreign direct investment; and that the private sector in developed countries would have a greater incentive to devote resources to the development of drugs against tropical diseases endemic to developing countries (World Bank, 1998). However, there is only weak evidence that technology transfers have increased through these mechanisms.

In certain industries, including pharmaceuticals, agricultural chemicals and software, reverse engineering and imitation can result in technology transfer irrespective of patents or the incentives to patent holders in industrial countries. However, in other sectors reverse engineering is not possible, hence the increased information offered through the patent regime is basically irrelevant. The same is true for technology transfer through foreign direct investment. Stronger IPR protection appears to be pertinent only in cases where technology is copied after a foreign patent owner has established production in a developing country. The empirical significance of such cases is unclear. In support of IPR protection the World Bank (1998) referred to findings of a report prepared before the TRIPS agreement. According to this report, 25 per cent of pharmaceutical and chemical firms in the US, Germany and Japan felt that IPR protection in a number of developing countries was too weak for them to invest in joint ventures or transferring advanced technology to a wholly owned subsidiary. A somewhat smaller proportion of machinery and electrical equipment industry in these countries felt the same.

The above arguments, however, can be looked at conversely: if 75 per cent of firms in the industries clamouring for the strengthening of IPR protection felt that more stringent IPR protection would make no difference to their investments or technology transfers, this suggests the limits of the argument and the importance of increased rent-seeking as a motive behind strengthened IPR protection. China offers a clear illustration: its IPR protection was weak before it became a WTO member, and yet it attracted huge foreign direct investment inflows since the early 1990s.[9]

Similarly, expectations that increased IPR protection would enhance pharmaceutical companies' efforts to develop drugs against diseases that are endemic in developing countries have, sadly, also not been realized. It is ironic that the international community has had to put together a major new initiative – The Global Alliance for Vaccines and Immunization – to provide an assured market for such drugs, when only a few years ago it was argued that if only the TRIPS Agreement were put in place, the private sector would take care of their research and development, given the enhanced incentives offered by strengthened IPR protection.

Trademarks and geographical indications

The strengthening of developing-country IPR regimes on trademarks and geographical indications is unambiguously serving to increase the rents that accrue to the holders/producers, which are mostly located in developed countries. Both trademarks and geographical indications involve producer efforts to establish product differentiation by claiming superior quality or standards and hence product value which permits the owner/producer to charge a higher price than similar competitive products. 'Pirates' that illegally use trademarks are typically able to undercut the official licensees with products whose quality may or may not be inferior to that of products made under licence.

Trademark piracy undoubtedly causes significant losses for producers, usually located in developed countries. The issue is primarily one of ethics and legal enforcement. By using false trademarks pirates are able to secure a higher price – and hence higher rents – than they can without the trademarks. The tightening of enforcement lowers the rents accruing to pirates and so offers gains to developing-country consumers (to the extent that they have been paying higher prices than the quality of the product warrants) and increases the transfers to the owners of the trademarks.

---

[9] The evidence of the effects of stronger IPR protection on trade flows also appears to be ambiguous, although there is some evidence that IPR market expansion effects may dominate the market restriction ones (Braga, 1996), but much more work on developing-country aspects of this issue is needed.

Geographical indications are important in the food, wine and spirits industries. In this case a product from a particular location is claimed to possess superior qualities (and hence can command a higher price) due to unique vegetative, climatic and/or soil conditions. With some exceptions in wines and spirits (for example Mexican tequila) and food (basmati rice) such product differentiation is of significance primarily in the developed countries, in particular the EU.

Under TRIPS, the treatment of wines and spirits is not identical to that of other products: whereas the former have explicit additional protection for geographical indications (Article 23), general protection for other goods (Article 22) is less rigorous. Some developing countries have become aware of the possible benefits to be had by extending the additional protection granted to wines and spirits to other products of interest to them, for example foods and handicrafts. Others, that are primarily consumers of such products, have resisted the extension of geographical indications to other goods.

In summary, IPRs 'are a compromise between preserving the incentive to create knowledge and the desirability of disseminating knowledge at little or no cost' (World Bank, 1998, p. 33). Whether the TRIPS agreement per se represents a good compromise for the developing countries is very much an open question. The agreement is probably unique among those negotiated in the Uruguay Round in that its implementation may well result in net long-term economic losses for developing countries as a group. By contrast, agreements involving the liberalization of trade in goods and services may result in short-term adjustment costs, but there is a strong presumption, based on extensive experience and empirical evidence, that more liberal trade regimes tend to be conducive to longer-term development (Harrison et al., 1996). The key issue in mutually liberalizing trade negotiations is the share of the overall gains that accrue to developed countries relative to the developing countries and to each country individually.

Given this conclusion, why did the developing countries sign the TRIPS Agreement? The answer lies partly in the pressure exerted by developed countries that were concerned about rent losses resulting from trademark piracy and copyright infringement. It was one of the areas in which developed countries were expected to obtain concrete benefits in exchange for gains by developing countries in other areas such as the general lowering of tariffs or the liberalization of developed countries' textile trade. To a certain extent, developing countries also felt that the agreement was of symbolic importance: their adherence to international IPR norms would demonstrate to foreign private investors that they were 'open for business'. Some countries felt that they should strengthen their IPR protection in order to share in the development of the new technologies of the future. Irrespective of what one thinks about the Uruguay Round compromise, the question facing developing countries is what to do about implementing the agreement in ways conducive to their long-term development.

Early implementation issues: 1995–2001

In implementing the TRIPS agreement, developing countries had to consider three issues: first, what steps were needed to strengthen their institutional capacity to meet their commitments when their transition periods expire; second, how to utilize the flexibility allowed under the agreement to pursue their development objectives; and third, what changes to seek in the agreement in order to further their economic development? The first two of these issues are discussed below. The proposed changes in the agreement are discussed in connection with the Doha Round.

Capacity constraints

Because developing countries were not required to implement most aspects of the TRIPS Agreement until 2000, attention was focused on the preparatory institution-building process that would permit them to meet their obligations under the Agreement on a timely basis. Notwithstanding the transition arrangements for developing countries, Article 70.8 stipulated that all members that did not currently provide patent protection to pharmaceutical and agricultural chemical products in line with Article 27 should establish 'a means by which such patents can be filed' and apply to them 'the criteria of patentability as laid down in the agreement'. Moreover, under Article 70.9, where products were subject to a patent application under the above procedures, members were required to grant exclusive marketing rights for five years, after obtaining marketing approval in the member country.

Early on, the US and the EU served notice that they would hold developing countries strictly accountable to their commitments under the agreement. First the US, in 1996, and then the EU, in 1997, lodged complaints against India for its lack of patent protection for pharmaceutical and agricultural chemical products and of any formal systems permitting the filing of patent applications and providing exclusive marketing rights on pharmaceutical and chemical products. India was thus accused of failing to meet its obligations under Article 70. To deal with the complaints the WTO set up dispute settlement panels which found for the complainants on the grounds that India had violated: Article 70.8 by failing to a establish a legal basis for the preservation of novelty and priority in respect of applications for product patents for pharmaceutical and chemical inventions; and Article 70.9 for failing to establish a system for the granting of exclusive marketing rights (WTO, 1997a, 1998a).

The broader institutional requirement for developing countries was to enact the necessary legislation and establish the necessary rules, regulations and implementation capacity to enable them to meet their commitments under the agreement. Implementation of the provisions under Article 27.3(b) was of special interest to developing countries for a number of reasons. First, this article was important for agriculture, a sector of prime social and economic significance in most low-income countries where a large proportion of the population lives in rural areas and where subsistence farming coexists in varying degrees with commercial agriculture. Second, developing countries feel they have a proprietary stake in biodiversity resources, most of which are located in their territories. Third, issues of biodiversity and agricultural research are central to the development prospects of many developing countries especially the low-income countries and LDCs.

Establishing proper institutional arrangements to meet the requirements of the TRIPS Agreement is a very difficult task for many developing countries. A patent system is costly to establish and implement. These costs include scrutinizing the validity of claims to patent rights and adjudicating in cases of alleged infringement. In developing countries, where resources are scarce and legal systems underdeveloped, the opportunity cost of setting up such a system is high. Initial capital expenditure may well be in the range of $1.5–2.0 million or even higher (Finger and Schuler, 2000), while operating costs may be in the $1 million per annum range (UNCTAD, 1996), although over time operating revenues, primarily from the administration of trademarks, may cover at least some of the costs.

Developing countries recognized that limitations in their judicial system and overall implementation capacity could result in delays or less effective enforcement of IPR protection than in developed countries. For this reason they insisted on Article 41.5 in the agreement which provides some additional flexibility in TRIPS implementation. The article essentially says that developing countries cannot be found in violation of TRIPS, if their enforcement of IPR protection is no worse than enforcement of other laws in general. It provides legal cover in case, for example, litigation over a patent takes a very long time. But this does not mean that their obligations under the agreement are different.

Consistent with Article 67 of the agreement which calls for *technical and financial assistance* to facilitate implementation of the Agreement to be provided by developed countries to all developing countries and LDCs on mutually agreed terms and conditions, the international community put in place a number of assistance efforts. Some of these efforts involved collaborative technical assistance efforts between the World Intellectual Property Organization (WIPO) and the WTO. The modalities of the technical assistance were varied, including organization of seminars and workshops for developing countries to understand the TRIPS Agreement and to review the relevant national legislation necessary for implementing it. Most developing countries, including but not limited to LDCs, felt that the assistance provided was very inadequate for the tasks at hand.

Many countries found themselves in a major quandary: on the one hand, they lacked the capacity to set up the institutions to implement the provisions of the TRIPS Agreement. At the same time, they were worried about the apparent willingness of the US and the EU – as evidenced by the India cases and several subsequent ones – to use the WTO dispute settlement mechanism to enforce the agreement. This situation led several WTO members to propose extensions of the transitional period for the implementation of the agreement.

Flexibility

There are various aspects of flexibility that developing countries needed to consider. Some pertained to legal interpretations of specific provisions. For example, regarding Article 27.3(b), important terms that are open to interpretation include 'micro-organisms', 'essentially biological processes', 'microbiological' or *sui generis* plant protection (Tansey, 1999). It may be to their advantage to limit the obligation to grant patents on micro-organisms only to genetically modified ones (Correa, 1998). Another aspect of flexibility involves the use of alternative policies – permitted under TRIPS – to pursue development objectives, such as price differentiation, parallel imports or compulsory licensing, which rigid IPR protection would impede.

On the granting of patents for pharmaceutical products, the most serious concerns of developing countries was that this will result in significant increases in the price of medicines that are essential for improving the health standards of the population as a whole, particularly the poor and vulnerable segments. However, the flexibility allowed by the TRIPS Agreement means that this can be prevented through the imposition of price controls, which are not prohibited under the agreement and have been used in the past by several European countries.

Similarly, compulsory licensing allows countries to compel the owner of a patent to license it to others for general social and other policy objectives and has the effect of limiting the monopoly power of the patent holder. Finally, as the agreement does not formally address the issue of global IPR 'exhaustion', parallel imports are permissible. If a patent holder charges a lower price in one country than in another, countries may be able to take advantage of the difference and obtain the product from the source with the lowest price (Correa, 1998).

In this connection, the South African Medicines Act of 1997 permitted compulsory licensing, parallel imports and domestic production of generic drugs against AIDS, as a means of combating the very high cost of such drugs under existing arrangements, even though patents on the brand-name drugs were still in effect. The US and the multinational pharmaceutical companies which had pushed for the establishment of TRIPS acted quickly to attempt to reduce the flexibility available under the agreement. The US Administration stated that, while in its view the Act did not conform to the TRIPS provisions on compulsory licensing, it would 'raise no objection to compulsory licensing or parallel importing of pharmaceuticals on the part of South Africa as long as it is done in a way that complies with TRIPS'.[10] Soon after, faced by widespread public outcry about the threat that AIDS poses to Africa, the US stopped harassing South Africa on the issue. However, the Act was challenged in the South African courts by 39 pharmaceutical companies, most of which were subsidiaries of multinational pharmaceuticals, only to have this challenge also fizzle out in early 2001, when under pressure from public opinion the drug industry dropped its suit.

Developing-country concerns to make certain that the TRIPS agreement is interpreted flexibly, so as to ensure the availability of drugs at reasonable prices to combat AIDS and other pandemics, were subsequently dealt with in the context of the Doha Round. But issues regarding the use of flexibility at the national level continue.

The Doha Round

A formal review of the implementation of the TRIPS Agreement was started in the TRIPS Council in 2000. This focused on the extension of

[10] US Congress (1999). In May 2000, the US, however, brought a complaint against Brazil on a related TRIPS issue (WTO, 2000b).

geographical indications beyond wines and spirits and the implementation of Article 27(3) on biodiversity. The Council discussions were soon overtaken by the preparations for and ultimately the launching of the Doha Round in 2001 (WTO, 2001a).

The Doha meeting had three important implications for TRIPS: first, it stressed the importance of flexible interpretation of TRIPS in the context of public health and agreed on a 'Declaration on TRIPS and Public Health'; second, it called for continuation of the TRIPS Council's work on geographical indications and of Article 27(3) which includes the link between TRIPS and the Convention for Biological Diversity; and third, it emphasized the relevance of special and differential treatment of developing countries under the agreement – which led to further consideration of transfer of technology commitments made by developed countries under Article 66.2.

By far the most important of these provisions was the 'Declaration on Health' in which it was agreed that, under the compulsory licensing provisions of TRIPS, each WTO member has the right to determine what constitutes a national emergency and that public health crises relating to HIV/AIDS, TB, malaria and other epidemics can represent a national emergency. But it became apparent, once again, that 'one size does not fit all' because provisions for compulsory licensing may not be very meaningful for developing countries that do not have the capacity to produce the drugs domestically. Hence the 'Declaration' also instructed the Council of TRIPS to find a solution to this problem and report to the WTO General Council by the end of 2002 (WTO, 2001b).

The TRIPS Council tried to develop a proposal, which would have permitted developing countries that did not have a capacity to produce drugs needed to combat epidemics to import them from low cost suppliers under carefully determined circumstances, which would protect against the danger that these drugs were re-exported into developed-country markets. The Council failed to reach agreement by the end of 2002 because the US wanted to limit the application of the exception to pharmaceuticals related to AIDS/HIV, malaria and TB rather than include the possibility that it may be extended to pharmaceuticals related to other possible diseases that may affect developing countries (based on Michalopoulos (2003).

An agreement was finally reached at the end of August 2003, under heavy political pressure to settle the issue before the fifth WTO Ministerial meeting in September 2003. This did not limit the exception to certain diseases but did introduce various reporting requirements on both exporting and importing countries that go beyond those in

TRIPS, initially as a waiver until the Agreement can be amended (see Michalopoulos, 2003, p. 10).

In December 2005, it was decided to amend the TRIPS agreement by making the waiver procedure agreed in 2003 permanent. It will be formally built into TRIPS once two-thirds of the membership agrees. Initially, WTO members gave themselves two years to 1 December 2007 to accept formally the agreement. This deadline was extended, originally to 2009 and later to December 2013. As of the end of 2012, only 71 members (counting the 27 EU members separately) had formally accepted the amendment. No doubt others will follow in due course and the deadline for acceptance will be suitably extended so that TRIPS will be ultimately amended in this important way for the developing countries.[11] Curiously, however, to date only one transaction involving the waiver has been notified – a sale from Canada to Rwanda. There are many alternative explanations offered as to why there have been so few transactions: it is possible that countries find cheaper alternatives are available through various assistance programmes; on the other hand, it may be that the procedure established is so cumbersome that few firms and countries are willing to go through with it.

Exclusions and alternatives to patents: Article 27.3(b)

The patentability of plants and animals, genetic materials and microorganisms is one of the most controversial aspects of the TRIPS agreement. It relates to matters of great importance to developing countries, such as sustainable agriculture, food security, access to plant genetic resources and the rights of indigenous peoples. Although in principle there should be no incompatibility between the objectives of conservation, access to and sustainable use of plant genetic resources for food and agriculture, and stimulating investments in plant development through IPRs (FAO/AITIC, 1998), the issue has given rise to much controversy in connection with Article 27.3(b).[12]

The general developing-country concern is that certain companies, particularly from developed countries, will be able to monopolize

[11] In the interim the waiver is still relevant for members that have not formally accepted the amendment.

[12] Several countries are implementing patent or *sui generis* protection for inventions of plants, animals and essentially biological processes for the production of plants or animals based on the principles of the 1991 Act of the Union for the Protection of New Varieties of Plants (UPOV) Convention, under which parties are free to protect plant varieties by plant breeders' rights.

and secure a lawful claim on genetic information from plant varieties obtained from farmers in developing countries, which would then be sold back to them with added royalties. They are also concerned about the discrepancy between some provisions in the TRIPS agreement and the UN Convention on Biological Diversity (CBD) and other related multilateral agreements, such as the FAO's International Undertaking on Plant Genetic Resources.[13] An example of apparent incongruity is that, whereas the TRIPS Agreement recognizes IPRs as private rights in such areas as micro-organisms and microbiological processes, the CBD affirms that a nation has sovereign rights over (implicitly all) its biological resources. Furthermore, the CBD explicitly espouses the equitable sharing of any benefits arising from the use of these resources and recognizes the usefulness of traditional knowledge, innovations and practices related to the conservation of biological diversity and its sustainable use.

Some developing countries also see a discrepancy between the TRIPS agreement and the FAO's International Undertaking on Plant Genetic Resources. The latter defines and recognizes farmers' rights, such as those to do with the past, present and future contributions of farmers to conserving, improving and making available plant genetic resources. At the same time, the International Undertaking recognizes that plant breeders' rights, as provided for in the Act of the Union for the Protection of Plant Varieties (UPOV) are not inconsistent with farmers' rights (FAO/AITIC, 1998). UPOV 1978 appears to correspond to the needs of developing countries better than UPOV 1991, which gives more protection to breeders' rights. But developing countries that wished to join UPOV but had not ratified UPOV 1978 were forced by trade agreements with developed countries to ratify UPOV 1991 (Dutfield, 2011).

In keeping with these concerns, the topics raised in the TRIPS Council discussions prior to the Doha Round included:

- How to apply the TRIPS provisions on whether or not to patent plants and animals and whether they need to be modified.
- The meaning of effective protection for new plant varieties (i.e. alternatives to patenting such as the 1978 and 1991 version of UPOV).
- To what extent invented life forms should be eligible for protection.
- How to deal with the commercial use of traditional knowledge and genetic material by those other than the communities or countries

[13] The CBD agreement has been signed by 175 countries. An important exception is the US.

where these originate, especially when these are the subject of patent application.
- How to ensure that the TRIPS agreement and the CBD support each other.

The Doha debate has focused on the last two of the above topics but without any success (see Chapter 9). In the meantime, there is a lot that the international community and the developing countries can do to deal with other issues of importance related to IPRs: (1) to increase technology transfer from developed countries; (2) to take advantage of existing TRIPS flexibilities by introducing appropriate national legislation and regulation; and (3) to guard against the reduction in flexibility that is often demanded by developed-country partners in preferential trade agreements.

Transfer of technology

Developing countries have drawn attention to the TRIPS declaration (Article 7) that IPR protection and enforcement should contribute to the promotion of technological innovation and the transfer of technology. In their view, not only has technology transfer not advanced significantly since the signing of the Agreement, but they are forced to pay exorbitant prices for the use of foreign technology. Early on developing countries and LDCs complained that developed countries have failed to implement Article 66.2 which requires them to provide incentives to their enterprises and institutions to promote technology transfer to LDCs.

To address LDC concerns, and in particular a request by the African Group, the TRIPS Council decided to establish a reporting and review procedure for developed-country actions implementing Article 66.2 (WTO, 2003b). According to the decision developed countries are asked to submit annual reports on 'actions taken or planned in pursuance of their commitments under Article 66.2'. More extensive reports are called for every three years. The reports should contain inter alia information on:

- The incentive regime put in place, including any specific legislative, policy and regulatory framework.
- The type of incentive and government agency providing it.
- Eligible enterprises and institutions providing the incentives.
- The type and mode of technology being transferred.

These developed-country reports are supposed to be reviewed by the TRIPS Council once a year so as to give an opportunity to WTO members to pose questions about their effectiveness.

Developed countries have produced voluminous reports on an annual basis which respond to the letter of the Council's decision but have little relationship to its intent. The reports have given the opportunity to developed countries to engage in another meaningless 'beauty contest' over their aid programmes not that different from their approach to more general 'aid for trade' programmes discussed in Chapter 5. They are typically wide ranging and cover everything that is remotely related to technical assistance to all developing countries and incidentally may have a bearing on aspects of technology transfer to LDCs. For example, the most recent report by the EU covers in detail an EU programme in Ukraine (see WTO, 2012e)! The US submission details all the drug testing and training programmes of the US National Institutes of Health (WTO, 2011a). The Japanese discuss the $12 billion that they are providing in aid for trade in the period 2009–11 (WTO, 2011b).

Undoubtedly amidst this vast array of developed-country projects there are some that might fill LDC needs for technology transfer. For example the EU reports a French programme for the development of seed certification in several African countries. Similarly, some of the US drug testing and training programmes may make important contributions to address health concerns in LDCs. But this is a far cry from the concrete targeted actions needed to address problems created by TRIPS. Developing countries, and LDCs in particular, must insist that the annual developed-country submissions to the TRIPS Council become more concrete and focus solely on programmes that affect them. Examples of such actions would be purchasing patents and granting them to developing countries (for example gene donations in the case of biotechnology) or tax reductions or exemptions for firms transferring technology in priority areas.

Domestic actions

There are three areas in which domestic efforts are needed:

- Adoption of an appropriate *sui generis* regime – under Article 27.3(b) – suited to each country's needs.
- Adoption of legislation and regulations that exploit the flexibility offered by the agreement with regard, for example, to price controls, compulsory licensing and parallel imports. These must be consistent

with the TRIPS provisions or they will face the unpleasant prospect of developed-country complaints raised through the WTO dispute settlement mechanism.
- The design and implementation of suitable competition policies that limit the opportunities for monopolization of domestic markets by foreign firms.

Developing countries should try to get as much technical assistance as possible from international organizations and bilateral donors in the design of the legislation, regulations and other institutional development needed for this purpose.

Developed countries have not tried to limit developing-country flexibilities through changes in the TRIPS agreement. Instead they have been trying to achieve the same objective through preferential trade agreements that require developing countries to accept what is commonly called 'TRIPS Plus' commitments. The US–Morocco FTA is an example. Under Article 15.10 of the agreement, Morocco is required to grant data exclusivity beyond what is provided under Article 39 of TRIPS; similarly, the FTA seeks to define patentability criteria so as to conform to the US standard as well as to restrict parallel importation. In the view of an African expert 'FTAs constitute the worst risk to utilization and enjoyment of TRIPS flexibilities by the developing countries. Those developing countries that have already entered into such agreements should find ways of mitigating the resulting damages. Those that are negotiating FTAs must be vigilant so that they do not lose the flexibilities provided by the TRIPS agreement' (Nkomo, 2011, p. 134; see also Vivas-Eugui, 2003).

In order both to negotiate effectively, and to implement the TRIPS provisions, countries need to place high priority on the development of national policy coherence. This will involve the establishment of mechanisms for information sharing and consultations between the public sector and its constituent parts as well as with the private sector and elements of civil society involved directly or indirectly with IPR protection. This will not be an easy task because TRIPS involves a variety of actors, for example ministries or other institutions dealing with international trade, agriculture, industrial development, competition policy, science and technology, public institutions of higher education and/or research, private entrepreneurs in industry and agriculture, the legislative branch and other elements of civil society.

8
Developing-Country Participation in the WTO

Introduction

The capacity of the developing countries to promote changes to the system of rules governing international trade that will benefit their development depends very much on the effectiveness of their participation in the WTO. Such participation has two main aspects: involvement in the ongoing activities of the Organization, including the DSM; and participation in the multilateral trade negotiations organized under the WTO's auspices.

As noted earlier, throughout the 1960s and 1970s, developing countries did not consider GATT as an institution through which they could promote their interests in international trade. Their representation in GATT reflected the low priority they attached to it: many developing countries were not members, and of those that were a large number did not maintain official representatives in Geneva, but instead used representatives in other European capitals to cover GATT matters – in the case of ACP countries, usually their missions to the EU in Brussels. Moreover, their participation in GATT negotiations prior to the Uruguay Round was passive in that they did not engage in a significant way in the mutual exchange of concessions on a reciprocal basis (Whalley, 1987).

Subsequently, however, their attitude towards participation in GATT (and later the WTO) changed significantly. Many developing countries played a very active role in the Uruguay Round negotiations and a large number decided to become members of the WTO. This attitude change was the result of a number of complex and interrelated developments. Developing countries in general became more effectively integrated in the international trading system, and several became major exporters of manufactures. The trade policies of many countries were liberalized, favouring outward orientation and lower protection. And there was growing appreciation of the importance of observing international rules in the conduct of trade as well as the need to safeguard trading interests through effective participation in the activities of the new organization.

The establishment of the WTO has resulted in further changes which place additional demands on developing countries for their effective participation. First, the WTO covers a variety of new areas, such as services, standards and intellectual property rights, all of which require additional institutional capacity in member governments both for more effective representation in Geneva and in their home capitals. Second, the WTO, unlike GATT, has been engaging in a variety of negotiations which have required active involvement by members. Negotiations on basic telecommunications, information technology products and financial services were concluded in 1997. Subsequently, there were a number of negotiations on TRIPS and agriculture, as part of the built-in agenda of the Uruguay Round; and in late 2001 the Doha Round was launched leading to off-and-on negotiations for more than a decade. Third, the new dispute settlement mechanism offers increased opportunities for developing countries to address grievances, but poses tremendous challenges because of their very limited institutional capacity in the field of international trade law.

A key question is whether developing countries' representation at the WTO is adequate for effective participation in WTO activities and promotion of their interests in the expanding range of issues being addressed. This question is of special importance because the WTO, like the GATT before it, is a member-driven organization, meaning that the bulk of the analytical work, the development of proposals and the negotiation of agreements and handling of disputes fall on the member countries and their representatives. The WTO Secretariat performs a support function for the effective consideration of topics at the different meetings. It does not normally initiate proposals or interpret rules (Blackhurst, 1998). A related question has to do with WTO decision-making processes in general and, in the context of multilateral trade negotiations, whether these processes permit effective representation of developing-country interests.

This chapter focuses on participation of developing countries at the WTO from 2000 onwards. The focus is on three main issues: (1) representation, as reflected in the existence or otherwise of a mission of adequate size in Geneva to deal with WTO matters; (2) participation in the affairs of the WTO, both in the formal and the informal processes that characterize WTO governance and decision making on day-to-day issues and in WTO ministerial meetings and the multilateral trade negotiations; (3) participation in the DSM. Based on this analysis, the last section in the chapter draws a number of conclusions and recommendations for the more effective participation of developing countries in the WTO.

Membership

Developing countries now account for 71 per cent of WTO membership compared to 56 per cent in 1982 (Table 8.1). Another 24 countries are applying for accession, most of which are developing economies (see Chapter 3).

During the period 1982–2000, a large proportion of the 47 new members were developing countries or, what in the 1990s were called, 'countries in transition'. Table 8.1 shows the GATT/WTO representation at different points in time, each associated with a distinct period in the organization's activity: 1982, before the start of the Uruguay Round; 1987, a year after the Uruguay Round was launched; 2000, several years after the establishment of the WTO; and 2012, several years after the Doha Round stalemate. The membership increased slightly – by seven countries – in the period 1982–87, notably with the addition of large developing countries such as Mexico; and it subsequently exploded with the addition of 62 new members mostly in the period 1987–2000 (Table 8.1).[1]

In 2012, WTO members accounted for over 97.5 per cent of world exports of goods and services, compared to slightly more than 80 per cent in 1982. There are few large trading economies that are not members, mostly in the Middle East and North Africa, e.g. Algeria, Iran, Iraq, Libya and Syria as well as a number of countries of the former Soviet Union such as Belarus, Kazakhstan, Turkmenistan and Uzbekistan.

During the same period, the proportion of world exports accounted by developing-country members of the WTO increased even more, from 14.5 per cent in 1982 to 40.4 per cent in 2012 (Table 8.1). This was because of the increase in developing-country membership and because of the very rapid expansion of developing-country exports in the 1990s and 2000s. Overall developing countries continue to constitute a much larger proportion of WTO membership than their proportionate share of international trade. However, contributions to the annual WTO

[1] As noted in Chapter 2, there is no formal developing-country definition and countries follow the principle of self-selection. The definition of countries or groups of members of the WTO as 'developed' and 'developing' for the purposes of this volume is shown in Appendix A.

Table 8.1 GATT/WTO membership and world trade, 1982–2012

Countries/ territories	GATT/WTO membership								World exports (goods and services)							
	Number				Per cent				Value in US$ billions				Per cent of world exports			
	1982	1987	2000	2012	1982	1987	2000	2012	1982	1987	2000	2012	1982	1987	2000	2012
Developed	32	32	40	45	36	34	29	29	1,504	2,222	5,351	12,283	85.5	84.4	75.3	59.6
Developing	56	63	100	112	64	66	71	71	254	412	1,752	8,393	14.5	15.6	24.7	40.4
Total GATT/ WTO members	88	95	140	157	100	100	100	100	1,760	2,634	7,103	20,676	80.5	86.4	88.8	97.5
Non-members									426	415	893	654	19.5	13.6	11.2	2.5
Total world									2,186	3,049	7,996	21,212	100	100	100	100

Source: GATT/WTO, COMTRADE.

budget are assessed on the basis of shares in international trade, with a minimum of about Swiss francs 29,000 in 2012. Thus the overall share of developing-country contributions to the WTO budget is not significantly different from their share of international trade.

The data on membership, nonetheless, disguise the fact that a significant number of developing countries have been in the past formally 'inactive' for not having paid their assessed contributions to the WTO budget for more than three years.[2] At the beginning of 2000, 15 developing countries/territories were so designated (down from 23 in 1997). Such a designation implies that their representatives cannot chair WTO bodies and that a number of other privileges, such as the distribution of documents, have been withheld from them.[3] In the last decade, the number of developing countries in serious arrears declined. Finally in 2011, in order to regularize the participation of ten countries (mostly LDCs) still in arrears, the organization agreed to write off about 22 per cent of their arrears and permit them to pay the remainder over time.

Representation

Location of missions

It is difficult for a country to represent its interests effectively in a member-driven organization such as the WTO without a significant presence in it. As late as 2000, 27 of 102 developing countries, or a little over a quarter, did not maintain WTO missions in Geneva. Most were represented by missions or embassies elsewhere in Europe, mainly Brussels, but also London and Bonn, and three were represented by people located in ministries in their own capitals (see Table 8.2(a)).[4]

The situation changed significantly in the last decade, in part because of the increased demands placed upon members by the Doha Round, in part because developing countries realized that more effective representation of their interests required greater presence in Geneva. As a result in 2012 only 14 of the 112 developing-country members did not have a mission in Geneva. Ten of these are small island economies with very few representatives abroad and which simply cannot afford

---

[2] These rules are contained in GATT (1994).

[3] After 1998, LDCs in arrears are not barred from receiving technical assistance from the Organization.

[4] The information used for analysing representation as well as leadership positions is based on GATT/WTO Directories issued in 1982, 1987, 2000 and 2012. A detailed discussion of the limitations of these can be found Michalopoulos (1999a).

Table 8.2 Country membership and representation in GATT/WTO, 1982–2012

8.2(a) By location, number of missions and number of mission staff

Countries/ territories	1982						1987						2000						2012					
	Geneva		Europe		Capitals		Geneva		Europe		Capitals		Geneva		Europe		Capitals		Geneva		Europe		Capitals	
	M*	Staff	M*	Staff	M*	Staff	M*	Staff	M*	Staff	M*	Staff	M*	Staff	M*	Staff	M*	Staff	M*	Staff	M*	Staff	M*	Staff
Developed	32	120					32	145					40	234		1		2	45	268		1		
Developing	38	115	14	15	4	5	43	140	15	21	5	5	73	320	24	73	3	4	98	534	14	18		7
LAC	11	33	3	3			12	43	4	4	1	1	22	118	9	19	1	1	22	117	10	13		5
Total	70	135	14	15	4	5	75	285	15	21	5	5	113	554	24	74	3	4	143	802	14	19		7

8.2(b) Staff per Mission

Countries/ territories	1982			1987			2000			2012		
	M*	Staff	Staff/ Mission	M*	Staff	Staff/ Mission	M*	Staff	Staff/ Mission	M*	Staff	Staff/ Mission
Developed	32	120	3.9	32	145	4.5	40	237	5.9	45	269	6.0
Developing	56	135	2.3	63	166	2.6	100	397	4.0	112	559	4.9
LAC	14	36	2.6	17	48	2.8	32	138	4.3	32	135	4.2
Developing (Geneva)	38	111	2.9	43	140	3.3	73	309	4.2	98	534	5.4
Total	88	255	3.4	95	311	3.3	140	634	4.5	157	828	5.2

Note: M*-number of missions.
Source: GATT/WTO Directory, 1982, 1987, 2000, 2012.

separate missions in Geneva. Many consider that their main international trade policy concerns involve the EU rather than the WTO and thus locate their representatives in Brussels, from where they also are supposed to follow WTO issues. There is little doubt that representation from Brussels or another mission in Europe can cause difficulties, delays and sometimes confusion. The limitations and constraints to effective participation in the WTO that derive from a lack of representation in Geneva were documented in detail for Sierra Leone, an LDC whose representatives in the WTO were based in Brussels early on (Chaytor and Hindley, 1997). To remedy the problems, the government changed its representation: while the formal head of the WTO delegation remains the ambassador to the EU in Brussels, now there is also a small office following WTO matters in Geneva.

Similarly, the small Caribbean islands have created a joint office in Geneva through which they follow WTO developments while they retain their ambassadors in Brussels as the formal heads of their WTO delegations. And many of the developing countries follow WTO issues through their embassies to the UN organizations in Geneva. Starting with 1999 the WTO launched the so-called 'Geneva Week', consisting of a series of lectures, seminars and other meetings whose objective is to inform non-resident members to learn about the latest developments and discuss the issues facing their delegations. AITIC was also especially helpful through its special programmes for non-resident missions – and its closing is likely to leave a gap. Still, the situation of developing-country representation in Geneva, while not perfect, is far better today than a decade ago.

Size of missions

In mid-2012 there were more than 800 mission staff formally listed as part of WTO delegations in Geneva and in European capitals, of whom 559 represented developing countries and 268 developed countries. This is more than triple the number that worked on GATT issues in 1982, with most of the increase occurring between 1987 and 1997, i.e. following the establishment of the WTO.[5] The increases between 1997 and 2012 were

[5] This is much larger than the expansion of WTO secretariat staff over the same period, which went from 340 in 1982 to 383 in 1987, to 515 in 1997, to about 540 in 2000, and to more than 600 in 2012 (using the Directory as the basis). The two listings are not comparable, however, because the Secretariat list includes all support staff. The professional staff in the Secretariat, excluding interpreters and translators, is less than 200. Thus both the absolute and the relative increase of WTO professional Secretariat staff has been much smaller than the expansion of mission staff.

partly due to increased membership and partly due to increases in the number of staff that developing countries in Asia, Africa and the Middle East devoted to WTO matters. By contrast, WTO staffing by developed and Latin American countries remained stable over the period.

The increase in the total head count was partly due to the increase in WTO membership but also because of an increase in the average size of missions dealing with WTO matters: from 3.4 persons per mission in 1982 to 4.5 persons in 2000, and 5.2 in 2012. The average size of a mission increased both for developed and developing countries. For developed countries the increase was from 3.9 persons in 1982 to 6.0 in 2012.[6] For developing countries the average rose from 2.3 in 1982 to 4.9 in 2012 with a large portion of the increase coming after 2000 (see Table 8.2(b)). Thus, the difference between the average size of the developed and developing-countries' missions declined between 2000 and 2012.

The fact that the average size of developing-country missions continues to be somewhat lower than that of developed countries, should not necessarily be interpreted as an indicator of relative capacity for effective representation on issues of interest at the WTO by the developing countries as a whole. This is because in this, as in so many areas, the average for developing countries disguises very large variations. At one extreme is a group of LDCs or small, low income countries as well as a large number of small island economies (for example, St Kitts and Nevis, St Lucia, St Vincent and Grenadines, Vanuatu) with little trade and basically only nominal representation. The average size of a mission for these countries was only 1.2 persons. At the other extreme are several economies, such as Brazil and China, whose WTO missions in Geneva are reported to be larger than the EU and about the same as Japan and the US. The Latin American countries average about six persons per Mission – about the same as developed countries – but which drops to 4.2 when the large number of smaller Caribbean countries is included.

Many developing countries are represented in Geneva by joint missions that also deal with a variety of UN institutions headquartered there. In such cases, even if some of the staff are listed as part of the WTO delegation, there is a strong likelihood they would have to deal with other international institutions and issues as well, and hence their capacity to deal with WTO matters would be diluted.

---

6 The decline in the average size of developed-country missions in the period 2000–12 is due to the accession of a number of smaller Eastern European countries classified as developed that maintain relatively small missions (Croatia, Montenegro, FYROM, Lithuania).

Discussions with mission staff from both developed and developing countries suggested that they are all hard pressed to cope with the increased number of meetings and activities at the WTO. According to some informal staff estimates there were approximately 60 scheduled WTO meetings in the average working week and even more during the period of multilateral negotiations. To this, one must add all the other informal gatherings for consultations that occur among delegations outside formal settings to develop a consensus.

Based on informal estimates developed in consultation with a number of missions, just to follow the topics of the various WTO bodies and attend their meetings requires a staff of at least four to five people, and the average is increasing.[7] If one uses this as a yardstick, it is clear that, as of mid-2012, a significant number of developing countries did not meet it. Fourteen developing countries and territories did not meet it because they did not have a mission in Geneva; another 23 had a mission, almost always as part of a joint UN mission, but with less than four assigned to WTO tasks. This gives a total of 37, or about a third of the total developing-country membership of the WTO, whose representation was handicapped in some or other fashion. Finally, a number of other countries, perhaps 10–15, had the minimum number of staff for adequate representation, but who also had to deal with a number of non-WTO issues.[8]

The situation has significantly improved compared to 2000 when almost 70 per cent of the total developing-country membership at the WTO was found to be handicapped (Michalopoulos, 2001, p. 159). The duality between developing countries that are WTO members in name only and others that are very active continues to exist, but it is definitely shrinking. And there are more countries that are becoming more involved in the affairs of the organization.

Decision-making

Any consensus-based institution such as the WTO, and GATT before it, must develop a variety of formal and informal decision-making processes. In principle, any single member can block a decision by casting a negative vote. It was clear even in the context of GATT, where the

[7] This is consistent with the estimate for a minimum size mission presented in Blackhurst (1997).

[8] Eleven developed countries also had staffing below the minimum; but most were smaller EU members (Bulgaria, Cyprus, Latvia, Lithuania and Malta) whose trade interests were represented primarily by the separate EU delegation.

developing countries had a majority of the votes but played a decidedly lesser role, that it would be futile to attempt to exercise voting strength either to block major progress or to force developed countries to implement obligations they had not freely accepted (Evans, 1968). In practice voting rarely takes place. This puts a premium on formal and informal consensus-building consultations.

As the WTO at present has more than 150 members, it is very difficult to conduct consultations, or for that matter any kind of business activity, when everybody has to be consulted about everything. Thus, while the General Council, the ultimate decision-making body where all members are represented, and the various subsidiary bodies and committees meet frequently, informal consultations take place even more frequently.

Leadership positions

The following analysis of leadership positions focuses on the country distribution of chairmanships in various GATT/WTO bodies and committees. Chairs have traditionally played a fairly active role in forging consensus in GATT and the WTO – their role has not been purely cosmetic. Operating according to consensus, when the countries represented are very different in terms of economic size, presents complex challenges when designing decision-making structures that will ensure equitable representation of the interests of all participants. Chairpersons play a role in the effort to forge consensus and to maintain a reasonable balance of interests. Thus the share of chairmanships and other offices held by the developing countries should shed some light on their involvement and potential influence in the organization, especially over time.

The analysis distinguishes between chairs of two main groups.[9] The 'important' chairs include those of the main constituent bodies, such as the GATT Council and later the WTO Council on goods, services and so on, as well as the chairs of the permanent organs of GATT and later of the Committee structure of the WTO.[10] The 'less important' chairs include those of various ad hoc working groups and other entities established under lesser 'authority' – for example, those under the

[9] For the period through 2000 vice chairs are also included in the totals.

[10] The chairman and vice chairman of the GATT Contracting Parties have been included in the list of 'important' chairmanships, although their functions were mostly ceremonial.

multilateral codes of GATT, under multilateral agreements of the WTO and the accession working parties.

The main findings are presented in Table 8.3. The table shows that over the last two decades, developing countries increased substantially the absolute number of 'important' chairmanships they hold. Indeed, starting with 1987 they held, in absolute terms, more important chairmanships than the developed countries. Since 2000 and especially in 2012 they hold far more leadership positions than the developed countries, almost as large as their proportion of the total WTO membership and much higher than their share of international trade.

The distribution of the very top leadership positions in GATT in 1982 seems to have been very carefully balanced: in each instance the chair was rotated annually and was alternately held by a representative of a developed and then a developing country. A similar balance existed at the very top of the WTO leadership positions in 2012 involving the positions of the Chair for the General Council (Norway), the Chair for the Councils of Goods (Kenya), the Chair for Services (Sweden) and TRIPS (Honduras), the Chair of the Dispute Settlement Body (Pakistan), the Chair of the Trade Policy Review Body (Colombia) and the Chairs of key Committees. Indeed, there is a pattern of informal rotation for the top positions, with the understanding that Chairs previously held by a developed country will be succeeded by a developing one and vice versa.[11]

Table 8.3 Country distribution of leadership positions in GATT/WTO, 1982–2012

Countries/ Territories	**GATT-1982**		**WTO-2000**		**WTO-2012***	
	Permanent Committees	**Other Com-mittees**	**General Council & Other Subsidiary Bodies**	**WP & Com-mittees**	**General Council & Other Subsidiary Bodies**	**WP & Com-mittees**
Developed	8	19	21	29	18	12
Developing	7	8	22	8	24	8
Total	15	27	43	37	42	20

* Chairpersons only.
Source: GATT/WTO Directory 1982, 2000, 2012.

[11] Very few of these top leadership positions are held by representatives of the EU, the US or Japan. The Chair of the Committee on Trade and Development, which deals exclusively with developing country issues, has traditionally been held by somebody from a developing country.

The picture that emerges in the case of the lesser chairmanships, however, is entirely different. In 1982 very few chairs went to developing countries. This was partly because most of the groups in question were focusing on the implementation of the multilateral codes in which developing-country participation was very limited. Developing countries focused their interest in – and maintained the chairs of – groups such as the Trade and Development Committee and similar entities that had been created to address primarily the interests of the developing countries and not the institution as a whole.

The situation has changed little in the WTO – the developing countries again hold proportionately few of the leadership positions in bodies dealing with the implementation of the two remaining multilateral agreements and very few of the chairmanships of the many working parties set up for accession of new members.

During the Doha Round there has been a proliferation of committees and working groups relative to the number of high level, experienced, developing-country representatives who have sufficient time to devote to the growing range of WTO tasks. If one judges that about 25–30 developing countries are active in WTO affairs, ambassadors or senior WTO representatives from developing countries hold the chairs of 32 WTO bodies or other Committees (Table 8.3). This is not a bad score, given that several ambassadors also have to represent their countries at other international organizations in Geneva. Fundamentally, it reflects an effort by WTO members to maintain a balanced representation in leadership positions.

The implications of the findings on leadership positions should not be exaggerated. They do suggest that the WTO as an institution is flexible enough to accommodate an increasing interest on the part of developing countries. Whether this translates into the promotion of issues of importance to the developing countries is a more complex issue, however. The preparation and presentation of issues does not hinge primarily on the holding of chairmanships or other leadership positions. It is based on a lot of preparatory work and institutional capacity in capitals in which developing countries face serious constraints (see Chapter 5 and Laker, 2011); it is also based on the development of points of common interest with similarly minded countries and delegations in Geneva.

Informal consultations

When issues of importance to the WTO as a whole require consultations, these usually involve the Director General and a smaller group of members that includes the major developed and developing trading countries, and others who are judged to be representative of the views of the remaining membership. The composition of this group (called the 'Green Room Group' because it meets at the Director General's green conference room) tends to vary by issue. In some cases during the Doha Round negotiations it consisted of as few as four to seven countries. But on issues of general importance to the organization it could consist of upwards of 30 members. Given that, in such meetings, the representative of the EU speaks on behalf of all EU member countries, developing countries may actually have the majority of 'voices' in some consultations.

During the late 1970s and early 1980s an effort was made to formalize the establishment of a smaller group of countries to engage in regular consultations in GATT. This so called 'Consultative Group of Eighteen' included ten developing countries. Although from time to time there have been proposals to revive such a group in the context of the WTO, it has not been possible to do so, in part because of difficulties in accommodating all the countries who would want to participate. As a consequence, the loose and flexible consultation formula has remained in place. Neither the weighted voting nor the related representation formula, whereby one country represents a number of others (frequently at a vastly different level of development) in the decision-making bodies of the IMF and the World Bank, has been in favour in the WTO.

Developing countries often do not have a common position on major issues before the WTO. There is a Developing Country Group that holds consultations from time to time; and the developing countries consult on trade policy issues of importance to them in UNCTAD. However, establishing a common developing-country position on various issues is becoming more of a challenge as there are growing disparities in their income levels, trading interests, degree of integration into the international economy, institutional capacities and participation in WTO affairs.

The only developing-country grouping that has received formal recognition in the WTO agreements and in the multilateral trade negotiations is a group of countries (currently 48) of which 32 are WTO members that meet the UN criteria as 'Least Developed'. There is also a large group of developing countries in Africa, the Caribbean and the Pacific (ACP) with 68 WTO members that receive preferential market access in the EU markets which coalesce on issues that affect those preferences – such as overall tariff liberalization. And there are regional groups, such as the African group (42 WTO members), the Asian developing countries (30 WTO members) and Mercosur (a common market for four WTO members: Argentina, Brazil, Paraguay and Uruguay). The

African group has been the most active, although its overall effectiveness has been questioned (Laker, 2011).

There is also a large group of developing countries, the so-called G-90, which includes the LDCs, the ACP group and the Africa group. Because of overlapping memberships, this group includes 66 WTO members as well as 24 non-members and is typically active on general developing-country issues, such as the preservation of special and differential treatment. And there is also the Small and Vulnerable Economies (SVE) group which consists of a number of small economies, primarily islands which have often pleaded for, but have not yet succeeded in, obtaining special treatment within the WTO rules.[12]

Some developing countries, for example Korea and Mexico, are also members of the OECD, and on some issues they share the outlook of the developed countries in that organization. Others also find that, on some issues, their interests tend to coincide with developed-country members and hence participate in groups with mixed developed-developing country memberships.

Agriculture is one such issue. The Cairns Group consists of a mixed membership of exporters of agricultural products and includes such countries as Australia, but also Argentina and Thailand – 19 WTO members in all. As discussed in Chapter 4, the interests of these exporters are often quite different from those of a large number of developing countries that are net importers of foodstuffs.

In the Doha Round a number of different groups emerged consisting of countries with similar interests on specific issues linked to the negotiations. Agriculture which is the most protected sector worldwide spawned the greatest number of groups. In addition to the Cairns group, the following groups have emerged in the negotiations. Several have overlapping memberships and not all continue to be active or relevant:

- The G-20, a group of 23 WTO members including developing-country members of the Cairns group, but also India and China, that has pressed for ambitious reforms in developed-country agriculture but retaining policy flexibility (i.e. greater protection) in developing countries.
- Cotton-4, a group of four low-income African cotton exporters (Benin, Burkina Faso, Chad and Mali), which seek reduced supports, tariffs and developed-country export subsidies on cotton.

---

[12] During the Doha Round the definition of the SVE group was significantly enlarged, but it is unclear whether this will form a precedent for the future.

- G-33, a coalition of 46 developing countries seeking to limit trade liberalization in agriculture.
- G-10, a coalition of primarily developed countries (Japan, Norway and Switzerland), but also including Mauritius and Korea, that wish to limit liberalization in agriculture because of the sector's special non-economic characteristics.

Several developing countries, such as Bolivia, Guatemala, Indonesia, Pakistan, Peru and the Philippines, saw no conflict between pushing for agricultural trade liberalization as members of the Cairns group and continued protection as members of the G-33.

There were also various groups focusing on liberalization in manufactures: some were dominated by developing countries wanting less; some were dominated by developed countries wanting more. And there were a number of other groups, consisting mostly of mixed members, focusing on specific issues such as: establishing geographical indicators (see p. 217); seeking reductions in export subsidies on fish; and recently acceded members seeking exceptions to liberalization commitments under the new Round because they had just undertaken major liberalization in connection with their accession.

It is unclear whether these groups will continue to function beyond the Doha Round negotiations. But their existence is indicative of the complexity of the issues and interests around which coalitions need to be built for effective representation in a body requiring decisions by consensus, demands for effective representation being placed on country representatives in Geneva, and demands for support being placed on trade institutions in capitals.

Agenda-setting and the ministerial meetings

In the aftermath of the Uruguay Round, many developing countries voiced concerns that the negotiating process did not give them an adequate voice to express their views. Some claimed that they had been railroaded into accepting commitments they were not even aware of. Prior to and during the Seattle ministerial meeting, developing countries voiced two complaints in respect of their capacity to influence the issues addressed by the WTO and ensure that the Agenda of future multilateral trade negotiations would reflect their interests. First, they were concerned that – partly because of their own institutional weaknesses, and partly because of the absence of an international institution such as the one provided by the OECD for the developed countries – they were unable to undertake research and analyses or to develop proposals of interest to a large group of developing countries, which could then be presented at the WTO for consideration by its full membership.[13] As it turns out, these concerns may not have been justified because developing countries submitted perhaps the bulk of the proposals for inclusion in the Seattle agenda.

The second set of concerns, which surfaced at the Seattle ministerial meeting, had to do with their perception that the processes used to develop consensus tended to ignore the interests of many developing countries. The problems derived fundamentally from the fact that WTO ministerial conferences (which take place at least once every two years), such as the one in Seattle which was expected to launch a new round of multilateral trade negotiations, put an especially heavy burden on processes to build consensus. This is because the conferences attempt to deal with a large range of issues in a very short period of time; and without adequate preparation and development of consensus in advance of the Conference, devising procedures that would permit both effective negotiation and full participation at the conference itself is extremely difficult, if not impossible.

Consensus decisions are essential for any actions that affect the legal rights and obligations of governments as they do under the WTO. No government will cede this right to others. On the other hand, serious negotiations are simply not practicable if every issue has to be discussed in a body as large as the General Council. 'Green Room' style meetings need to be kept small enough to allow effective negotiations to take place but, at the same time, all major developed and developing countries need to be present, if the results are to command consensus support. This means that very few of the many small developing countries are ever included in such consultations, prompting many to complain that their interests are not being taken into account. Even when they are present, negotiations tend to take place in English, translation services are inadequate, and francophone delegates have felt handicapped (Narlikar, 2001).

At Seattle, there was inadequate advance preparation for the ministerial meeting. In particular the US and the EU were not in agreement on many important issues. And there were many other problems with

---

[13] For a long time many developing countries looked to UNCTAD as an institution in which such analyses and positions could be developed. UNCTAD has also provided a forum for discussion of broader aspects of a trade policy agenda for developing countries. More recently UNCTAD's role in this area appears to have declined and been taken over by NGOs.

the meeting, including the role played by the massive demonstrations and local government. But Mike Moore, then WTO Director General, states in his memoirs: 'I insisted that there was always a majority of developing countries in the Green Room in Seattle too, although a few developing countries at that Ministerial chose to ignore this because alleged non-transparency played better in their home capitals' (Moore, 2003, p. 129).

The Doha Ministerial was obviously much better prepared and organized. There was apparently good chemistry between the US and EU negotiators and extensive consultations with 'facilitators' and 'friends of the chair' who transmitted the deliberations in the smaller groups to their constituencies, permitting governments to express their views promptly. And there were 22 ministers present at the final Green Room negotiations, of whom 16 (73 per cent) were from developing countries and six (27 per cent) from developed countries – not an unreasonable distribution given that this was supposed to be a Round focused on development.

Although the subsequent WTO ministerial meeting in Cancún was basically a failure, and there were complaints about the role played by the meeting's chairman, Mexico's foreign minister Derbez, there was less grumbling about the transparency of the process. This issue has essentially disappeared in subsequent ministerial meetings – for which Pascal Lamy, former WTO Director General, and his staff deserve considerable credit.

The Secretariat

The fact that the WTO is a member-driven institution implies that the Secretariat plays a smaller, supportive role compared to that of other international organizations. It has been argued earlier that this puts developing countries at a disadvantage in participating in the WTO operations. Developing countries, however, have resisted a substantial expansion of the Secretariat's size or functions. In part they do not trust that an enlarged Secretariat will serve their interests (Narlikar, 2001). This is in turn driven to an extent by their concerns about the Secretariat's staffing – which is predominantly composed of staff with developed-country nationality. Developing countries have pushed recently for a resolution co-sponsored by Brazil, China, India, South Africa and other leading emerging economies seeking to establish a WTO recruitment policy that parallels that of other international organizations which aims at giving preference to developing-country nationals among equally qualified applicants.

In reviewing the composition of WTO staff in 2012 compared to that of 2000, one gets the impression that, indeed, there has been an increase in developing-country nationals among the Secretariat – though the overall staffing continues to be dominated by developed-country nationals. The most noticeable change, however, has been in the allocation of staff among various types of issues. In 2000, barely a dozen staff could have been classified as occupying themselves with issues related to developing countries. In 2012 this number had increased by at least five times through the addition of the staff of the EIF, aid for trade, the technical standards fund, staff dealing with technical assistance and training, trade facilitation, LDCs, etc. This is of course as it should be. After all WTO membership has shifted drastically in favour of developing countries; and the allocation of its staff resources should reflect the interests of its constituents.

Dispute settlement

Both developed and developing-country members have utilized the new WTO DSM far more actively than the GATT mechanism for settling disputes. As of 2011, developing countries had made 207 requests for consultations (or 42 per cent of the total). Roughly two-thirds of these were against developed countries (see Table 8.4). Developing countries were the respondents to 112 complaints by developed countries (or 40 per cent of the total).[14] The EU and the US have raised by far the largest number of requests for consultation. On the

Table 8.4 WTO disputes, 1995–2011 (number of requests for consultations)

	1995–mid-2000			Mid-2000–2011			
	Developed	**Developing**	**Total**	**Developed**	**Developing**	**Total**	**Grand total**
Complaint by							
Developed	79	67	146	92	45	137	283
Developing	33	20	53	107	47	154	207
Total	112	87	199	199	92	291	490

Source: WTO Dispute Settlement database.

[14] Developing countries had also joined developed countries in raising complaints against a number of developed countries, e.g. the banana issue brought by several Central American countries and the US against the EU.

developing-country side the countries with the largest number of complaints have been Brazil, India and Mexico. Other heavy users of the system (more than ten complaints each) were Argentina, Chile, Korea and Thailand.

Table 8.4 shows some interesting patterns. First, it is clear that over time developed countries decreased the number of cases they brought to the DSM. They had 151 total requests for consultation in the period 1995–2000 compared with only 110 in the period 2000–11. By contrast developing-country consultation requests tripled in the later period and their cases against developed countries almost quadrupled. In the first five years of WTO's existence, it appeared that an asymmetry was emerging in the use of the DSM between developed and developing countries: developing countries were being the target of far more complaints through the DSM (46 per cent) than their relative share in developed-country exports would suggest. Just over 50 per cent of the developing countries' complaints were lodged against developed countries, which was considerably less than the latter's share of trade with developing countries. The situation has changed drastically since 2000. In the period 2000–11, developed countries were by far the main target, accounting for over two-thirds of developing-country complaints while developing countries were the target of only about a third of developed-country complaints, much less than their share in trade. The increased use of the DSM reflects only to a small extent the entry of China and Chinese Taipei in the WTO: these two countries accounted for only ten requests for consultation – mostly against the EU and the US.

The number of developing countries increased both as complainants and as respondents: 29 filed requests for consultations and 24 were the targets of complaints.[15] The number of developing countries using the system essentially doubled in the last decade, compared with the period 1995–2000. Just as in the earlier period, however, the same countries tend to appear on both sides of disputes: 22 developing countries were both the targets of complaints and the initiators of consultations. This included not only major trading economies like China, Brazil, India and Mexico, but others like the Dominican Republic, Ecuador, Guatemala, Pakistan and Thailand. Latin American countries are especially frequent users of the DSM: 21 of the 34 developing countries that have used it are in Latin America. Brazil has raised the most complaints whereas China has been the most frequent target. South Africa is the only

[15] A significant number of other developing countries have joined disputes as third parties.

sub-Saharan African country that has used the system (as a respondent) and Bangladesh the only LDC (as a complainant).

In the period 1995–2000, it appeared that developing countries fared reasonably well in cases which have been completed or which have been settled following consultations between the parties involved. Of the 38 cases where legal action was completed, in the sense that Panel and or Appellate Body reports were adopted by decisions of the Dispute Settlement Body (DSB), 13 involved complaints by developed countries against developing countries, seven were complaints by developing countries against developed, three were between developing countries, and one by a combination of developed and developing countries against a developed country (WTO, 2000b). The record in these cases shows that a fair number of legal points were decided in favour of developing countries (either as complainants or as defendants), and both developed and developing countries have taken action to implement the decisions or to deal with issues that gave rise to the complaints.[16]

Developments since 2000 show a slightly differentiated picture. Developing countries including Brazil, China and India have had a significant rate of success at around 50 per cent in cases they brought against the EU and the US, but a much lower rate of success in cases they brought against other developed countries (around 30 per cent). On the other hand, the EU and the US have a very high rate of success (70–80 per cent) against developing countries (Horn *et al.*, 2011).

Active developing-country participation in the DSM gives them the opportunity to address trade issues of concern to them. This opportunity is being seized by an increasing number of countries with reasonable amounts of success. Without doubt others will follow as more and more develop the institutional capacity for doing so. The effective integration of developing countries in this WTO dimension is part of the larger question of developing countries' capacity to design and implement trade policy. Unfortunately, this is not the end of the story, as the design of sanctions in the DSM contains features that inherently disadvantage small and low income trading economies (Mavroidis, 2012). And unless these are addressed these developing economies will not be able to get a fair deal in international trade.

There are several distinct problems that place developing countries at a disadvantage: (1) remedies are prospective (i.e. damage caused from the time that rules are broken to the finding of fault is not compensated) and thus there is a premium to discovering the breaking of the rules

[16] For examples, see Michalopoulos (2001, p. 175).

early; but (2) developing countries are at a disadvantage because they do not have the institutional capacity at home nor the trade diplomats abroad to monitor the practices of developed countries that may be breaking the rules; (3) the main inducement to comply with decisions of the DSM is the threat of suspension of concessions, e.g. reduction of access to one's markets by raising tariffs against an offending member, though there is an asymmetry in the threat: 'it is one thing for the EU to excluded from the Ecuadorian market and another for Ecuador to be excluded from the EU market' (ibid.); (4) the increase in protection that is the main remedy for a rules infraction may hurt the aggrieved party more than the perpetrator.

Some of these inherent disadvantages can only be remedied through the long-term strengthening of developing countries' institutional capacity. This is happening in some of the emerging trading powers as is evidenced by their increased use of the system. And there have been some proposals to address the problem of asymmetric bargaining power in enforcement through the development of a system of 'tradable remedies' (Bagwell et al., 2005) which, however, have not gained much acceptance.

Capacity constraints and institutional integration

The developing countries' increased presence in Geneva combined with the strengthening of their representation has resulted in far greater participation in WTO affairs and especially in the Doha Round. They have submitted hundreds of proposals, attended literally thousands of meetings and made tens of thousands of interventions. And in the last set of Green Room negotiations in 2008 – which essentially resulted in a deadlock that has not been broken to this date – Brazil, China and India played a critical role as three of the G-7: the others were Australia, the EU, Japan and the US.[17]

The question of course is how effective has this increased participation been in promoting developing-country interests. Effective participation in the WTO and proper representation of their interests depends crucially on the development of an adequate institutional capacity in the developing countries themselves. As noted in Chapter 5, the ever increasing range and complexity of issues handled by the WTO, some of which are very technical, means that the capacity of developing countries to participate effectively in the work of the WTO will depend

---

[17] For a lively discussion of this and other Doha Round meetings, see Blustein (2009).

very heavily on the analytical capacity and strength of governmental and other institutions handling WTO issues in capitals. The evidence suggests that in many developing countries, especially in sub-Saharan Africa, there are still serious constraints. The quality of the representation in Geneva also seems to be handicapped by lack of significant legal expertise (Laker, 2011).

In 2000 I had argued that only perhaps 15–20 developing countries were effectively integrated in the WTO as an institution and that there was a large group of countries that was not, including all LDCs (with the possible exception of Bangladesh) and most low-income countries (Michalopoulos, 2001). This conclusion was reached in part on an analysis that used the following three criteria as indicators of institutional integration:

- Whether a country has initiated an anti-dumping action, which is a complex task requiring the implementation of complex administrative procedures.
- Whether it has initiated a complaint under the DSM, which is also a difficult and expensive task, as discussed above.
- Whether it has adequate representation as measured by the presence in Geneva of a WTO mission of at least four staff (including the head of the mission).

Twenty developing countries met these criteria in 2012 compared to 13 in 2000. The list is shown in Table 8.5.

Table 8.5 Institutionally integrated WTO developing-country members

Argentina	Malaysia*
Brazil	Mexico
Chile	Pakistan*
China*	Peru
Chinese Taipei*	Singapore
Colombia*	Thailand
Costa Rica	Uruguay*
Dominican Rep.*	Venezuela
Guatemala	
India	Bangladesh**
Indonesia	Egypt**
Korea	Hong Kong, China**
	South Africa**

*New in 2012. **Meet two of three criteria and/or judged to be integrated on other grounds.

Obviously, institutional integration in the WTO is a continuum and any listing that uses discrete criteria will exclude some countries which should not be excluded or include others that may not have been included had different criteria been used. Other obvious additions to the list which satisfy two of the three criteria include Bangladesh, Egypt and South Africa (the latter two having never instituted a DSM complaint) and Hong Kong, China which has neither a DSM nor an anti-dumping case, but whose position as a leading international trade participant is undeniable.

One can disagree about the indicators chosen to define this list or a few of the countries on it, but the core of developing countries that are effectively integrated in the WTO is obviously increasing, and a number of them are emerging powers whose agreement is essential for any major decision. Still the participation of a large number of developing countries is minimal. Strengthening the institutional capacity of these countries through international assistance, as discussed in Chapter 5, is essential for effective participation in the WTO. The focus of such assistance should be on strengthening the capacity at home. There is no point in trying to strengthen the representation of a country's interests in Geneva without improving the institutional capacity in the home country.

A number of observers have also been critical of the involvement of developing countries in the Doha Round by pointing out that they have focused too much of their attention on obtaining special and differential treatment (SDT) as opposed to participating in the negotiations for mutual reductions in trade barriers (Ismail, 2007; Laker, 2011). The developing-country issues in the Doha Round will be discussed in detail in Chapter 9. Suffice it to state here that maintaining SDT has been a critical developing-country objective. One may disagree with whether specific aspects of SDT are actually beneficial to developing countries, but the principle is explicitly imbedded in the WTO. And although the overall Doha Round negotiations have failed so far, developing countries have ensured that SDT has been accepted in all major negotiations: in agriculture, in non-agriculture market access (NAMA), in services, in trade facilitation, etc. This reflects their role as emerging powers in the WTO in the 21st century.

On a number of issues developed countries have agreed to provide SDT – for example by exempting LDCs from offering any trade concessions – not because this is in the interests of these countries' development, but because these countries' markets are of little commercial interest. On other issues, for example in the area of special safeguards for developing countries in agriculture, developed countries balked at specific developing-country demands for SDT, thus contributing to the failure to reach agreement. But it cannot be said that developing countries were not effective in negotiating their positions.

Policy implications

The analysis suggests that the duality in the participation of developing countries in the WTO is shrinking: the number of these countries that have significantly increased their capacity to participate in WTO activities and whose representatives are playing an active role in the decisions of the organization is increasing. Their participation in formal and informal decision-making processes is substantial, although they frequently do not speak with one voice as their interests sometimes diverge, resulting in the formation of different coalitions.

There is still a large group of primarily smaller and lower income developing countries for which effective representation and participation in the Organization's activities is a major challenge. Their situation has improved since 2000, but not sufficiently to cope with the complex issues, the number of meetings and the obligations in the WTO. Institutional development is a lengthy process that takes a great deal of time. As a consequence, solving the problem of effective developing-country participation is not amenable to quick, stroke-of-the-pen changes in policies or rules. That said there are a number of things that can be done, some of which should start now, although their payoff may be long term.

First, developing countries need to ensure that the effectiveness of their participation is not impaired by such matters as failing to pay their membership dues. The amounts involved are typically very small and falling into arrears in their payments is not cost effective even in the face of serious budget constraints.

Second, ensuring adequate representation in Geneva is a thorny issue for which there are no general solutions. For some countries with a very small international representation in general, setting up a mission may not be the optimal use of scarce human and material resources. The main objectives of such countries should be to ensure that they have adequate information flow on the issues handled by the WTO and how these affect their interests, and to identify like-minded countries or groups, which do have effective representation, and to engage in regular consultations with them thereby obtaining some assurance that their interests are reflected on an on-going basis. Pooling resources and representation in Geneva through the regional groupings to which they belong is an obvious answer to some of these problems.

For all countries, measures to increase effective representation in Geneva should be taken *pari passu* with measures to strengthen their institutional capacity at home, as part of the broader process of becoming more effectively integrated into the international trading system. Likewise an adequate information flow to the appropriate ministries or other decision-making bodies in capitals is essential and should be addressed at the earliest opportunity. At the same time, they need to strengthen the policy making and implementation capacity of these institutions seeking assistance for this purpose from international donors and the WTO itself.

It is important to recall in this context the discussion in Chapter 5 on trade-related technical and other assistance. Efforts by the international community to help strengthen developing countries' overall capacity to trade will go a long way towards helping them participate more effectively in the WTO.

9
The Doha Round Negotiations

Introduction

The multinational trade negotiations launched in Doha in 2001 have lasted the longest of any other. It is unclear how and whether they will ever be concluded. But however they end, they are unlikely to ever be repeated. Over a decade a great deal of effort has been expended to achieve very little in liberalization while over the same period world trade has expanded manyfold supported by unilateral reduction of trade barriers or preferential trade arrangements. The failure to agree has weakened the WTO as an institution and has led to a great deal of soul searching about how to change the way it operates.

Over time, the scope of the negotiations was narrowed at the insistence of the developing countries which, for good reasons discussed in detail in the volume I wrote before Doha, did not want to negotiate an agreement on three of the so-called 'Singapore Issues' (foreign investment, competition and government procurement) but were prepared to consider an agreement on the fourth, trade facilitation (Michalopoulos, 2001, pp. 220–5). The negotiations focused on two sets of issues: non-agriculture market access (NAMA) and agriculture. There were negotiations on other issues as well: services, TRIPS, trade facilitation and rules, especially as they relate to anti-dumping and preferential trade agreements – all these received differing degrees of attention. But the negotiating dynamic which developed required that fundamental agreement was reached in NAMA and agriculture before tackling seriously the other issues. In the end, while total agreement on these two major areas was not possible, a great deal of progress was made and many points were agreed leaving a lot of potential trade liberalization on the negotiating table.

The concept of special and differential treatment (SDT) and policy flexibility imbued all discussions and was imbedded in all agreed texts, as was to be expected from a Round that was supposed to focus on developing-country issues. Unfortunately its application in the design of the Special Safeguard in Agriculture and elsewhere also contributed to the final break in the negotiations.

This chapter will not review the tortuous ups and downs of the various discussions. Rather it will summarize the main issues and points of agreement and contention in each of six different areas: NAMA; agriculture; services; trade facilitation; TRIPS; LDCs, with a passing reference to the negotiations on rules. Further sections review some of the analyses of what could have been achieved if a deal in agriculture and NAMA had been reached and the reasons why it was not, and the prospects for the conclusion of the Round.

NAMA

The main aspects of the agreements reached during the discussions on market access for non-agricultural products had to do with the formula that would be used to reduce tariffs and the flexibility that would be introduced for different groups of developing countries in applying the formula. It was agreed to use the so-called 'Swiss' formula (see Chapter 2, Note 6) whose essential feature is that it tends to reduce the highest tariffs the most. Since the higher the tariff the higher the economic cost, adoption of the formula implies reductions in tariff peaks and suggests significant potential for economic benefits. At the same time, such reductions are likely to cause significant pain to industries that have been functioning behind high protective barriers. Still, developed countries agreed to apply significant formula cuts on all their bound tariff rates, which typically are close to their applied rates.

As discussed in Chapter 4, developing countries have bound much less of their tariff schedule and the bindings are typically at much higher rates than those applied. In the course of the negotiations, developed countries tried to obtain developing-country commitments to bind more of their tariff schedule as well as to reduce their bound rates consistent with the Swiss formula. Developing countries agreed, and were able to introduce a number of flexibilities and exceptions consistent with the principle of special and differential treatment. The main flexibilities agreed were as follows:

- The coefficient to be used in the Swiss formula for developing countries would result in smaller proportional cuts than for developed countries (Laborde and Martin, 2011a).

- Developing countries would have the flexibility of choosing between various options regarding the proportion of total tariff lines/or percentage of their total imports they would cut using alternative Swiss formula coefficients and the proportion of total tariff lines/ percentage of imports they would retain without cuts.
- LDCs were exempted from any cuts.
- Small and vulnerable economies (defined very loosely to include 39 countries, including Guatemala, Mongolia, Paraguay and Uruguay) were exempted from Swiss formula cuts but were expected to cut their average bound rates by certain amounts depending on their previous bound level – with higher proportional cuts for those with higher previously bound averages.
- Twelve countries which have bound less than 35 per cent of their tariff lines were also exempted from any tariff cuts; instead they were to commit to bind up to 80 per cent of their tariff lines.
- Also exempted from any tariff cuts were 11 very recently acceding countries, including Saudi Arabia and Ukraine.

After all the exemptions and flexibilities were taken into account, roughly 20 developing countries would have been expected to make formula cuts under NAMA. These would have included most countries/ territories which have been effectively integrated into the WTO as listed in Table 8.5.[1]

If the formula cuts were to be applied throughout the WTO membership without any flexibility, they would have decreased average applied tariffs worldwide by about one-third from 2.9 to 2.0 per cent. After the flexibilities introduced for developing countries are taken into account, the reduction in the overall tariff level would have been reduced to 2.3 per cent (Laborde and Martin, 2011a). However, the low overall world tariff averages are misleading, as a great number of products are exchanged duty free worldwide. The main beneficiaries of the NAMA agreement would have been developing countries in Asia such as Bangladesh, China, India and Pakistan whose exporters face tariff peaks in developing countries in sectors such as textiles.

The introduction of flexibilities would tend to hurt developed countries such as the US and the EU less than developing countries in sub-Saharan Africa and LDCs which depend for a larger share of their

[1] See Laborde and Martin (2011a, Table 3.2). Korea was classified as 'developed' for NAMA negotiations, while Turkey and Israel were classified as 'developing'. Korea was classified as 'developing' for agriculture.

exports on developing-country markets. Still, at the end of the day, it was the US that felt that NAMA would not have benefited its exporters significantly. It felt that its main exporting interests were in other manufacturing sectors in which it hoped to eliminate all applied tariffs through sectoral initiatives. Lack of support for these initiatives by other countries, especially China, became one of the factors that contributed to the overall breakdown of the negotiations in 2008.

Agriculture

WTO negotiations in agriculture have three dimensions: market access, domestic support and export subsidies. In agriculture, it is the developed countries that typically introduce more significant distortions to trade through border restrictions and farm support programmes. Their export subsidies for dairy and farm products have also undermined developing-country efforts to reduce poverty (see p. 139). On the other hand, there are major agricultural exporters in both developed and developing countries as reflected in the Cairns group. And there are several countries both in the North and the South that consider rural life and agricultural activities worthy of protection, almost irrespective of economic costs. Finally, developing countries are concerned about food security and ensuring both that they have access to adequate supplies of foodstuffs and that their farm communities – where typically poverty is the highest – are not adversely affected by price fluctuations.

The interplay of this complex set of interests produced a set of agreements of extraordinary complexity, again designed to take special and differential treatment into account but also to permit flexibilities for developed countries who wished to maintain significant agricultural protection. Perhaps the easiest part of the negotiations related to export subsidies. Developed countries agreed early on – at the Hong Kong Ministerial in 2005 – to eliminate export subsidies by 2013. This would have formally ratified a decision most of them, and in particular the EU, had made to abandon such subsidies essentially for budgetary reasons.

On market access, the basic principles underlying the Swiss formula used in the NAMA negotiations, namely that higher tariffs would be cut proportionally more than lower ones and that developing countries would cut their tariffs less than developed ones, were implemented in agriculture as well. Four tariff bands (A, B, C and D) were agreed upon. For developed countries the 'A' band referred to tariffs up to 20 per cent; the 'B' band to 20–50 per cent; the 'C' band to 50–75 per cent; and the

'D' band to 75 per cent and more. The lower the band, the smaller the percentage cut. The developing-country bands were higher and wider, with the percentage cut for each band being smaller.[2] Developed countries were to implement the cuts in equal annual segments over five years and developing countries over 11 years.

The tariff formula would have resulted in much deeper tariff cuts than those implemented during the Uruguay Round. There were also additional provisions favouring developing countries, including special additional reductions in specific processing chains in order to reduce tariff escalation, and deeper than formula cuts for tropical and diversification products of interest to developing countries. As in NAMA a variety of special and differential provisions were agreed upon:

- LDCs were exempted from all cuts.
- SVEs would have been able to make smaller reductions than other developing countries.
- Some 'very recently acceded members' were exempted from all cuts – while some 'recently acceded members' which included China could make smaller than formula cuts.
- Developing countries would be able to designate a set of 'special' products up to a certain number of tariff lines that would be subject to no or limited reductions; these would be products which a country would consider critical to its food security, livelihood or rural development.

All members would have been able to make smaller cuts on 'sensitive' products. There was no agreement, however, on how many of these products (or the special products permitted to developing countries) there could be.

There was also agreement in principle on the need to modify the Special Safeguard for Agriculture (SSA). The one agreed under the Uruguay Round permits countries (mostly developed that had tariffied previous non-tariff barriers) to raise tariffs above their Uruguay Round bound levels. As few developing countries had done such tarrification, they were essentially unable to use the SSA. The intention of the Doha negotiations was to create an instrument that would help insulate developing countries from volatility in world prices of foodstuffs. How this would be done

[2] Contrary to the smooth tariff reductions that result from using the Swiss formula, using the bands may lead to situations where the larger reductions in higher bands will result in lower tariffs than the smaller reductions in the next lower band.

was not agreed – nor whether countries would be permitted to impose duties above the Uruguay Round bindings.

Finally, there was a lot of discussion but no agreement on what to do about cotton. This is a major export of a number of very poor developing countries in Africa. The so-called 'Cotton Four' (Benin, Burkina Faso, Chad and Mali) have been pushing very hard with the support of the African group and others to improve market access and reduce domestic support for cotton in both developed and developing-country markets. China and the US, the main countries with protective policies, have agreed to do so in principle but have not offered significantly more access for cotton than for other agricultural products.

Given the complexity of the arrangements and the lack of agreement on certain important issues (the extent of sensitive and special product exceptions and the SSA), it is difficult to judge by how much the agreed provisions would have liberalized agricultural trade. But making some reasonable assumptions, the estimates obtained are very different than those for NAMA. According to one study (Laborde and Martin, 2011b), tariffs in developed countries would have been cut by more than half, from 15.4 to 7.0 per cent. But the reductions would have been substantially less if there were significant exceptions due to a large number of 'sensitive' products claimed by these countries. Tariffs in developing countries would have been cut by less and, if all the flexibilities for special and sensitive products were allowed, market access for agricultural products in these countries would barely change.

On the issue of domestic support, the negotiations succeeded in agreeing on a measure that contains a comprehensive definition of measures that distort trade, 'overall trade-distorting support' (OTDS), that includes domestic programmes previously excluded (for example payments made to farmers without requiring supply control). There was also consideration but no final agreement on additional measures to help poor cotton producers in Africa.

The EU and the US markets are of critical importance for developing-country exporters as these countries maintain the largest measures of support for their farmers. During the decade of the 2000s there were reductions in both the EU and the US programmes of domestic support – primarily for budgetary reasons. And world prices on agricultural commodities remained at historically high levels during this period. As a consequence, and if prices were to stay at the same high levels, the limits on OTDS discussed in the Doha negotiations would not have had a serious constraining effect on the domestic farm support policies of the US and the EU (Blandford and Josling, 2011). The main problem that the US had with the agricultural negotiations related to the fact that there were limited opportunities to its own exporters and whatever opportunities there were would have been further eroded if it had agreed to an SSA that would have permitted increases in tariffs beyond the Uruguay bound level as was being proposed by India.

In 2012, a number of proposals were made in order to try to reach some agreements that would be formally concluded at the 2013 WTO Ministerial thus putting a formal end to the Doha Round. Several such proposals were being considered in agriculture. The first is intended to assist developing countries to address food security issues by shifting measures taken for this purpose from the so-called 'amber' list of products which are potentially distorting to the 'green' list of non-distorting supports; the second aims at essentially permitting greater flexibility for developed countries to maintain tariff quotas; the third is focused on export competition. None of these proposals would make a great deal of difference in the overall scheme of protection in agriculture. Still, it was not clear as to whether these proposals would be agreed upon.

Services

The services negotiations were far less intense than the ones on NAMA and agriculture. As shown in Table 4.11, there is a large gap between the commitments made under the Uruguay Round and the restrictiveness of actual policies on services pursued by all countries; and the gap is larger for developing countries than for developed ones.

In the Doha negotiations, countries made commitments additional to those in the Uruguay Round, but the gap relative to actual policies remained quite large. Many low income countries especially in sub-Saharan Africa did not submit offers and those that did excluded major sectors such as financial services. Developed countries put somewhat more liberal offers on the negotiating table, as did countries in South Asia whose actual policies are at present somewhat more restrictive than those in Africa.

The sectoral distribution of the Doha offers is not significantly more promising. The financial sector is relatively open and the Doha offers would liberalize it further – but the gap with actual policies is still large. Retail services are even more open, but the gap with actual policies would be greater. In professional services, actual policies, especially those involving mode 4 which is of great interest to developing countries, are quite restrictive and hence the present gap between commitments and actual policies is already small. But it did not narrow significantly at Doha as developed countries' offers were limited. Putting aside these differences among countries and sectors, on the whole it can be said that the Doha offers on services as they stood at the time the negotiations were stopped did not entail anywhere as much liberalization as those on goods (Borchert et al., 2011).

Developing countries have found it difficult to make more extensive commitments for a variety of reasons. Some are similar to the traditional infant industry protection argument in goods. But there are other concerns as well: they do not have adequate domestic regulatory regimes which make them apprehensive of the implications of liberalization; and there is inadequate international regulatory cooperation which would help them realize the benefits of liberalization (Martin et al., 2011). On the other hand, the rise of anti-immigration sentiment in developed countries has made it even more difficult for these countries to be more forthcoming on all aspects of mode-4 liberalization.

It could be argued that the evolution of the overall Doha negotiations constrained progress in the negotiations on services: if a deal could have been made on NAMA and agriculture, countries may have been willing to engage more in services. There is no doubt that there are ample opportunities to do so. This has been demonstrated by the progress made in the negotiations for a preferential agreement in services in which 46 countries (counting the 27 EU countries) are participating under WTO auspices in Geneva. The agreement is supposed to be consistent with Article V of the services which covers 'economic integration' in this sector and parallels Article 24 in GATT which deals with customs unions. The group includes practically all the OECD countries, but also Colombia, Chile, Costa Rica, Hong Kong and Taiwan (China) – but none of the BRICS – and negotiations have focused, among others, on distribution and communication services. The agreement is likely to result in significant benefits to members but at the same time it will represent one more important deviation from the MFN principle which is central to the operations of the WTO.

Trade facilitation

As formal trade barriers decline, the importance of the environment and procedures for the conduct of international trade increases. This is not simply the logistics of moving goods through ports or customs. It relates to the whole set of activities, practices and formalities involved in collecting, presenting, communicating and processing information both at the border and behind the border regarding the movement of goods in international trade as well as the procedures for adjudication of disputes regarding this movement.

On average about 60 documents are used in an international trade transaction, and they often differ from country to country. This is compounded by antiquated official clearance procedures. Lack of transparency and predictability is a major source of uncertainty in terms of the costs and time incurred for delivery of commercial transactions. The problems are typically much greater in developing countries with weak or non-existent automated procedures in customs administration.

There is little doubt that adherence to standardized and transparent rules and procedures would be of great benefit to developing countries by reducing transaction costs and delivery times both for their exports and their imports. The key questions relate to the capacity of developing countries to introduce improvements, their costs, as well as what happens if a developing country fails to adhere to a particular procedure to which it has committed.

Following the agreement to initiate negotiations, a very extensive list of rules and commitments relative to the procedures to be followed has been developed, ranging from commitments to publish information in a non-discriminatory and easily accessible manner (Article 1) on a large number of laws, policies and regulations affecting international trade; to the use of the internet (Article 2); to disciplines on the fees and charges imposed in connection with importation or exportation (Article 6); to procedures related to the release of goods (Article 7); to requirements for temporary admission (Article 10) (WTO, 2012f). In the several years of negotiations, a number of studies have concluded that what was included in the proposed agreement would result in large gains to developing countries amounting to $131 billion ($47 billion from exports, $84 billion from imports) compared to $94 billion for developed countries ($40 billion from exports, $54 billion from imports) (Hufbauer et al., 2010). These are large numbers in absolute terms which represent about 1 per cent of developing and half a per cent of developed countries' trade in 2010. Another study has argued that aid to trade which focuses on the kinds of commitments contemplated in the draft agreement promises to have significant benefits both to exporters and importers in developed and developing countries (Taylor and Wilson, 2011).

Thus, there is little disagreement on the benefits that can be obtained from trade facilitation. The main issues have to do with developing-country concerns about their capacity to implement the provisions in the draft agreement. Various estimates suggest that implementation of most aspects of the agreement would require $5–10 million plus the recurrent costs in operating the new systems (McLinden et al., 2011). Developing countries have wanted to avoid repeating the mistakes of the Uruguay Round when they committed themselves to a variety of agreements which they lacked the capacity to implement and relied on vague promises of technical assistance which did not materialize or transition periods which had little to do with the time it takes to implement institutional capacity. They also wanted to avoid being found responsible for violating WTO rules in the context of a dispute proceeding when they had been unable to fulfil an obligation because of inadequate capacity. This was actually foreseen in paragraph 27 of the Doha Ministerial Declaration which calls for 'identifying the trade facilitation needs of members, in particular developing and least developed countries, and the assurance of corresponding technical assistance and support for capacity building' (WTO, 2001a).

These legitimate developing-county concerns have led to a variety of proposals to introduce special and differential treatment in the agreement. It has been agreed that the commitments made by developing countries and LDCs would be organized in three categories: 'A' 'B' and 'C'. Category A commitments would involve rules that the developing country or LDC would accept at the time the agreement enters into force; category B includes provisions that would be implemented after a specified transition period; and category C relates to provisions that could be implemented only after the country has received technical (or financial) assistance that would enable it to meet its commitments. While the basic principle has been agreed, many of the details have not, including how to assure the developing country that it would get the assistance it needs to meet category C provisions, when the developing country has to decide as to which provisions it will place in the various categories, whether it would be possible to shift provisions from category B to category C, etc. Another major issue has to do with the grace periods for the avoidance of disputes with regard to the implementation of provisions in categories B and C.

The basic problem in this and other trade-related assistance has to do with the way assistance agencies – both bilateral and multilateral – function relative to the WTO. The WTO involves legal commitments. The aid agencies cannot guarantee in advance that they will provide assistance to a particular country to meet its commitments as they have their own rules and conditions that an aid recipient must meet before a project is approved and implemented. Moreover, even if a project is approved, there is no guarantee that the improved capacity needed to implement certain provisions will be in place on time. Thus, the only way that an individual country can commit to implement a category C provision is after the capacity has been put in place through the use of assistance or other resources. It is unclear at this point how the draft text of the trade facilitation agreement will evolve before it is fully agreed, if it ever is. But the trade facilitation agreement raises some fundamental issues of collaboration between the WTO and assistance agencies – which are more fully discussed in Chapter 10.

TRIPS

A large group of developing countries led by India, Brazil, the African group and several others have tabled a proposal to amend the TRIPS agreement so that patent applicants are required to disclose the country of origin of genetic resources and traditional knowledge used in the inventions, evidence that they received 'prior informed consent' (a term used in the CBD) and evidence of 'fair and equitable' benefit sharing.

The developed countries have opposed amending the TRIPS agreement and refused to discuss the substance of the developing countries' proposals. Instead they have offered procedural solutions: the Swiss have proposed dealing with the issue by amending WIPO's Patent Law Treaty; the EU has proposed that all patent applicants disclose the source or origin of genetic material – but with the remedies lying outside the scope of patent law; the US by using national legislation.

The discussions have been deadlocked essentially for almost five years with only some procedural proposals emerging – which have also not been accepted (see p. 217). It may well be that progress in the area of protection of traditional knowledge is more promising in WIPO as evidenced by preparation of a draft text establishing a legal instrument that addresses issues of concern to developing countries.

Protection for geographical indications of goods

Many WTO members, in particular the EU, but also several developing countries wish to extend the greater protection provided by geographical indications for wine and spirits under Article 23 to other food products. A number of agreements to which developing countries participate (the Cartagena Agreement for the ANDEAN Community, the Bangui agreement on a possible African Intellectual Property Organization) provide protection for a wider range of products, including beverages, dairy and other food products, such as basmati rice, Darjeeling tea, alphonso mangoes and Amazonian nuts as well as handicrafts. A related issue also discussed in the Doha Round has been the creation of an international register for wines and spirits.

It is unclear whether an extension of the geographical indications to other products would be a net benefit to developing countries as a group. It would also result in increases in such designations for products originating in developing countries for which other developing countries are consumers. In addition, developing countries with a comparative advantage in imitating these products, or producing like-products, may not wish to go along with a broader definition of geographical indications, which would result in higher protection.

On this issue the divide is not North–South. This is reflected in the proposals and the debate so far. In 2005, the EU supported by a number of developing countries proposed to amend the TRIPS agreement (by adding an annex to Article 23.4) so that when a geographical indication is registered this would establish a 'rebuttable presumption' that the term is to be protected in other WTO members except in detailed described circumstances.

The US supported by Australia, Canada and a number of developing countries from Central and Latin America (but not including Brazil) opposes amending the TRIPS agreement. They have proposed instead to establish by action of the TRIPS Council a voluntary system where notified geographical indications would be registered on a database.[3]

In 2008, in order to break the deadlock in the separate geographical indications and in the Article 27.3 discussions, a proposal was made to negotiate the two sets of issues jointly in the hope that the discussions would provide additional opportunities for trade-offs and compromises. This proposal also failed to gain acceptance in good part because there are different groups of countries with opposing views in each of the two sets of issues.

LDCs

Throughout the Doha Round, a variety of initiatives were introduced to provide SDT for LDCs. It is doubtful whether the main initiative agreed

---

[3] Hong Kong has also made a proposal in which it attempted, unsuccessfully, to find a compromise by combining elements of the CBD proposal with that of the geographical indicators.

by all would be beneficial to the LDCs. This was the agreement that LDCs would not be asked to liberalize any of their trade restrictions in either manufactures or agriculture. On the part of the developed countries this was not done because they believed that this was good for development. Rather it was because the LDC markets are so small that they do not matter to developed-country exporters, either of goods or services. On the part of the LDCs, this was done primarily because it gave them more 'policy space' to pursue whatever trade policy they believed would be helpful to their development unconstrained by international commitments. It is also true that in Geneva developing-country representatives tend to be more enamoured with the traditional infant industry arguments for protection – irrespective of their validity or the policies actually pursued back home. As a consequence of excluding LDCs from liberalizing commitments, the potential benefits these countries would have obtained from liberalizing their own policies – which could have been quite substantial – were lost, with significant effects on the potential overall balance of gains and losses from the Round (see p. 220).

On the other hand, neither the developed countries nor the more advanced developing countries provided substantial SDT to LDCs in the area they should have – market access. There was an early proposal to provide DFQF access to LDCs agreed by a number of countries (for example the EU and Canada). But the US would only agree to provide DFQF access to 97 per cent of the tariff lines of imports from LDCs. Several studies showed that the remaining 3 per cent could include so many products that the market access improvement would be miniscule (Laborde, 2008).

A number of other proposals have also been made to deal with the institutional constraints LDCs face both at accession and after they have become WTO members. The agreement about accession was discussed in Chapter 3 – and it does not provide much help in the area needed most, namely institutional weaknesses. The proposed trade facilitation agreement also provides for SDT to LDCs – which in this instance appears quite suitable as it attempts to address institutional constraints. A proposal was made in early 2013 to permit LDCs not to implement any of the TRIPS agreement as long as they continue to be classified as LDCs. Developed countries have objected, partly because there are few countries that ever graduate from LDC status. Only three countries have done so in almost 40 years. The criteria used by the UN are supposed to be quantitative and objective, but the process is undeniably political and there are very few incentives for a country to graduate from the list. In the end, as noted earlier, it was agreed to give LDCs another eight years to implement TRIPS.

Rules

The Doha Round has also engaged in fruitless discussions on a number of WTO rules, notably anti-dumping and trade preferences. On anti-dumping the focus has been on the issue of 'zeroing' – a US (and formerly EU) practice of estimating dumping margins that tends to produce larger margins and hence greater protection than justified by the actual firm pricing policies.[4] On preferences the idea was to develop a more effective system of notification and review of the consistency of preferential arrangements with the WTO provisions.

The zeroing issue has been the subject of an increasing number of anti-dumping disputes involving the US and mostly developed-country trading partners. The US has typically lost most of the disputes but has not changed its practices. This has a potentially damaging impact on the dispute settlement system – although the actual number of cases involved has so far been small. Given this background there is absolutely no reason to believe that discussion of this matter in the Doha Round will go anywhere.

Similarly, as noted earlier, there is absolutely no interest on the part of any member to tighten WTO rules on preferences. Japan had shown the most interest in doing something on this issue. But its decision to join the discussions for a Trans-Pacific Partnership agreement suggests that it too has joined the mass preferences movement.

How much was left on the table?

As noted above, the exhaustive discussions on NAMA and agriculture reached a certain degree of consensus – which was not formalized because of the break-up of the negotiations on other matters. As a consequence, it is possible to estimate what would have been the impact of the agreed provisions on these two areas on the trade and welfare of WTO members. Clearly these estimates would have been the minimum likely as they do not take into account the impact of other negotiations

[4] Recall that dumping is supposed to occur when prices in the domestic market of the exporter are higher than the price charged in a foreign market. 'Zeroing' means that in calculating the weighted average of a firm's prices in the domestic and foreign market, the US assigns a value of zero for all transactions where the margin is negative, i.e. the foreign price is *higher* than the domestic price. This practice results in an upward bias of the estimated dumping margin which is supposed to take into account all transaction prices in the domestic and foreign market for a particular firm whose practices are investigated.

which may also have had a positive effect, such as on services and trade facilitation. They also do not take into account the benefit to exporters from increasing the proportion of bound tariffs and reducing the differences between applied and bound.

The most recent comprehensive estimates (Laborde et al., 2011) show that if the formula cuts were implemented throughout, the benefits would be in the range of $160–271 billion. However, the benefits would decrease almost by half as a consequence of the introduction of 'flexibilities' (i.e. primarily special and differential treatment for developing countries) to a range of $94–161 billion. This sounds like a large number but it is not. It is actually less than the estimated benefits from the trade facilitation agreement cited earlier.[5]

In addition, the distribution of benefits would favour developed countries and higher income developing countries. According to the above study (ibid., Table 10.1), in the flexibility scenario which was the one agreed, the EU and Japan would get about half of the benefits, while the largest beneficiaries among developing countries would be Korea, China, Brazil, India and Mexico in that order – large countries with a lot of exports. Sub-Saharan Africa would barely have a positive gain while many individual countries and the LDCs as a whole would lose. The reason for the estimated losses is that, under the 'flexibilities' scenario, low income developing countries and LDCs do not liberalize their own trade regimes – hence they forego the efficiency gains from their own liberalization, while they face losses through the erosion of their preference margins in developed-country markets and, since they are net importers of food, a slight increase in the prices of agricultural imports (Bouet and Laborde, 2011a). It is of course disingenuous to argue, as some developing countries' delegates in Geneva have, that the Doha Round would not be beneficial to them at the same time that they push for special and differential treatment which contributes to the adverse result.

There is another angle to the Doha Round, namely that as long as countries engage in liberalization discussions, they do not engage in trade wars or raise trade barriers unilaterally to their bound levels. If the counterfactual is significant increases in protection for whatever reason, then the 'benefits' from even fruitless negotiations would be much higher. Moreover, the countries that would be most hurt by increased protection would be middle-income developing countries and LDCs (Bouet and Laborde, 2011b). But as we have seen, even during the last

[5] The methodology used in making the estimates is similar but not identical – so the results are not strictly comparable, but the orders of magnitude are similar.

financial crisis there is low likelihood of large increases in protectionism. Thus, the expected value of benefits from the Doha Round for avoiding cataclysmic events should be judged to be small.

The blame game

The world cannot engage in fruitless negotiations for more than a decade without somebody to blame. In the Doha Round there are many countries large and small, developed and developing, that can be blamed for the failure to reach agreement.

To begin with the negotiations were launched soon after 11 September 2001, when there was a large amount of international good will in support of the US following the terrorist attacks. Developing countries agreed to the Doha Agenda despite a lot of misgivings about what they saw as lack of implementation of developed countries' Uruguay Round commitments. The agenda contained the Singapore issues on which developing countries were not interested in negotiating. Early on there was also disappointment over the limited willingness by the EU to liberalize agriculture.

Over time developing countries asserted themselves in the negotiations as they never had before, especially concerning their prerogatives (contained in the WTO) to seek special and differential treatment in all aspects of the negotiations. Starting with the biggest protagonists, it is clear that the US failed to see an advantage in the negotiations: its benefits from liberalization in manufactures would have been modest, especially as there was no agreement on initiatives to eliminate all tariffs on sectors of interest; the offers for prospective service liberalization were also miniscule; and the potential benefits from agricultural exports would have been threatened by the proposed SSA. The EU saw limited benefits in both NAMA and services and its main stance was driven by efforts to safeguard its agricultural policies. In both the US and the EU there was a failure to mobilize the private sector which had in the past played an important role in supporting trade negotiations.

On the Indian side, it became clear early on that there were no prospects of using the negotiations to achieve liberalization in the movement of natural persons. This was also combined at the last moment with narrow political concerns by its main negotiator resulting in a rigidly defensive stance. China was not interested in further liberalization, as it had just gone through a large amount of liberalization in connection with its accession – although it was likely to benefit significantly from the NAMA liberalization. Brazil was the country which at the end was the most supportive of the deal that was put on the table by Lamy at the last G-7 negotiations.

The developed countries have blamed the main developing countries in the negotiations – Brazil, China and India – for not showing proper leadership commensurate to their large and rising importance in international trade. The fact of the matter is that the WTO negotiations were a clear example of the rising strength of emerging powers such as China and India, which do not accept the legitimacy of the US and EU-led international trade and finance system while they continue to seek greater power within it. Brazil is closer to the OECD countries in its approach to trade and finance but is still fiercely protective of its industrial policy. All three countries, as well as South Africa, insist on a greater voice in the functioning of the system while continuing to benefit from SDT.

The only way that developing countries could have overcome the entrenched protectionism in developed countries in agriculture, textiles or maritime services was to take advantage of the pressure that export interests in the developed countries would have brought to bear on their own governments to negotiate in order to open up developing-country markets. But this presupposed a willingness to reduce their own applied tariffs and protection in agriculture and services. This they did offer – but either because protectionism in developed countries was too entrenched or because the offer was not sufficiently attractive or most likely a combination of the two, the result was no deal.

Finally, it is fair to say that the loading of the negotiations with too many topics as well as the principle that nothing is agreed unless everything is agreed was also in part to blame for the Doha Round failure. Before the start of the Doha Round I had warned (Michalopoulos 2001, p. 226), using the old bicycle analogy, that the momentum of a new Round is needed to push the bicycle forward, but that the bicycle should not be loaded with so much baggage that it collapses under the excess weight. Unfortunately, the bicycle was overloaded, and although the developing countries succeeded in lifting the weight of the Singapore issues from the agenda, the remaining burden proved too much, the bicycle collapsed and is in urgent need of repair.

Where do we go from here?

As this is being written, there are feverish preparations for the next WTO ministerial in Bali at the end of 2013. A consensus appears to be emerging that the ministerial should provide a conclusion to the Doha

Round. But there is no agreement as to what this conclusion will consist of. There are still some voices that are seeking an ambitious result which covers all the areas in NAMA, agriculture, etc. It is interesting that it is primarily the developing countries that are now seeking a comprehensive agreement. But it is clear that there is far too little time to negotiate a full package.

A limited package may emerge – although the dimensions of the package are still unclear. As noted there are a number of proposals on agriculture – but it is not certain that any of them will be agreed on. Trade facilitation is supposed to be the centrepiece, but even this is not fully agreed. Some of the sticking points are very real: for example, commitments on the so-called category B are supposed to be time limited but not conditioned on the provision of assistance. This is very risky for developing countries, since if they are not able to meet a commitment at the time of entry, they will probably need some kind of assistance to meet it at a later date. Thus, developing countries should have some flexibility in shifting commitments between categories B and C, after the agreement has been negotiated. Similarly, developing countries should be exempted from any disputes for all commitments they make under categories B and C, as it is not possible to judge in advance the time it will take for individual countries to make the institutional improvements necessary for the implementation of their commitments.

There are also a number of proposals dealing with LDCs: the changes in the accession procedures were noted above in Chapter 3, but are of limited value. It has been agreed that the LDCs will get a further extension – to 2021 – from applying the TRIPS agreement, although it may have been preferable to have adopted a procedure similar to the one proposed under the Trade Facilitation agreement with different categories of commitments conditioned on the provision of assistance for strengthening the institutional infrastructure.

Whatever is done in Bali it will be necessary to get the WTO to move away from the doldrums resulting from the stalled Doha Round. But it will not be sufficient to make the WTO play its role as the main multilateral trade institution. For this a more radical rethinking is necessary concerning WTO rules affecting international trade and the role to be played by developing countries.

10
The Future of the WTO in Global Governance

Introduction

In mid-2013, with the accession of Russia, the imminent accession of Kazakhstan and only a few LDCs and several Arab and former Soviet Union states left outside its fold, the WTO could reasonably claim almost universal membership. Ironically, as WTO membership approached universality, its *raison d'être* as the multilateral institution charged with global governance responsibilities in international trade was very much in question.

The failure of the Doha Round has broken WTO's first leg: its usefulness as a forum for multilateral trade negotiations aimed at liberalizing trade. The unfettered proliferation of regional and other preferential trade agreements – 'termites' in the language of Bhagwati (2009) ostensibly consistent with WTO provisions – is undermining the edifice of WTO rules based on the MFN principle, and thus weakening the second leg on which the WTO stands, that of the institution in which the rules governing international trade are made. More and more trade is subject to rules made in Brussels, Washington and the myriad other centres of preferential agreements in developed and developing countries alike, scattered throughout the globe. These agreements also threaten the third leg on which WTO stands: dispute settlement, as disputes arising from rights conferred by PTAs are extended only to their members and may be adjudicated by them rather than the WTO: 'Can the WTO save itself from irrelevance?', *The Economist* asked in early 2013 (16 March, p. 74).

The provisional agreements reached in the context of NAMA and agriculture during the Doha negotiations were characterized by another development, also eating away at WTO rules: the extraordinary complex special and differential provisions (SDT) proposed to be granted to various groups of developing countries. As noted earlier (p. 37), the SDT principle is enshrined in the WTO and earlier GATT agreements. There is no doubt that there are many legitimate reasons for providing substantial and meaningful SDT as well as technical and financial assistance to lower income developing countries and LDCs which do not have the institutional capacity to implement WTO rules. Policy space is needed for these countries to build capacity and transform their economies to meet the challenges of the 21st century. But the rising power of developing countries in the WTO resulted in provisional agreements for treating developing countries arbitrarily and in ways, which if implemented, would have deleterious effects both on the countries themselves and the WTO as an institution.

Whatever happens with the Doha Round – whether it is given a decent burial, or parts of it are agreed upon and others kept alive – and there are many variations that are feasible, the role of the preferential trade agreements and SDT is critical to the future of the WTO and the role developing countries play in it. The purpose of this chapter is to review these issues in the context of the future role of the WTO as the institution entrusted with global governance responsibilities in international trade. How can the WTO survive as a serious centre for rule making and as a forum for trade liberalization? What can be done about providing meaningful SDT for countries that need it and deserve it? What should be the relationship between the WTO and other multilateral institutions also entrusted with global governance responsibilities, such as the World Bank and the IMF? And finally what can be done to promote policy coherence in the sphere of trade and finance for development?

Preferences

It is well understood that under certain circumstances preferential arrangements can have a net positive effect on international trade. While they are never going to be better for global welfare than multilateral trade liberalization on an MFN basis, they could be better than no liberalization at all. But their dynamics are protectionist and discriminatory: they are designed to gain advantage against a competitor in a third market, or to safeguard a value chain and the related investment. Their multiplicity results in a fragmented trading system with rising global inefficiencies.

Agreements between smaller developing countries and developed ones such as those pursued by the US and the EU pose an additional major problem for developing-country participants: the developed-country partners propose and usually obtain through these agreements commitments which they have not been able to obtain in WTO negotiations. These include commitments on IPRs, which go beyond TRIPS, as well as in areas such as labour standards, environmental considerations as well as capital account controls and protection of investments. Developing countries correctly blocked consideration of many of these issues in the Doha Round. But this has not stopped developed countries from obtaining similar objectives through preferential arrangements by dangling preferential market access in exchange:

> Bilateral Agreements typically involve much deeper tariff concessions from the developing countries and make demands on issues like intellectual property rights that go far beyond what WTO members require of each other and can threaten the health and livelihoods of the poor. Many countries would do well to resist the immediate temptations of a bilateral embrace and build up slower but ultimately more productive multilateral relationships that can lead to more durable human development outcomes. (UNDP, 2006)

Preferential agreements existed before the WTO and have been pursued in parallel with multilateral trade liberalization for many decades. Their supporters have always argued that they could be used as steppingstones for broader multilateral agreements. And indeed the efforts to rationalize the overlapping preferential arrangements in Africa involving 26 countries (members of Common Market for East and Southern Africa (COMESA), East African Community (EAC) and Southern African Devlopment Community (SADC) are a step in the right direction. But the announcements of the Transatlantic Trade and Investment Partnership (TTIP) between the US and the EU in early 2013 and the Trans-Pacific Partnership appear to be aimed against China; while the Regional Comprehensive Economic Partnership launched earlier appears to be an effort by Asian countries to hedge their bets by promoting their own preferential trade relationships against the rest of the world.

Negotiation and ultimately implementation of all these agreements will undermine the WTO as a forum for multilateral trade negotiations for years to come – unless a political decision is made in the US, the EU and a number of the BRICS as well as groups of developing countries such as the LDCs to revive the Geneva negotiating process. The chances that this will occur in the near future are becoming increasingly remote as the US and the EU, accounting for half of the world's trade, are busily engaged in hard negotiations on TTIP. As long as these negotiations continue, there will be little political impetus for either the US or the EU to engage in meaningful multilateral negotiations in the WTO. If in the end the negotiations succeed, the implications are unclear: they could either result in a blow to the WTO from which it will not recover, or provide the impetus for a new deal with the emerging powers. But the longer they drag on, the more entrenched the interests, supported by the preferential arrangements, become, and the weaker the WTO becomes – to the detriment both of developing countries and the global economy.

Unfortunately, the WTO and trade liberalization (in general and of the multilateral kind) have no constituencies in practically all countries – other than that of economists and a few bureaucrats. Multilateral trade liberalization involves the creation of global public goods. As such it is necessary for governments to take the lead in mobilizing support (Michalopoulos, 2006).

In previous Rounds developed-country governments were able to mobilize their exporters as the main constituencies in support of multilateral trade liberalization – although the private sector pushed for the Services and TRIPS agreement in the Uruguay Round. This did not happen in the Doha Round. How such constituencies can be developed and mobilized in developed and now in emerging countries, whose trading strength is large and rising, is a major task that would fall in part on the new WTO Director and on the political leadership, especially in the US, but also the EU and the BRICS – none of which have been willing to spend any political capital for this purpose. If they do not do so soon, the future of the WTO will be grim.

Negotiations

The basic change that is needed in the area of negotiations is to take steps to ensure that the outcome of the multilateral negotiations on liberalizing trade and changing the rules for its conduct is more balanced – or as balanced as possible, recognizing that completely equitable distribution is impossible to ensure. But some things can be done.

The first step is to separate the negotiations for trade liberalization from those involving changes in the rules. Lumping the two sets of negotiations together makes it impossible for most developing countries – all except members of the G-20 and a few others – to participate meaningfully, simply because the negotiations are too complex and most countries do not have the capacity to represent themselves adequately. Hard as it is to evaluate the benefits that result from trade liberalization, it is virtually impossible to compare them to the benefits accruing from changes in rules, especially rules which many developing countries have limited capacity to implement. Also, it is unnecessary to hold the one set of changes hostage to the others. Combining the two is not needed to provide opportunities for 'balancing' the outcome of a 'single undertaking'. There are plenty of balancing opportunities within the negotiations on goods and services. If anything, the 'Singapore issues' which related to rules were a hindrance to progress in the Doha Round.

Over the course of the Doha Round negotiations, country positions on the issue have shifted: in the beginning of the Round it was the developed countries that championed the single undertaking. As developing countries succeeded in dropping issues of interest to the developed countries from the Doha Round agenda, they instead became the champions of the single undertaking.

Another important step is to strengthen the role of the Secretariat in the presentation of information and in analysing the implications of different liberalization proposals. The Secretariat should spend more time analysing the proposals submitted by various members and less in providing summaries of their precious statements in the various meetings. Analyses of the implications of various alternative proposals are made primarily by NGOs or the World Bank or other research institutions. This situation results from the sacrosanct principle that the WTO is a 'member driven' organization. But this principle essentially means that the developed countries and the more advanced developing countries that have the capacity to do the analyses have an unfair advantage over the others, mostly the poorer developing countries and the least developed.

The weak secretariat role in analysis of proposals is a relic of GATT's past when negotiations consisted of efforts to outwit your opponent based on superior information and make him or her (usually him as there were very few women negotiators those days) sign a deal which was not to his or her advantage. There is no place for this kind of approach if the WTO is to have any future.

In the past, developing countries have not been supportive of a strengthened role for the Secretariat, and with good reason. The Director General (with one short-lived exception) had always been a developed-country national, and the vast majority of Secretariat staff were also recruited from these countries. This has changed. The new Director General is a Brazilian who should be able to increase the diversity of the Secretariat.

To ensure balanced outcomes in the negotiations, all developing countries must participate in trade liberalization, and not only the more advanced countries. Developing-country markets are important to other developing countries whose access is impeded by trade barriers. In the Doha negotiations, a deal in agriculture and NAMA required detailed agreement from the G-20 and a number of so-called small and vulnerable economies (SVEs) – though only mere acquiescence from the LDCs, who had been bought off by the prior agreement that they would not have to reduce their own trade barriers. As a result (noted in Chapter 9), the LDCs could not benefit from the Doha Round (and did not benefit much from the Uruguay Round), because they opted out of liberalizing their own trade. By opting out, LDCs are emulating the behaviour of most developing countries which in earlier periods opted out from the negotiations in GATT. It was only in the 1980s when the developing countries started to participate more actively – even become members of GATT – that they started to benefit more from trade, and barriers to developing-country exports started to come down.

Special and differential treatment

A revitalized WTO negotiating process has to take into account the reality of the growing importance of developing countries in international trade as well as the strengths and weaknesses of their economies. This will require a drastic rethinking of how SDT is implemented.

Beneficiaries

Previous chapters have shown that there are still vast differences in developing countries' institutional capacity and degree of integration in world markets. Because of the principle of self-selection, under WTO rules on SDT the treatment of all developing countries by developed countries is supposed to be the same: Singapore and the Republic of Korea are supposed to be treated the same way as Ghana and Saint Lucia; Argentina and Brazil the same as Nicaragua and Honduras. A policy is needed that more narrowly defines which countries are eligible for SDT.

The present system has created a 'pretend' culture in the WTO. The developing countries pretend that they are all the same, except the LDCs. The developed countries pretend that they provide meaningful SDT to all, but in practice do so only for LDCs, because the latter are so small in trade terms that they do not have a serious impact on their commercial interests – or to their 'friends' in regional or bilateral agreements.

During the Doha Round actual differences among developing countries were handled on an ad hoc bargaining basis and produced economically counter-productive results. Turkey, a participant of a customs union with the EU, and Israel were considered 'developing' countries – because they said so and were supported in their claims by the US and the EU. Korea was considered to be 'developing' in the agriculture negotiations but 'developed' in NAMA. A number of countries were considered to be small and vulnerable on a self-selection basis, without the use of systematic criteria: Uruguay (population of 3 million, 2011 income per capita of $11,860) was considered SVE in NAMA; but Costa Rica (population of 4 million, 2011 per capita income of $7640) was not. But, irrespective of the individual choices, this meant that smaller countries were permitted to have higher trade barriers than larger ones contrary to all teachings on international trade which suggest that the costs of protection are higher the smaller the country.

The SVE list includes small islands, such as Saint Lucia but also Sri Lanka and Cuba, and landlocked countries, like Mongolia and Paraguay, but also Uruguay which is neither. Higher tariff protection will not solve these countries' problems. It will probably only result in raising domestic costs with possible adverse effects on the poor. Small and remote islands need cheaper transport links and not to be charged monopolistic rates by maritime shipping conferences. Landlocked countries need better regulation of trucking cartels and infrastructure assistance to reduce their transport costs as well.

Many problems of institutional capacity are common to LDCs and other lower-income and small and vulnerable developing economies with more limited participation in international trade. These problems are not faced by more advanced developing countries – the emerging powers.

There is an obvious need to rationalize this system through the use of income and size criteria. Developing countries have opposed this in the past because they perceive that such a system will dilute their political strength in the WTO. But their rising strength should permit them to develop a system which makes more economic sense and is beneficial to the less advanced economies which would reap more benefits if the higher income countries were excluded from SDT consideration and they themselves provided SDT to poorer developing countries and LDCs – as some have started to do.

Per capita income (for example $4,000 per capita) and share of world trade indicators (for example countries with more than 0.5 per cent of world trade in goods and services) need to be introduced to differentiate developing countries in terms of transition periods, scope of implementation and access to assistance. SDT should be extended to this group of roughly 70–80 countries, including LDCs but excluding the more advanced developing countries and trade powers like India.[1] There is no magic to any single number or set of criteria: the point is simple, LDCs are not the only group that faces capacity constraints in transforming their economy. This should be recognized by using systematic economic/social criteria, but not bargaining or 'self-selection'. Substantial differentiation exists regarding financial flows from all the international financial institutions and from the UNDP. In the World Bank, some developing countries get no assistance; others are eligible only for loans on hard terms; still others for soft loans; and yet others for a mix. Why cannot this principle that has been accepted without serious difficulty on issues of finance be also acceptable for trade?[2]

Market access

It is absurd for developed countries to provide preferential market access to such global trading powerhouses as Brazil, China, Korea, Mexico or Singapore. Their commercial strength is taken into account and they are excluded from preferential treatment through the so-called Generalized System of Preferences (GSP) which is neither generalized nor systematic anymore (see Chapter 2).

But a case can be made that LDCs and lower income developing countries continue to face institutional weaknesses in their capacity to expand exports, especially manufactures, and continue to need preferential market access in both developed and advanced developing countries. At present there is a hotchpotch system of preferences provided to these countries. The major developed countries have systems which differ with regard to beneficiaries and product coverage, degree of liberalization and rules of origin. The EU provides DFQF for all products, but only to LDCs, and different, regionally determined preferences to ACP countries; the US provides DFQF for 97 per cent of products, to a mixed group of LDCs and lower income countries; and so on for other developed and some developing countries (Laird, 2012). There is a strong need to rationalize these systems to cover all products and all LDCs and lower income countries as well as devise more liberal rules of origin so as to enhance their utilization rate (Herfkens, 2013).

---

[1] A somewhat more restrictive definition would result from using LDCs plus countries scoring 'low' in the UNDP's Human Development Index (UNDP, 2013).

[2] Per capita income has also been used to differentiate among developing countries in the provision of assistance through the Advisory Center and in the WTO on the provision of subsidies – though the economic rationale for doing so in the latter instance is quite dubious.

Rules

There are some basic rules that all countries should adhere to if their membership in the organization is to have any meaning: the MFN principle, the elimination of quotas as instruments of trade policy, the binding of all tariffs, are examples of such rules. But there are other rules whose observance depends very much on the institutional infrastructure of different countries. LDCs and lower income developing countries need the policy space to address the constraints they face in transforming their economies. They need special and differential treatment in observing these rules (Hoekman et al., 2004).

The major change that needs to be made regarding rules is not to set up different ones for different groups of countries, but to ensure that countries have the capacity to implement whatever rules they have agreed to. In the past developing countries would be asked to agree to rules in standards, in intellectual property rights, in customs valuation and in other areas without any evaluation of the implications of these rules for their economies, their capacity to implement them or the needs for assistance to bring their institutions into compliance. Vague promises for technical assistance were made, which were not legally enforceable nor were they specifically related to developing-country needs. This pattern cannot continue.

The trade facilitation negotiations made a promising break to the pattern by making an explicit link between developing-country commitments, implementation capacity and assistance requirements. The details for this arrangement must be spelled out more precisely and be related to the overall trade for aid initiative; as should all future changes in rules whose implementation faces capacity constraints in developing countries.

Monitoring implementation and dispute settlement

The Trade Policy Review (TPR) mechanism, introduced with much fanfare in the late 1980s as one of the major innovations of the Uruguay Round, has been receiving less and less attention. TPR meetings have been relegated to the smaller WTO meeting rooms with attendance primarily by lower level staff. And the Secretariat, which prepares the Reviews, rarely presents critical remarks or recommendations for policy improvements. A much more serious system of monitoring and evaluation of members' policies is needed which would include for developed countries and the larger and more developed of the developing countries a review of their policies and assistance efforts in the field of trade, as well as an assessment of the impact of their policies on other countries and the system as a whole. The focus of reviews for the poorer developing countries should be on the effects of their own policies on development, the constraints they face in further integrating into the trading system and priority assistance needs. Finance ministers have accepted a surveillance role for the IMF regarding the world financial system; they are prepared to have an international secretariat review their own policies and recommendations for change. What makes trade ministers so special or so sensitive that they should refuse a similar surveillance role for the WTO Secretariat?

By comparison to the TPR system, the Dispute Settlement Mechanism (DSM) is faring much better: it is being taken seriously and countries are participating, including some developing ones, both as defendants and as complainants. Practically all disputes in which developing countries were defendants and most of those in which they were complainants involve a small number (20–25) of the emerging powers. Poorer countries are not targets of complaints because their markets are so small they are not worth the trouble. Thus, there is a degree of mismatch between the mandate of the Advisory Center to help poorer developing countries and its actual use: most of its clientele appear to be relatively advanced developing countries – those likely to be involved in the DSM. But at least a significant number of developing countries have received some help in their cases.

Some additional improvements had been under the discussion in the Doha Round. Among these, the question of 'zeroing' in anti-dumping cases is quite important: the continued US insistence on its interpretation sets a dangerous precedent for other countries on issues which would weaken the DSM – the star WTO performer so far. But the major issue that faces smaller and poorer developing countries under the DSM system is different: it involves the remedies that are available to members which are adversely affected by the trade policies of other members.

As noted in Chapter 8, if a member fails to comply with a final DSM a decision, the offended party has as an ultimate recourse the imposition of a counter-measure that limits imports from the offending country. But with a few notable exceptions (Brazil) developing countries are not likely to use counter-measures; and for good reason: developing countries typically have relatively small markets and their restrictions are not likely to impose significant damage on large developed countries' exporters and have no deterrent effect on their actions. It is necessary to develop some alternatives that are more suitable to developing-country circumstances more broadly than to the few with large enough markets to take meaningful counter-measures.

Policy coherence

Trade liberalization is not the ultimate goal to be pursued for its own sake. The ultimate goals which international institutions are committed to pursue is reduction of poverty through increased employment in better jobs resulting in more income and improvements in health, education and other dimensions of well being as articulated in the Millennium Development Goals (MDGs) and subscribed to by all countries at the highest level in the UN in 2000. Trade and trade liberalization are means to achieving these ends.

To achieve the MDGs, policy coherence is necessary at both the national and the international level. Thus, trade policies need to be integrated at both these levels with other policies which are in the domain of other domestic and international institutions.

Issues of policy coherence both antedate the MDGs and the establishment of the WTO and post-date them. There have always been tensions between the trade policies of developed countries at the national level and their efforts to promote development, especially through technical and financial assistance. Issues of coherence at the national level also arise in developing countries, where trade policy implementation, by typically weak ministries of trade, sometimes runs counter to overall policy directives formulated by ministries of planning or finance, often in the context of agreements with the IMF and the World Bank.

At the international level issues of policy coherence arise very frequently in the context of the relations between the organizations dealing with trade, such as GATT/WTO, and those dealing with finance, such as the IMF, the World Bank, the Bretton Woods Institutions (BWIs) and other aid giving entities such as the UNDP. The increased attention directed to Aid for Trade has raised the importance of this issue in the last decade.

National policy coherence

Developed-country aid objectives have always been very complex. Political/security objectives and the pursuit of domestic economic and commercial interests, sometimes very narrowly defined, often combine and dominate the objective of promoting the development of the recipient or global humanitarian objectives. A good example is the practice of tied aid that characterizes significant portions of the bilateral aid programmes of almost all donors.

Aid policy is usually formulated by the foreign ministry, an 'aid' agency, which may be independent, but usually has some links to the foreign ministry and the ministry of finance. The relative importance of each in policy determination and representation tends to be different in various donors and for various programmes. With regard to the IMF, policy formulation/representation usually rests in a combination of ministries of finance and central banks, with ministries of foreign affairs typically playing a subsidiary role and 'aid' agencies, with few exceptions, having very small inputs, if any. With regard to the World Bank, policy formulation/representation has traditionally been dominated by ministries of finance, because of the Bank's involvement in borrowing in developed-country capital markets. Coordination mechanisms among these agencies in major donors tend to vary both in their nature and in their effectiveness. These mechanisms generally include some agencies involved in setting trade policy, such as ministries of commerce or trade. But the links with agencies or units dealing with WTO matters are minimal.

Trade policy in all countries is dominated by commercial objectives, frequently narrowly defined to reflect the interest of particular producer groups and formulated and implemented by ministries of commerce or trade (which sometimes are incorporated in ministries of the economy), with various arrangements made for formulation of policy and representation at the WTO. Coordination of positions on trade policy is done by the ministries of trade, with some participation of ministries of finance and foreign affairs, but in most cases very limited inputs or influence by 'aid' or 'development' agencies. The establishment of the WTO has resulted in the need for far greater interagency coordination as the WTO agreements include many sectors/activities previously considered the sole domain of 'domestic agencies'.[3]

Mutatis mutandis, the situation in developing countries parallels the arrangements in developed countries. Ministries dealing with a country's overall development or planning tend to be the counterparts to aid agencies for economic assistance – with ministries for finance also playing a role with either one of the two ministries usually representing

[3] In the case of the EU, commercial policy and WTO representation rests with the European Commission, which has its own Commissioner for Trade, as well as separate aid programmes. Thus, the impact of 'aid' or 'development' agencies on trade formulation becomes more complex: they can try to influence their own trade ministries and through them the Commission; or those parts of the Commission which concern themselves with 'development' have to influence their colleagues on the trade side. Agriculture has traditionally been a special case, with the Commissioner for Agriculture playing a very important role in EC trade policy formulation.

governments at the World Bank. For many developing countries, however, the most senior officials in Geneva are from foreign ministries rather than from ministries of trade. Coordination of economic policy at the national level tends to be directed by the ministries of development (planning) in cooperation with the ministries of finance. Trade ministries are charged with implementation of trade policy but are often not in charge of its design or coordination, especially in the context of the WTO commitments which involve a variety of other agencies/ministries.

By far the most serious problems in developed countries arise from the domination of narrowly defined commercial objectives, which involve private benefits to a specific sector or group of producers, at the expense of domestic consumers and the development objective. The result usually is a waste of national resources made available through the aid budget (for examples see Michalopoulos, 2001, pp. 231–2).

In developing countries, the problems of incoherence derive from a different source. In many cases trade policy reforms have been instituted by the government without 'ownership' by important stakeholders, inside and outside the government. In earlier periods many reforms were initiated, especially in Africa, under the pressure of 'conditionality' imposed by the BWIs. Frequently, the negotiation of particular trade policies had occurred primarily between these institutions and ministries of planning or finance, which were keen to gain access to the external financing provided to meet urgent needs, with other ministries, including trade and foreign affairs, which were not part of the decision-making process.

In the last 20 years, a consensus has developed that the impact of trade policy on poverty hinges on a lot of other policies and institutions that are internal to the country undertaking the trade reforms. It is well understood by now that if governments and stakeholders do not own the reforms, they will neither last nor succeed.

The increased international attention paid to aid for trade and the establishment of local focal points for the coordination of such assistance has been a major innovation in recent periods. But there is still dissonance: representatives of developing countries in both Geneva and New York, usually from their foreign ministries, continue to use rhetoric based on traditional import substitution through protection rationale, even when their governments have fully espoused liberalizing trade reforms or are trying to attract foreign investment in value chain activities. Moreover, trade policy in both developed and developing countries tends to be dominated by producer interests and lobbies. In the Doha Round negotiations, the criteria used to determine the lists of products chosen as 'sensitive' by developing countries have little to do with poverty issues. Also, little attention has been paid by developing countries to strengthening the explicit WTO provisions that permit them unlimited domestic support to programmes that help small farmers.

There is a need to increase policy coherence both in developed and developing countries: AFT in all its aspects, but especially bilateral programmes, require much closer coordination between the bilateral aid agencies and trade policy officials. In developing countries, trade officials, both in capitals and in Geneva, must be better integrated and reflect the views of the ministries of planning or the economy on overall development strategy and policies.

Issues of international coherence

The Bretton Woods Institutions and the WTO

Issues of lack of coherence between the BWIs and the WTO are far less significant than incoherence of trade and development policies at the national level. The BWIs' staff and management are typically concerned with economic efficiency issues and hence tend to be strongly supportive of liberal trade policies, which has been the objective that governments have also pursued within the WTO. Moreover, governments are represented at these institutions primarily by finance ministries, which on the whole tend to have far more liberal views on trade policy than trade ministries in either developed or developing countries. The latter, in most cases, are strongly influenced by domestic producer interests that frequently lobby for protection. Some problems arise, however, because the influence of the BWIs is asymmetric: they have far more influence on trade policy in developing countries than in developed ones.

The Uruguay Round and the WTO

The link between trade and finance received explicit recognition at the launch of the Uruguay Round. A negotiating group on the functions of the GATT system (FOGS) was established with the mandate to increase the contribution of GATT to achieving greater coherence in global policy-making through strengthening its relationships with other international organizations responsible for monetary and financial matters (Croome, 1995).

One of the issues that were taken up in FOGS (the results of which were inconclusive) is whether and how developing countries which undertake autonomous trade liberalization can obtain 'credit' for such liberalization in the context of subsequent multilateral trade negotiations. In the years leading up to the launching of the Uruguay Round in 1986, developing countries viewed the role the World Bank and the IMF were playing in trade with suspicion. They were concerned that these institutions had far more leverage in promoting trade liberalization in developing countries, which were subjected to the conditionality of their loans and credits, than in developed countries whose trade restrictions appeared to be on the rise during this period. Also, some felt that their 'autonomous' liberalization (in the context of World Bank/IMF programmes) tended to reduce their negotiating leverage in the trade negotiations that were to be launched.

It was to allay these concerns that the World Bank management first proposed during this period the idea that 'credit' should be given in subsequent GATT negotiations for any autonomous liberalization undertaken in the context of World Bank/IMF programmes (Balassa and Michalopoulos, 1986; Krueger and Michalopoulos, 1985). During this period contacts between staff and management of the BWIs and GATT were starting to get closer. As a symbol of this strengthened relationship, in 1984 Arthur Dunkel, then Director General of GATT, was asked, for the first time ever, to address the World Bank/IMF Development Committee, a practice which would continue in subsequent years,[4] and in the same year there was a first visit of GATT staff to the World Bank.

The 'credit' idea was negatively received by many developing countries in the run-up to the Uruguay Round because they perceived it as putting more pressure on them to liberalize. No action was taken in the context of trade in goods. But in GATS the principle received explicit recognition in Article XIX:3 which states that 'for each Round ... negotiating guidelines shall establish modalities for the treatment of liberalization undertaken autonomously by Members since previous negotiations'. No guideline was set for the Services negotiations which started in 2000 or in the subsequent Doha Round.[5]

---

[4] At a meeting with the author in December 2000, Dunkel recalled that his appearance before the Development Committee was strongly opposed by the EU.

[5] For a fuller discussion of the issue see Michalopoulos (2001, pp. 235–8). It is difficult but not impossible to devise a rule through which developing countries could get 'credit' for autonomous reductions in *applied* rates when the tariff negotiations deal with commitments involving *bound* rates even where tariff reductions are agreed using a Swiss formula: developing countries which have reduced their applied rates autonomously (since the WTO Agreements took effect on 1 January 1995) could be given the option to postpone the time in the future when tariffs are cut under the Swiss formula adopted by a number of years and for product coverage equal to the number of years, (since 1 January 1995), during which the autonomous applied tariff reductions had been in place.

The WTO period

Article III.5 of the WTO agreement makes direct reference to achieving greater coherence in global policy-making. And the Ministerial meeting in Marrakesh in April 1994 instructed the senior management of the World Bank, the IMF and the WTO to review coherence issues and report to WTO members on coherence issues in global policy-making. In the aftermath of the establishment of the WTO, a High Level Group on Coherence was set up with representatives from senior managers in the secretariats of the three institutions. At the same time the three organizations launched into extended discussions focused almost exclusively on procedural issues which had to do with: what official meetings of the WTO could be attended by staff of the IMF and the World Bank and vice versa; the exchange of documents and databases; and possible collaboration in research and training, as well as staff exchanges.[6]

These lengthy discussions led eventually to agreements formally adopted by the two institutions. There has also been an increase in cooperative efforts in research, training and technical assistance, areas where the staff and management of the three institutions could collaborate most effectively (WTO, 1998c).

These agreements were fundamentally procedural in nature, and some have questioned whether they really were worth the time the staff spent in negotiating them (Winters, 2000).

Developing countries, in particular, were concerned that very close coordination among the three institutions would result in greater cross-conditionality being imposed on them. Nonetheless, over time, the need for strengthened collaboration in providing technical assistance has increased, especially in connection with the EIF for LDCs (see pp. 125–7). Both the World Bank and the IMF have played key roles in the provision of assistance and coordination of the EIF programmes. The Bank in particular has launched a massive programme of support of trade facilitation, an area of important negotiations for the Doha Round (World Bank, 2009).

The management of both institutions has been strongly supportive of all aspects of the Doha Round negotiations and in particular of the negotiations for the conclusion of an agreement on trade facilitation. The Bank has also produced a vast amount of research analysing various aspects of the Doha Round negotiations, much of which has been used in the preparation of this volume. Finally, the Bank, working with the

---

[6] The author was the first member of the World Bank staff to be seconded to the WTO in 1997–99, as part of this effort.

WTO/UNCTAD International Trade Center, is helping to develop and disseminate improved databases related to the prevalence of NTMs in developed and developing countries.

The staff of the three institutions have continued informal consultations on policy issues at the level of individual developing countries. In recent periods, the most common issue has been that developing countries have made WTO commitments which they are unable to meet without additional assistance, as the WTO has not always been accommodating in permitting countries to modify their legal commitments.[7]

The WTO Secretariat by virtue of its mandate in a 'member driven organization' has far less leeway in coming forward with specific initiatives or policy proposals than the management of the World Bank and the IMF. Characteristically, the WTO Secretariat takes no official position on any specific WTO policy issues and there is no official clearance procedure for Secretariat documents or statements. The main reason is that if clearance procedures existed, then members would want to get involved, there would be differences in interpretation and nothing would be cleared!

The management of the IMF and the World Bank *does* have the capacity and authority to take independent initiatives, but unless developed-country governments develop more coherent policies such initiatives are not likely to succeed.

The experience with debt relief for the Highly Indebted Poor Countries (HIPC) is instructive in this respect. Following the agreement reached in the IMF/World Bank meetings in the autumn of 1999 to increase the international effort in support of debt relief for the HIPC, and in advance of the Seattle WTO Ministerial, the Managing Director of the IMF and the President of the World Bank proposed that market access preferences provided to LDCs should be extended to HIPC. This proposal was an extension of earlier proposals by the Director General

---

[7] A specific problem arose in the early 1990s when Bank/IMF programme conditionality in Egypt contained requirements that Egypt liberalize its trade through the elimination of restrictive licensing and import bans. To cushion the impact of the programme on domestic producers, the Bank/IMF proposed increases in the tariffs of a number of products. Egypt had bound the tariffs on some of these products at low levels in earlier GATT Rounds; but the tariffs were meaningless as an instrument of protection because of the existence of the restrictive NTMs. Nonetheless Egypt was legally obliged to offer compensation for any such increases or seek a waiver (author's files). It did the latter and the issue was closed. No similar problems have occurred since.

of the WTO which had been supported by many countries to extend duty and quota free treatment for all LDC exports.

The BWIs argued that as export growth in the HIPC countries was an important determinant of their capacity to service debt, it would make sense that the HIPC got as good access as any country, for example that quota and duty free treatment be extended to them as well. The two lists coincide to a large extent, as 30 LDCs also appeared on the HIPC list of 40. The difference was 10 lower income countries: Bolivia, Honduras and Nicaragua in Latin America; Cameroon, Congo, Ghana, Ivory Coast, Kenya and Senegal in Africa; and Vietnam in Asia – with total exports of $25 billion or 0.47 per cent of world exports in 1999. Even with the two lists together, the countries involved accounted for less than 1 per cent of world exports.

Both the EU and the US signalled non-support for the proposal, in the EU case by referring to concerns that such preferential treatment would have adverse implications for other low income countries – alluding to the ACP countries which may have wished to be included in any such extension of preferences – but most probably because the extension of any such duty and quota free treatment would not have been acceptable to EU farmers.

The BWIs attempted to formalize this proposal as part of the joint declaration of the heads of the three institutions in advance of the Seattle Ministerial. The WTO Director General balked and the proposal was dropped.

As argued elsewhere in this book, there is little reason to believe that the problems faced by LDCs are significantly different from those of other low-income countries. The measures which the international community takes should address both. In this case, the internationally community and the BWIs had exhaustively analysed the problems of the HIPC. But the trade ministers of the same governments could not be convinced that it would be useful to reduce trade barriers to them. Continuation of trade restraints on HIPC exports means that the consumer in developed countries was hurt twice: first by having to pay higher prices on imports from these countries and second by having to pay more in aid and debt relief to assist them to recover. The effect that such preferences would have on exports of other low-income developing countries appears to have been no more than a convenient excuse for doing nothing in an area where all logic suggests that concerted international action was urgently needed.

No other major initiative of this kind was undertaken by the management of the BWIs in the period since. Throughout the Doha Round, however, developing countries have been attempting to introduce links between the trade negotiations and finance issues – most recently related to the issue of exchange rate valuation. Developed countries have resisted these efforts, wishing to keep the discussion of finance and exchange rates in the IMF where the governance structure favours them.

The emerging powers and governance of international institutions

The growing economic and trading strength of the emerging powers from the developing world has resulted in the establishment of new international institutions that play a role in global economic governance as well as in shifts in the power relations between groups of countries within existing institutions. The most important new institution is the G-20. It is important because it gives a global voice to all the major economic and trading powers and it addresses both trade and finance issues. Another development that bears watching is the institutionalization of the economic cooperation among the BRICS.

The WTO governance structure has not changed, but the power relations within the existing structure have, as a result of Russia's accession in combination with the rising strength of the other BRICS and the developing countries in general. The QUAD can no longer drive the negotiating agenda. Negotiated outcomes need to be more balanced. Yet, in order for the WTO to survive and flourish, both the traditional OECD powers and the emerging powers among the developing countries need to show more flexibility in their positions on many issues.

The OECD countries cannot continue to drag their feet in reducing agricultural protection for products of importance to poor countries, such as cotton, while asking them to join in duty free sectoral agreements in manufactures; they cannot continue to propose liberalization in services while maintaining controls on mode four.

The emerging powers need to show restraint. If they push too hard on some aspects of SDT, the traditional OECD powers have decided that they will take their game elsewhere – essentially PTAs. This has happened before: the OECD countries agreed to the establishment of UNCTAD. But when UNCTAD's political processes and its secretariat became dominated by developing countries, developed countries progressively withdrew their financial support and UNCTAD has withered away as an institution with a significant role in global trade and development. The same could happen to the WTO. It will not die – international institutions rarely if ever do. It would wither away. It could continue to play its dispute settlement function. However, it is questionable whether that role alone would be sufficient to keep it going or whether it too will be pre-empted by the rising importance of PTAs – which would be detrimental to the system as a whole and to the smaller and poorer developing countries.

The growing importance of the emerging powers in trade and finance received formal recognition in 2010 when the IMF agreed to change its governing structure in ways that would give greater voice – and votes in its weighted voting system of governance – to emerging powers, in conjunction with a significant increase in its resources through a large quota increase. All developed countries agreed to this change – including the US government and EU countries that would lose the most voting power. Unfortunately, as of mid-2013 both the change in the IMF governance structure and the related quota increase has been blocked by the US Congress which has to ratify the proposed change.

Convergence between the OECD and the emerging powers requires more coherence (see WTO, 2013). Both in trade and in finance, weakening and splintering of the multilateral system hurts the global economy and the poorer developing countries. Over the last decade these countries have made significant progress in attaining the MDGs. They have weathered the storm created by the 2008 financial crisis. Yet globalization has been unbalanced with a lot of unequal outcomes especially within countries. The burden of eradicating poverty through appropriate policies, including on trade, rests squarely on the shoulders of the developing countries themselves, though the international trade architecture and related financial assistance can be supportive of their efforts.

11
Conclusions and Recommendations

Conclusions

The main conclusion of this book is that during the last 30 years integration of the developing countries in the international trading system has been in many ways impressive, but uneven. A significant number of countries, 20–25, have made giant strides in their institutional integration into the WTO system. A few emerging trading powers are exercising significant influence in the WTO and in the global economy more broadly. And the developing countries as a group played a much greater role in the Doha Round negotiations than in previous Rounds.

This increased integration is in part a result of increased liberalization of trade regimes in both developed and developing countries undertaken in the context of the Uruguay Round of multilateral trade negotiations or, for some developing countries, as a consequence of unilateral liberalization and, in still others, as a product of preferential arrangements which have multiplied at a dizzying pace in the last decade. Applied tariffs as well as traditional core NTMs, such as non-automatic licensing, have declined significantly over time as instruments of protection in both developed and developing countries.

Indeed, the means of protection used by developed and developing countries – especially middle and high income ones – are becoming increasingly similar: trade remedies, especially anti-dumping, are becoming the instruments of choice for all except low income developing countries. SPS and TBT measures are also being increasingly used, but their protective intent as well as their effect are difficult to gauge.

Liberalization in services has lagged behind liberalization in goods. This suggests that the service sectors are the most promising area where efforts for further liberalization may produce results. Protection did increase somewhat following the 2008 financial crisis. But the increase was far less than feared and had been experienced in even milder previous recessions.

It would have been impossible to achieve the large rates of growth of exports in the last 20 years unless markets were becoming more open. Increased integration has also resulted from stronger institutional development in many countries and a strengthening of developing-country representation in the WTO.

But progress has been uneven. Sub-Saharan Africa's exports have boomed in the last decade due to favourable developments in primary commodity markets, while growth of manufactured exports has been much less robust. These countries have also not benefited from the growth of value chains that has been critical to trade expansion worldwide.

Low-income countries tended on the whole to have higher levels of protection and also were characterized by serious institutional weaknesses which undermined their capacity to participate effectively in international trade and transform their economies as well as in meeting their obligations in the WTO. Capacity constraints were especially pronounced in LDCs, but they are present in other lower income countries as well. And while poverty is being reduced globally, averages disguise increased inequalities within and between countries, resulting in continued marginalization of poor countries and people.

To what extent have the policies of the developed countries affected this uneven performance of the developing countries? The evidence in Chapter 6 shows that developed countries have been liberalizing their trade regimes. But it also shows that their regimes are on the whole more closed towards developing-country exports of goods and services than for products and services of interest to other developed countries. Their tariffs are on the average higher for products of developing countries; their remaining non-tariff barriers are concentrated in agriculture which is of primary interest to developing countries; and the incidence of their 'trade remedies', especially through anti-dumping, is skewed against developing countries.

Unfortunately, the protective actions of developing countries are also skewed against themselves. China in particular has been singled out as a target for anti-dumping actions by both developed and other developing countries. LDCs on the other hand have not suffered from trade remedies taken by either developed or other developing countries. Indeed these countries have benefited from a hotchpotch of uncoordinated unilateral preferences offered by developed and some developing countries. These preferences have not been fully utilized in part because of continued supply constraints and in part because of the administrative complexity and restrictive nature of rules of origin required for product eligibility.

The explanations of the uneven performance of developing countries must be primarily sought in the capacity constraints and policy deficiencies of the developing countries themselves; although trade liberalization in developed countries would undoubtedly make a contribution to the welfare of all countries, including their own. But it is the more advanced and higher income developing countries with the stronger institutional and human capacities that have been able to take advantage of the opportunities offered by a liberalizing international trade environment.

There is a never-ending debate as to whether a liberal trade policy is a cause or an effect of growth and sustainable development. The preponderance of the evidence supports the proposition that for a liberal trade policy to be successful in helping to alleviate poverty it has to be complemented by a variety of other policies, both at the macro and micro-level, for example to improve the operation of factor and product markets. A number of successful 'integrators' in the international markets, such as Korea and, most certainly, India, maintain protection, in some cases at rather substantial levels. But they have offset the disincentives created by protection through policies, for example tariff rebates (and earlier through export subsidies) that minimize the cost of protection on their exporters. For such a strategy to be effective, however, it is necessary to develop the institutional capacity to implement the required policies.

Capacity development is the *sine qua non* for developing-country integration in the international trading system and for grasping the opportunities and reaping the benefits that such a system can provide. Trade-related institutional capacity involves:

- The capacity to design and implement trade policy and to represent the country's interests effectively in international fora such as the WTO.
- Trade-related human and physical infrastructure that affects the capacity to export.
- Supporting institutions to maintain quality standards and provide finance, insurance and marketing for exports.
- Appropriate safety nets to ensure that trade reforms, that may benefit the country as a whole, do not cause severe damage to the poor that can ill afford it.

As this is being written, the future environment is clouded by slower growth of trade during 2012–13 and weak economic prospects in major economies, including the EU but also China and India. So far the experience with increased protection has not been too bad. Whether it will continue in the future remains to be seen.

The international community missed an opportunity to consolidate ongoing liberalization and further reduce tariff and non-tariff barriers in goods and services when it failed to reach agreement after a decade of negotiations on the Doha Round. Developing countries, especially the emerging powers, participated actively in the negotiations and share in the blame for their failure. The failed negotiations have undermined the stature of the WTO and have raised serious questions about its future.

The proliferation of regional and other partial preferential arrangements are both a cause and a result of the lack of progress in the multilateral trade negotiations. But whatever their origin and motivation they violate the basic WTO tenet of MFN and thus pose a potential threat to the multilateral system. While it has been argued that such arrangements can also provide a potential stimulus to further multilateral collaboration, this has not proved to be the case so far. Regional and other partial preferential trade arrangements with developed countries also pose serious dangers for developing countries which may be forced to make commitments in excess of those required of them from the WTO.

The one positive development of the Doha Round is the increased attention and resources that have been channelled to aid for trade. While the statistics measuring aid for trade leave a lot to be desired, and there is a need for better coordination among the multiple programmes that have been put in place in order to increase their effectiveness, there is little doubt that the Doha Round had a catalytic effect in focusing attention on developing-country needs in aid for trade. Increased attention to these needs requires greater policy coherence between aid and trade agencies in aid-giving countries and ensuring trade policy and programmes are consistent with poverty reduction strategies in recipient countries. The proliferation of agencies and activities poses an administrative burden on poorer developing countries and should be rationalized to increase programme effectiveness.

Other aspects of special and differential treatment for developing countries fared less well during the Round. Many developing countries were exempted from reducing significantly, if at all, their own trade barriers – to their own detriment. At the same time improved market access for LDCs through the provision of DFQF for all their products did not materialize; nothing was done to deal with the problems of market access and producer support for cotton – to the detriment of poor countries in Africa; and the need to modify LDCs' and other lower income countries' commitments in areas such as TRIPS, SPS and TBT was only partially addressed.

A well functioning WTO in all its dimensions – as a forum for negotiations, rule setting and dispute settlement – is good for the international community and for the weakest of its members. The next section contains a 12-point agenda to strengthen the WTO and the world trading system.

Agenda for action

WTO negotiations

1. Agree on a package that concludes the Doha Round. This package ideally should have two components: first, a group of agreements that could be implemented immediately, which should include the trade facilitation agreement, three agreements presently being considered in agriculture (public stockholding for food security and domestic food aid, export competition/restrictions, tariff rate quota administration) and for LDCs, and 100 per cent DFQF; second, agreement now to renew negotiations later on other aspects of the Doha Round, specifically NAMA and agriculture.
2. Envisage modalities for the future NAMA and agriculture negotiations that include participation in reciprocal liberalization by all WTO members, including LDCs and countries characterized as SVEs. LDCs, SVEs and other lower income developing countries need policy space to implement programmes and policies that would address capacity constraints and transform their economies. They do not need policy space that excludes them from tariff bindings and commitments to reduce tariffs. If it proves politically impossible to get LDCs to commit to reduce tariffs, they should at least be required to bind the bulk of their tariffs with some flexibility as to the proportion bound and the level of the binding in relation to the actually applied rates. Such flexibility is not needed for so-called SVE.
3. Complete a reciprocal services liberalization agreement open to all countries. However, the negotiations should also consider liberalization of mode-four service provisions which are of interest to developing countries.
4. Conclude discussions towards achieving zero-for-zero sectoral accords on a reciprocal basis. These discussions should be an important complement to NAMA discussions.

Rules

5. Initiate discussions aimed at substituting the GSP by 2018 with a new DFQF system of preferences that covers all products from LDCs and all countries with per capita income of less than $4,000, except those with a share of more than 0.5 per cent of world trade for goods and services on average for a three-year period, with simple common rules of origin involving low local content and generous cumulation requirements.
6. Permit all LDCs and developing countries with per capita income less than $4,000 and less than 0.5 per cent of world trade after appropriate notification to create more policy space by opting out of aspects of the TRIPS, SPS, TBT and Customs Valuation agreements that they are unable to implement because of institutional constraints; adopt rules similar to those in the projected Trade Facilitation agreement that enable countries to commit to additional aspects of these agreements as they establish appropriate institutional capacity in conjunction with aid-for-trade.
7. Develop a package of reforms in the agreement on agriculture that is aimed at helping the poor as follows: (a) introduce special safeguard provisions for crops produced predominantly by small and poor farmers; (b) expand the measures of support for small and poor farmers who are excluded from producer support limitations; (c) exclude from limitations the support measures that help the urban poor; (d) improve market access and reduce producer supports for cotton.
8. Develop in WIPO or in the WTO a legally binding agreement according to which patent applicants are required to disclose the country of origin of genetic resources and traditional knowledge used in the inventions, evidence that they received prior informed consent and evidence of fair and equitable benefit sharing.

Dispute settlement

9. Introduce an option other than retaliation that would permit a developing-country member to obtain compensation for non-compliance to a finding by another member. Monetary damages or tradeable rights of retaliation are examples of alternative approaches to counter-measures in the case of non-compliance which are more suitable to developing-country circumstances.
10. Provide a grace period for a number of years in the application of dispute settlement provisions – as in the proposed trade facilitation agreement – for provisions in TRIPS, SPS, TBT and Customs Valuation agreements temporarily waived (see 6 above) for lower income countries and LDCs.

Trade policy reviews

11. Strengthen the capacity of the WTO Secretariat to review and recommend policy changes in the context of Trade Policy Reviews both for developed and developing countries.

Aid for trade

12. Establish a new World Trade Fund (WTF) that would be open to LDCs and lower income countries and would substitute for several existing funding mechanisms, including the EIF, the TBT Fund and trust funds for trade-related work provided to the World Bank, the WTO and other multilateral institutions. The existing multilateral funds with overlapping objectives and responsibilities only create coordination burdens for recipients that reduce their effectiveness. Setting up a single fund that integrates several existing ones would rationalize and streamline multilateral assistance: see box.

World Trade Fund

The objective of the new World Trade Fund (WTF) would be to promote the more effective integration of developing countries in the world trading system through the provision of predictable and reliable technical and related financial assistance. An initial Fund of $1 billion for five years is proposed with a review in the fourth year to determine if and by how much it needs to be replenished. The primary purpose is not to stimulate additional funding but to integrate existing facilities and programmes.

Scope of Activities. The WTF would support strengthened institutional capacity in: (a) trade policy and regulation, design and implementation; (b) trade support services; (c) trade facilitation; (d) trade adjustment. Funding in these areas would be provided for training and human resource development, diagnostic studies, expert advice and software but also for related hardware and some limited construction.

Beneficiaries. WTF beneficiaries would include LDCs as well as other lower income countries and small and vulnerable island economies but exclude large trading nations such as India.

Terms. Grants for LDCs, ODA loans for others; public/private partnerships.

Governance. A three-tiered structure composed of a 'Governing Body', a 'Programme Board' and a Secretariat. The Governing Body would be a political body with representation from governments, donors and recipients who should take ultimately responsibility for the activities of the WTF. The main functions of the Governing Body would be to review the overall policies and programmes of the WTF, approve changes in its functions as well as approve any new replenishment. The Programme Board would be composed of a subset of the overall membership as well as representatives from the six implementing agencies (ITC, IMF, UNCTAD, UNDP, the World Bank and the WTO) as observers. The main functions of the Board would be to: (a) review and approve the work programme submitted to it by the Secretariat; (b) establish operational strategies for the WTF, such as directives and criteria for project selection and execution; (c) ensure that WTF policies are pursued and that projects and programmes are monitored and evaluated; (d) direct the utilization of funds, review the availability of WTF resources and seek to mobilize additional resources as necessary; (e) review and approve the administrative budget of the WTF. The main functions of the Secretariat would be to: help identify and, in collaboration with national authorities, prepare projects for funding by the WTF; monitor and evaluate project implementation; disseminate best practices; and undertake the daily operations of the WTF.

Location. Logically, a global fund focusing on trade and development should be established in UNCTAD. However, that institution does not have the confidence of the major donors; the World Bank, with a lot of capacity and experience in trade-related activities and trade facilitation, is not acceptable to the developing countries; and the WTO is not viewed as an appropriate development assistance institution by either group. Thus, a new independent fund needs to be set up with its secretariat housed in one of the six EIF implementing agencies for administrative purposes, salaries, pensions, etc.

Local presence. The WTF would need to strengthen its local presence in developing countries and create a more direct and efficient link between the action plans from diagnostic studies and the funding of projects. Action plans need to become more focused and prioritized.

Mainstreaming trade in developing country programmes and strategies can be promoted by: the establishment of national 'steering committees'; early involvement of the ministry of finance as well representatives of the private sector that stand to benefit from proposed programmes; and the establishment of a focal point, 'a champion' for trade, possibly located in a visible high level position, not identified with an individual ministry.

Link to the WTO. Greater policy coherence in addressing developing-country concerns arising from the WTO negotiating process require the allocation of WTF resources so that developing countries will be better able to meet WTO commitments. The WTF will develop procedures in collaboration with the WTO under which developing countries notify the WTO Secretariat and the WTF of technical assistance requirements to meet specific obligations under WTO agreements. The WTF, in collaboration with the governments, would then develop specific projects to address these problems.

To achieve this agenda, a great deal of effort and compromise are needed from the developed OECD members, the emerging powers and the many lower income countries. Even in the best of times, trade policy reform is not politically easy. It is extraordinarily difficult at times of economic uncertainty. Always, it takes time to put in place. Some of the above actions are short term. Others can only be implemented over time. All are needed for sustainable development and the achievement of the Millennium Development Goals.

Appendix A: Country Groupings

There is no formal 'developing country' definition in any of the major international organizations such as the World Bank or the WTO. The former uses for statistical purposes a per capita income grouping which does not distinguish between developed and developing countries and which is used in part in this analysis. The WTO has no official breakdown of developed versus developing countries. For operational purposes 'developing' countries use the principle of self-selection. The breakdown between developed and developing countries used in this analysis follows roughly the breakdown used by the WTO for statistical purposes with a few changes to be noted below.

Developed countries in my analysis include 47 countries in Europe (including Belarus, Kazakhstan, Russia and Ukraine, but not Armenia, Azerbaijan, Georgia or Moldova), Australia, Canada, Israel, Japan, New Zealand, Turkey and the USA. This is pretty close to the WTO definition with the exception that South Africa, which the WTO classifies as 'developed', in our case is in the developing-country group – while Turkey, classified by the WTO as 'developing', is in our analysis in the developed-country group, as it is applying for association with the EU. Also, Armenia, Georgia and the Kyrgyz Republic classify themselves in the WTO as 'transition' economies – a category that had been used in the past but which is of doubtful usefulness in this analysis. All three countries are classified as 'developing', as is Moldova, Tajikistan, Turkmenistan and Uzbekistan.

All remaining countries and territories are considered 'developing'. For merchandise trade, the analysis has data for 145 countries. Forty-six are in sub-Saharan Africa, 42 in Asia, 35 in Latin America and the Caribbean, and 22 in Europe, the Middle East and North Africa. The latter region includes the five North African countries (Morocco, Algeria, Tunisia, Libya and Egypt) and stretches all the way east to include Iraq and Iran (but not Afghanistan, which is in Asia). It also includes Armenia, Azerbaijan, Georgia and Moldova. Far less service data are available for developing countries. In this case our analysis includes information for 132 developing countries, 46 in sub-Saharan Africa, 33 in Latin America and the Caribbean, 33 in Asia, and 20 in Europe, the Middle East and North Africa.

OPEC consists of 12 members: Algeria, Angola, Libya, Nigeria, Indonesia, Iran, Iraq, Venezuela, Kuwait, Qatar, Saudi Arabia and the United Arab Emirates.

The income level analysis uses the same definition for developed countries as above. Developing and transition economies are then grouped into five categories using basically the World Bank definitions of groupings and per capita income in 2012 for 192 economies/countries, except: LDCs, which are the 48 countries in the UN list, are shown as a separate category; low income countries are those with per capita income less than $1,025 (except LDCs); lower middle income countries are those with $1,026–4,035; upper middle income countries are those with $4,036–12,475; and high income countries are those with $12,476 or more.

For merchandise trade sectoral breakdown data are available for 161 countries from UN COMTRADE with 42 LDCs (six LDCs are missing data); information for service sectors is available for 173 countries in 2010, though only for 46 developed countries and 127 developing economies. Similarly, the low income group includes 22 countries for merchandise trade but only 32 for services. The number of developing countries in the other groups is as follows: lower middle income: 41 for merchandise trade and 44 for services; upper middle income: 34 and 37; and high income: 17 and 14 respectively.

Appendix B: Methodology in Estimating Frequency Ratios

The TPR data permitted us to estimate frequencies in the applications of these NTMs at the Harmonized System (HS) two-digit level involving 97 product categories. Thus, the frequency ratios (f) calculated from the TPR relate to the proportion of HS2 product categories out of the total which is affected by a particular measure. The weakness of this indicator is that it gives equal weight to the presence of a measure in a country that could affect only one or a few lines in an HS2 category, for example HS72, Iron and Steel, with the presence of the same measure in another country which affects a large number of tariff lines, for example all steel products.

Formally, let N_{qm} be an NTM imposed by country m on a product or group of products q. Then the frequency ratio for that measure, $f_{nm} = \Sigma N_{qm}/\Sigma Q_m$, where Q_m is the total number of products, measured in total tariff lines or product groups. Thus, for the calculation of (f), using the HS2 product breakdown employed in most of the analysis, $Q_m = 97$. Where tariff line information was available, as for example in the case of tariff quotas for the calculation of (f'), a standard HS six-digit tariff line classification of approximately 5,200 lines was used.

It may appear at first glance that f would always be larger than f'. This is not the case, however. The two different frequency ratios show different aspects of a country's trade regime: if a specific NTM involves a large number of tariff lines concentrated in one or two groups of products, f may be smaller than f'; the converse will be the case if a particular measure applies to a few products in a large number of groups. A simple example from one of the countries, Thailand, in which tariff line and broader category measures are available for the same year, can be used to illustrate this point. In 1997 Thailand applied non-automatic licensing on a total of 25 product categories, involving 713 tariff lines. In this case, $f = 26$ per cent while $f^1 = 14$ per cent. For the same year, Thailand's prohibitions were concentrated in six product categories involving 613 tariff lines. In this case $f = 6$ per cent while $f^1 = 12$ per cent.

References

ACWL (Advisory Centre for WTO Law) (2011) *The ACWL at Ten: Looking Back, Looking Forward* (Geneva: Advisory Centre for WTO Law).

Adhikari, R. (2011) *Evaluating Aid for Trade Effectiveness on the Ground: A Methodological Framework* (Geneva: ICTSD).

Adhikari, R., P. Kharel and C. Sapkota (2011) *Evaluating Aid for Trade on the Ground: Lessons from Nepal* (Geneva: ICTSD).

Aminian, N., K.C. Fung, and F. Ng (2009) 'A Comparative Analysis of Trade and Economic Integration in East Asia and Latin America,' *Economic Change and Restructuring*, 42(1): 105–137.

Ancharaz, V. (2012) *Trade Preference Schemes for LDCs* (Geneva: ICTSD).

Anderson, K., W. Martin and D. van der Mensbrugghe (2005) 'Distortions to World Trade: Impacts on Agricultural Markets and Farm Income' Policy Research Working Paper 3736, (Washington, DC: World Bank).

Arvis, J. *et al.* (2012) *Connecting to Compete: Trade Logistics in the Global Economy* (Washington, DC: World Bank).

Bachetta, M., J. Richtering and R. Santana (2012) 'How Much Light Do WTO Notifications Shed on NTMs?' in O. Cadot and M. Malouche (eds), *Non-Tariff Measures: A Fresh Look at Trade Policy's New Frontier* (Washington, DC: CEPR and World Bank).

Bagwell, K., P.C. Mavroidis and R.W. Staiger (2005) 'The Case for Tradeable Remedies in WTO Dispute Settlement' in S.J. Evenett and B.H. Hoekman (eds), *Economic Development and Multilateral Trade Co-operation* (Washington, DC: World Bank).

Balassa, B. and C. Michalopoulos (1986) 'Liberalizing Trade Between Developed and Developing Countries', *Journal of World Trade Law*, 20(1).

Bhagwati, J. (1978) *Anatomy and Consequences of Exchange Control Regimes* (New York: National Bureau of Economic Research).

—— (2009) *Termites in the Trading System: How Preferential Agreements Undermine Free Trade* (New York: Council of Foreign Relations).

Bhagwati, J. and T. N. Srinivasan (1999) 'Outward Orientation and Development: Are Revisionists Right?' Center Discussion Paper 806, Economic Growth Center: Yale University.

Binswagner, H. and E. Lutz (2000) *Agricultural Trade Barriers, Trade Negotiations and the Interests of Developing Countries* (Bangkok: UNCTAD).

Blackhurst, R. (1997) 'The WTO and the Global Economy', *World Economy*, 20, 527–544.

—— (1998) 'The Capacity of the WTO to Fulfill its Mandate' in A. O. Krueger (ed.), *The WTO as an International Organization* (Chicago, IL: University of Chicago Press).

Blandford, D. and T. Josling (2011) 'The WTO Modalities Proposals and Their Impact on Domestic Support in the EU and the US' in W. Martin and A. Mattoo (eds.), *Unfinished Business? The WTO's Doha Agenda* (Washington, DC: CEPR and World Bank).

Blustein, P. (2009) *Misadventures of the Most Favored Nations* (New York: Public Affairs).

Borchert, I., B. Gootiiz and A. Mattoo (2011) 'Services in Doha: What's on the Table?' in W. Martin and A. Mattoo (eds), *Unfinished Business? The WTO's Doha Agenda* (Washington, DC: CEPR and World Bank).

Bouet, A. and D. Laborde (2011a) 'Duty Free, a Round for Free and Least Developed Countries' in W. Martin and A. Mattoo (eds.), *Unfinished Business? The WTO's Doha Agenda* (Washington, DC: CEPR and World Bank).

—— (2011b) 'The Hidden Gain of the Doha Round: Lowering the Cost of Trade Wars by Reducing Binding Overhang' in W. Martin and A. Mattoo (eds.), *Unfinished Business: The WTO's Doha Agenda* (Washington, DC: CEPR and World Bank).

Bown, C. and H. L. Kee (2011) 'Developing Countries, New Trade Barriers and the Global Economic Crisis', in M. Haddad and B. Sheppard (eds), *Managing Openness* (Washington, DC: World Bank).

—— (2012) 'Emerging Economies and the Emergence of South-South Protectionism', *Policy Research Discussion Paper 6162* (Washington, DC: World Bank).

—— (2013) 'Emerging Economies and the Emergence of South-South Protectionism' *Journal of World Trade*, 47(1): 1–44.

Braga, C. A. (1996) 'Trade-related Intellectual Property Rights: The Uruguay Round Agreement and its Economic Implications' in W. Martin and L. A. Winters (eds), *The Uruguay Round and the Developing Countries* (Cambridge: Cambridge University Press).

Braga, C. A. *et al.* (1999) 'Intellectual Property Rights and Development', TechNet Working Paper (Washington, DC: World Bank).

Cadot, O. and M. Malouche (2012) 'Overview' in O. Cadot and M. Malouche (eds) *Non-Tariff Measures: A Fresh Look at Trade Policy's New Frontier* (Washington, DC: CEPR and World Bank).

Cadot, O., M. Malouche and S. Saez (2012) *Streamlining Non-Tariff Measures: A Toolkit for Policy Makers* (Washington, DC: World Bank).

Cadot, O. *et al.* (2012) 'Evaluation of AFT: From Case-study Counting to Measuring', paper presented for the FERDI-World Bank-ITC workshop on Aid for Trade, mimeo, Geneva, December.

Cattaneo, O. and C. A. Braga (2009) 'Everything You Wanted to Know about WTO Accession' Policy Research Working Paper 5116 (Washington, DC: World Bank).

Chang, W. and L. A. Winters (2002) 'How Regional Blocks Affect Excluded Countries: the Price Effects of Mercosur' *American Economic Review* 92(4): 889–904.

Charnowitz, S. (2008) 'Mapping the Law of WTO Accession' in M. E. Janow, V. Donaldson and A. Yanovitz (eds) *The WTO: Dispute Settlement, Governance and Developing Countries* (New York: Juris Publishing).

Chaytor, B. and M. Hindley (1997) *A Case Study of Sierra Leone's Participation in The World Trade Organization* (London: Cameron).

CIPR (Commission on Intellectual Property Rights) (2002) *Integrating Intellectual Property Rights and Development Policy* (London: Commission on Intellectual Property Rights).

Correa, C. M. (1998) *Implementing the TRIPS Agreement* (Penang: Third World Network).

—— (2013) 'Reflections on the IP System: A Development Perspective' *South Bulletin*, February.

Croome, J. (1995) *Reshaping the World Trade System* (Geneva: WTO).
CUTS (2008) 'Trade Openness: The Only Path to Sustainable Growth', Briefing Paper (Jaipur: CUTS International).
Dadush, U., S. Ali and R. Odell (2011) 'Is Protectionism Dying?' The Carnegie Papers (Washington DC: Carnegie Endowment).
Daly, M. and H. Kuwahara (1998) 'The Impact of the Uruguay Round on Tariff and Non-Tariff Barriers to Trade in the Quad' *The World Economy* 21: 207–234.
Das, J. (1998) *The WTO Agreements: Deficiencies, Imbalances and Required Changes* (Penang: Third World Network).
Deardorff, A. V. (1990) 'Should Patent Protection Be Extended to All Developing Countries?' *The World Economy*, 13, 497–508.
—— (1992) 'Welfare Effects of Global Patent Protection', *Economica* 59.
Dollar, D. (1992) 'Outward-Oriented Developing Countries Really Do Grow More Rapidly: Evidence from 95 LDCs, 1976–1985', *Economic Development and Cultural Change*, 40: 23–44.
—— and A. Kraay (2001) 'Trade, Growth and Poverty', paper presented at the World Bank-EU Conference on Trade and Poverty, Brussels, 6 March.
Dornbusch, R. (1992) 'The Case for Trade Liberalization in Developing Countries', *The Journal of Economic Perspectives*, 6 (1).
Drabek, Z. and S. Laird (1998) 'The New Liberalism: Trade Policy Developments in Emerging Markets,' *Journal of World Trade* 5(3): 241–269.
Duran, E. and C. Michalopoulos (1999) 'Intellectual Property Rights and Developing Countries in the WTO Millennium Round', *Journal of Intellectual Property*, 2 (6).
Dutfield, G. (2011) *The Role of the International Union for the Protection of New Varieties of Plants* (Geneva: Quaker United Nations Office).
Economist, The (2013) 'Can the WTO Save itself from Irrelevance?', 16 March.
Edwards, S. (1993) 'Openness, Trade Liberalization and Growth in Developing Countries,' *Journal of Economic Literature*, 31: 1358–1393.
EIF (2013) www.enhancedif.org.
Evans, J. (1968) 'The General Agreement on Tariffs and Trade', *International Organization* XXII, 72–98.
Evenett, S. J. (2009) *Global Trade Alert 1st Report* (London: CEPR).
—— (2012) 'Summary,' *Debacle: The 11th GTA Report on Protectionism*, www.global trade alert.
Evenett, S. J., B. M. Hoekman and O. Cattaneo (2009) 'Effective Crisis Response and Openness: Implications for the Trading System' in S. J. Evenett, B. M. Hoekman and O. Cattaneo (eds) *Effective Crisis Response and Openness* (Washington, DC: CEPR and World Bank).
FAO/AITIC (1998) 'The Relationship between the FAO International Undertaking on Plant Genetic Resources, the Convention on Biological Diversity and TRIPS', Uruguay Round Agreements – Implications for Agriculture, Forestry and Fisheries in the Less-advantaged Countries (Geneva: AITIC).
Farole, T. (2011) *Special Economic Zones in Africa* (Washington, DC: World Bank).
Finger, J. M. (1993) *Anti-dumping: How It Works and Who Gets Hurt* (Ann Arbor: Michigan University Press).
Finger, J. M. and L. Schuknecht (1999) 'Market Access Advances and Retreats since the Uruguay Round', Policy Research Working Paper 2232 (Washington, DC: World Bank).

Finger, J. M. and P. Schuler (2000) 'The Implementation of Uruguay Round Commitments: The Development Challenge' Policy Research Working Paper 2215 (Washington DC: World Bank).

Finger, J. M. and L. A. Winters. (1998) 'What Can the WTO Do for Developing Countries,' in A. O. Krueger (ed.), *The WTO as an International Organization* (Chicago IL: University of Chicago Press).

Folleti, L. *et al.* (2009) 'Smoke in the Water' in S.J. Evenett, B.M. Hoekman and O. Cattaneo (eds) *Effective Crisis Response and Openness* (Washington, DC: CEPR and World Bank).

Francois, J. and I. Wooton. (1999) 'Trade in International Transport Services: the Role of Competition,' mimeo, Erasmus University, Rotterdam, August.

Francois, J. *et al.* (2011) 'Opening Markets for the Poorest Countries: Assessing the Effects of Duty-Free, Quota-Free to the G20', mimeo (Washington, DC: World Bank).

Frankel, J. and D. Romer (1999) 'Does Trade Cause Growth?' *American Economic Review*, 89(3): 379–399.

Gabunia, G. (1998) 'Reasonable Protectionism' *Expert* (Russia) 33, September.

Gay, D. (2005) 'Vanuatu's Suspended Accession Bid: Second Thoughts?' in P. Ghallaher, P. Low and A. Stoler, *Managing the Challenges of WTO Participation*, pp. 590–606, (Geneva: Cambridge University Press and WTO).

GATT (1948) *Preamble to the Establishment of GATT.*

—— (1954) *Basic Instruments and Documents (BISD)*, 3rd Supplement.

—— (1955) *Report of the Review Working Party on Quantitative Restrictions*, L/332/Rev.

—— (1958) *Trends in International Trade* (Geneva: GATT).

—— (1964) *BISD* 12th Supplement.

—— (1972) *BISD* 18th Supplement.

—— (1979) *The Tokyo Round of Multilateral Trade Negotiations*, Report of the Director General, (Geneva: GATT).

—— (1980) *BISD* 26th Supplement.

—— (1982) *Directory* (Geneva: GATT).

—— (1987) *Directory* (Geneva: GATT).

—— (1989–94) *Trade Policy Review* for 29 developing countries, various years (Geneva: GATT).

—— (1994) 'Measures to Deal with Members in Category IV of the Administrative Arrangements on Arrears', PC/7, L/7578, December.

—— (1995) 'A Description of the Provisions Relating to Developing Countries in The Uruguay Round Agreements, Legal Instruments and Ministerial'.

Gorter, H. D., L. Ruiz and M. Ingco (2003) 'Export Competition Policies,' in M. Ingco and J. Nash (eds), *Agriculture and the WTO* (Washington, DC: World Bank).

Goswami, G., A. Mattoo and S. Saez (2012) *Exporting Services: A Developing Country Perspective* (Washington, DC: World Bank).

Gourdon, J. and A. Nicita (2012) 'NTMs: Interpreting the New Data' in O. Cadot and M. Malouche (eds) *Non-tariff Measures: A Fresh Look at Trade Policy's New Frontier* (Washington, DC: CEPR and World Bank).

Grimmett, J. (2012) *US Trade Remedy Laws and Non-Market Economies: A Legal Review* (Washington, DC: Congressional Research Service).

Hallaert, J. J., R. C. Cepeda and G. Kang (2013) *Succeeding with Trade Reform: The Role of Aid for Trade* (Paris: OECD).

Hanson, G. (2011) 'Sources of Export Growth in Developing Countries,' in M. Haddad and B. Shepherd (eds), *Managing Openness* (Washington, DC: World Bank).

Harrison, G. *et al.* (1996) 'Quantifying the Uruguay Round' in W. Martin and L. A. Winters (eds) *The Uruguay Round and the Developing Countries* (Washington, DC: World Bank).

Herfkens, E. (2013) 'Harmonized Trade Preferences for Low Income African Countries', mimeo, SAIS, Johns Hopkins University, Washington, DC.

Hertel, T. and W. Martin (1999) 'Developing Countries Interests in Liberalizing Manufactures Trade,' CEPR Workshop: London, 19–20 February.

Hertel, T. W. and L. A. Winters (2006) 'Poverty Impacts of a WTO Agreement: Synthesis and Overview,' in T. Hertel and L. A. Winters (eds), *Poverty and the WTO* (Washington, DC: World Bank and Palgrave Macmillan).

Hertel, T.W., F. Zhai and Z. Wang (2004) 'Implications of WTO Accession for Poverty in China' in D. Bhattasali, S. Li and W. Martin (eds) *China and the WTO: Accession, Policy Reform and Poverty Reduction Strategies* (Washington, DC: World Bank).

Hoekman, B. (1996) 'Assessing the General Agreement on Trade in Services', in W. Martin and L. A. Winters (eds) *The Uruguay Round and the Developing Countries* (Washington, DC: World Bank).

—— (2009) 'Aid for Trade: Helping Countries Benefit from Trade Opportunities' in D. Njinkeu and H. Cameron (eds) *Aid for Trade and Development* (New York: Cambridge University Press).

—— (2011) 'Aid for Trade: Why, What and Where Are We?' in W. Martin and A. Mattoo (eds) *Unfinished Business? The WTO's Doha Agenda* (Washington, DC: World Bank).

Hoekman, B., C. Michalopoulos and A. Winters (2004) 'Special and Differential Treatment of Developing Countries in the WTO' *World Economy* April.

Hoekman, B., W. Martin and C. A. Primo Braga (2009) 'Quantifying the Value of Preferences and Potential Erosion Losses,' in B. Hoekman, W. Martin and C.A. Primo Braga, (eds.) *Trade Preference Erosion: Measurement and Policy Response* (Washington, DC: Palgrave Macmillan and World Bank).

Horn, H., L. Johannesson and P. C. Mavroidis (2011) 'The WTO Dispute Settlement System (1995–2010): Some Descriptive Statistics' *Journal of World Trade* 45(6): 1107–1138.

Hudec, R. E. (1987) *Developing Countries in the GATT Legal System* (Hampshire: Gower Publishing).

Hufbauer G. *et al.* (2010) *Figuring out the Doha Round* (Washington, DC: Peterson Institute for International Economics).

Hynes, W. and P. Holden (2012) 'What Future for the Global Aid for Trade Initiative', IIIS Discussion Paper 421.

IOB (2005) *Aid for Trade?* IOB Evaluation 300 (The Hague: Netherlands Ministry of Foreign Affairs).

IMF/World Bank (2007) *Aid for Trade-Harnessing Globalization for Economic Development,* staff study prepared for Development Committee meeting (Washington, DC: IMF/World Bank).

Ismail, F. (2007) *Mainstreaming Development in the WTO* (Jaipur: CUTS and Geneva: Friedrich Ebert Steiftung).

ITF (International Task Force on Commodity Risk Management) (1999) *A Proposal for a Market Based Approach* (Washington, DC: World Bank).
Jensen, J., T. Rutherford and D.G. Tarr (2007) 'The Impact of Liberalizing Barriers to Foreign Direct Investment in Services: The Case of Russian Accession to the WTO', *Review of Development Economics* 11(3): 482–506.
Karsenty, G. and S. Laird (1987) 'The Generalized System of Preferences: A Quantitative assessment of the Direct Trade Effects and of Policy Options', Discussion Paper 18 (Geneva: UNCTAD).
Keesing, D. B. (1998) *Improving Trade Policy Reviews in the World Trade Organization* (Washington, DC: Institute for International Economics).
Kemper, R. (1980) 'The Tokyo Round: Results and Implications for Developing Countries' Staff Working Paper 372 (Washington, DC: World Bank).
Kessie, E. (2000) 'Enforceability of the Legal Provisions Relating to Special and Differential Treatment under the WTO Agreements', paper presented at WTO Seminar on Special and Differential Treatment of Developing Countries, Geneva, 7 March.
Krueger, A. O. (1974) 'The Political Economy of the Rent Seeking Society', *American Economic Review*, 64(3).
—— (1978) *Liberalization Attempts and Consequences* (New York: National Bureau of Economic Research).
—— and C. Michalopoulos (1985) 'Developing-country Trade Policies and the International Economic System', in E. Preeg (ed.) *Hard Bargaining Ahead: US Trade Policy and Developing Countries* (Washington, DC: Overseas Development Council).
Krueger, A. O. *et al.* (1988) 'Agricultural Incentives in Developing Countries: Measuring the Effects of Sectoral and Economy-wide Policies', *World Bank Economic Review*, 2 (7).
Laborde, D. (2008) 'Looking for a Meaningful Duty Free Quota Free Market Access Initiative in the Doha Development Agenda' ICTSD, Issue Paper 4 (Geneva: ICTSD).
Laborde, D. and W. Martin (2011a) 'Non-Agricultural Market Access' in W. Martin and A. Mattoo (eds) *Unfinished Business? The WTO's Doha Agenda* (Washington, DC: CEPR and World Bank).
—— (2011b) 'Agricultural Market Access' in W. Martin and A. Mattoo (eds) *Unfinished Business? The WTO's Doha Agenda* (Washington, DC: CEPR and World Bank).
Laborde, D., W. Martin and D. Van der Mensbrugghe (2011) 'Potential Real Income Effects of Doha Reforms' in W. Martin and A. Mattoo (eds) *Unfinished Business? The WTO's Doha Agenda* (Washington, DC: CEPR and World Bank).
Laird, S. (2012) *A Review of Trade Preference Schemes for the World's Poorest Countries* (Geneva: ICTSD).
Laker, J. (2011) 'African WTO Member Participation', PhD Dissertation (Geneva: Graduate Institute).
Lerner, A. (1936) 'The Symmetry between Import and Export Taxes', *Economica* 3, 306–13.
Leutwiler, F. *et al.* (1985) *Trade Policies for a Better Future: Proposals for Action* (Geneva: GATT).

Liebrechts R. and P. Wimenga (2004) 'The IF for Trade Related Technical Assistance to LDCs' Country Reports of Ethiopia and Yemen (Rotterdam: ECORY/NEI).

Lindbland, J. (1997) 'The Impact of the Uruguay Round on Tariff Escalation in Agricultural Products', ESCP 3, FAO: Rome.

Little, I., T. Scitovsky and M. Scott (1970) *Industry and Trade in Some Developing Countries* (London: Oxford University Press).

Mangellsdorf, A., A. Perez and J. Wilson (2012) 'Do Better Standards Facilitate Exports? Evidence from China,' in O. Cadot and M. Malouch (eds) *Non-Tariff Measures: A Fresh Look at Trade Policy's New Frontier* (Washington, DC: CEPR and World Bank).

Martin, W. and L. A. Winters (1996) 'The Uruguay Round: A Milestone for the Developing Countries,' in W. Martin and L. A. Winters (eds.), *The Uruguay Round and the Developing Countries* (Cambridge: Cambridge University Press).

Martin, W., A. Mattoo and D. Winkler (2011) 'Introduction' in W. Martin and A. Mattoo (eds), *Unfinished Business? The WTO's Doha Agenda* (Washington, DC: CEPR and World Bank).

Mascus, K. (1990) 'Intellectual property Rights', (mimeo) paper presented for conference on 'The Uruguay Round: What can Be Achieved', Washington, DC: Institute for International Economics, June.

—— (2000) *Intellectual Property Rights in the Global Economy* (Washington, DC: Institute for International Economics).

Mattoo, A. (1998) 'Financial Services and the WTO', Policy Research Working Paper 2184 (Washington, DC: World Bank).

—— (2005) 'Economics and Law of Trade in Services, mimeo, Washington DC: World Bank.

Matusz, S. J. and D. G. Tarr (1999) 'Adjusting to Trade Policy Reform', Policy Research Working Paper 2142 (Washington, DC: World Bank).

Mavroidis, P.C. (2012) 'On Compliance in the WTO: Enforcement Amongst Unequal Disputants', Briefing Paper 4/2012 (Jaipur: CUTS).

McLinden *et al.* (eds) (2011) *Border Management Modernization* (Washington, DC: World Bank).

Messerlin, P. (2009) 'A Significant Slippage in Protectionism? Not Yet,' in S.J. Evenett, B. Hoekman, and O. Cattaneo (eds.), *Effective Crisis Response and Openness* (Washington, DC: CEPR and World Bank).

Michalopoulos, C. (1999a) 'Developing Countries in the WTO', *The World Economy* 22 (1).

—— (1999b) 'Trade Policy and Market Access Issues for Developing Countries', *Policy Research Working Paper* No. 2214, World Bank.

—— (2001) *Developing Countries in the WTO* (Basingstokes: Palgrave Macmillan).

—— (2003) 'Special and Differential Treatment of Developing Countries in TRIPS', TRIPS Issues Papers 2 (Geneva: Quaker United Nations Office).

—— (2005) 'Enhancing the Integrated Framework: A New Approach', mimeo, prepared for the UK Department for International Development.

—— (2006) 'The World Trade Organization: An Assessment' *Expert Paper Series Four: International Trade* (Stockholm: Secretariat of the International Task Force on Global Public Goods).

—— and F. Ng (2013a) 'Trends in Developing Country Trade, 1980–2010' Policy Research Working Paper 6334 (Washington, DC: World Bank).

—— and F. Ng (2013b) 'Developing Country Trade Policies and Market Access Issues' Policy Research Working Paper 6463 (Washington, DC: World Bank).
—— and L. A. Winters (1997) 'Summary and Overview,' in P. D. Ehrenhaft *et al.* (eds), *Policies on Imports from Economies in Transition*, Studies of Economies in Transformation, No. 22 (Washington, DC: World Bank).
Miranda, J., R. Torres and M. Ruiz (1998) 'The International Use of Antidumping: 1987–1997,' *Journal of World Trade* 32(5): 5–71.
Moore, M. (2003) *A World Without Walls* (Cambridge: Cambridge University Press).
Narlikar, A. (2001) 'WTO Decision Making and Developing Countries', Working Paper 11 (Geneva: South Centre).
Nkomo, M. (2011) 'The Under-Utilization of TRIPS Flexibilities by Developing Countries: The Case of Africa,' in WTO-WIPO (eds), *Colloquium for Teachers of Intellectual Property* (Geneva: WTO).
Nogues, J. J. (1993) 'Social Costs and Benefits of Introducing Patent Protection for Pharmaceutical Drugs in Developing Countries', *The Developing Economies*, 31(1).
—— , A. Olechowski and L. A. Winters (1986) 'The Extent of Non-Tariff Barriers to Industrial Countries' Imports,' *World Bank Economic Review* 1(1): 181–199.
OECD (1997) *Indicators of Tariff and Non-Tariff Barrier* (Paris: OECD).
—— (2000) *Outlook* (Paris: OECD).
—— (2012) 'The Costs and Challenges of Trade Facilitation Measures', TAD/TC/WP (2012) 25, November.
—— (2013) *Aid For Trade in 2010: Continued Growth, Modest Outlook* (Paris: OECD).
OECD/WTO (2011a) *Aid for Trade 2011: Results Emerging from the Case Stories* (Paris: OECD).
—— (2011b) *Aid for Trade at a Glance 2011: Showing Results* (Paris: OECD).
OECD/WTO/UNCTAD (2013) 'Implications of Global Value Chains for Trade, Investment, Development and Jobs', mimeo prepared for G-20 Summit, St Petersburg, September.
Otsuki, T., J. Wilson and M. Sewadah (2001) 'What Price Precaution? Europe's Harmonization of Aflatoxin Regulations and African Groundnut Exports,' *European Review of Agricultural Economics*, 28(3): 263–84.
Oyejide, A. T. (1990) 'Africa and the Uruguay Round', *The World Economy* 13(3).
Palmeter, D. N. (1998) 'The WTO Antidumping Agreement and the Economies in Transition' in T. Cottier and P. C. Mavroidis (eds.) *State Trading In the Twenty First Century* (Ann Arbor: University of Michigan Press).
Panagariya, A. (2000) 'Preferential Trade Liberalization: The Traditional Theory And New Developments', *Journal of Economic Literature* 38(2).
—— (2004) 'Miracles and Debacles: In Defense of Trade Openness,' *World Economy* 27(8): 1149–1171.
Portugal-Perez, A. and J. S. Wilson (2008) 'Why Trade Facilitation Matters for Africa', Policy Research Working Paper 4719 (Washington, DC: World Bank).
Prebisch, R. (1950) *The Economic Development of Latin America and Its Principal Problems* (Santiago: UN ECLA).
Rodriguez, F. and D. Rodrik (1999) 'Trade Policy and Economic Growth: A Skeptic's Guide to the Cross National Evidence', NBER Working Paper 7081, April.
Rodrik, D. (1992) 'The Limits of Trade Policy Reform in Developing Countries', *Journal of Economic Perspectives*, 6(1): 87–105.
Rose, A. K. (2004) 'Do We Really Know that the WTO Increases Trade?' *American Economic Review*, 94(1): 98–114.

Rutherford, T. and D.G. Tarr (2008) 'Poverty Effects of WTO's Accession: Modeling Real Households and Endogenous Productivity Effects', *Review of International Economics* 18(1): 30–46.

Sachs, J. D. and A. Warner (1995) 'Economic Reform and the Process of Global Integration,' Brookings Papers on Economic Activity, Brookings, Washington DC.

Said, J. *et al.* (2011) *Evaluating Aid for Trade on the Ground: Lessons from Malawi* (Geneva: ICTSD).

Sapsford, D. and V. N. Balasubramanyam (1999) 'Trend and Volatility in the Net Barter Terms of Trade', *Journal of International Development*, 11(6).

Schiff, E. (1971) *Industrialization without Patents: The Netherlands, 1869–1912, Switzerland, 1850–1907* (Princeton: Princeton University Press).

Singer, H. (1950) 'The Distribution of Gains between Investing and Borrowing Countries', *American Economic Review, Papers and Proceedings* 11: 473–485.

Smeets, M. and C. Fournier (1998) *Trade and Tariffs in Leather and Leather Products* (Geneva: WTO).

Sok, S. *et al.* (2011) *Evaluating Aid for Trade on the Ground: Lessons from Cambodia* (Geneva: ICTSD).

South Center (1997) *The TRIPS Agreement: A Guide for the South* (Geneva: South Center).

Srinivasan, T. N. (1998) *Developing Countries and the Multilateral Trading System* (Oxford: Westview Press).

Stiglitz, J. E. (2000) 'Two Principles for the Next Round or, How to Bring Developing Countries in from the Cold,' *World Economy*, 23(4): 437–454.

—— and A. Charlton (2006) 'Aid for Trade', *International Journal of Development Issues* 5(2): 1–41.

—— and A. Charlton (2012) *The Right to Trade: A Report to the Commonwealth Secretariat* (London: Commonwealth Secretariat).

Subramanian, A. (1995) 'Trade-Related Intellectual Property Rights and Asian Developing countries: An Analytical View', mimeo, Asian Development Bank, Manila.

—— and S. J. Wei (2007) 'The WTO Promotes Trade, Strongly but Unevenly', *Journal of International Economics* 75(1): 151–175.

Tansey, G. (1999) *Trade, Intellectual Property, Food and Biodiversity* (London: Quaker Peace and Service.

Tarr, D. G. and N. Volchkova (2010) 'Foreign Economic Policy at a Crossroads' in A. Aslund, S. Guriev and A. Kutchins (eds) *Russia after the Global Economic Crisis* (Washington, DC: Peterson Institute for International Economics and Center for Strategic and International Studies), pp. 200–222.

Taylor, D. and J. Wilson (2011) 'Doha and Trade Facilitation: Lending Specificity to the Multilateral Trade and Development Agenda' in W. Martin and A. Mattoo (eds) *Unfinished Business? The WTO's Doha Agenda* (Washington, DC: CEPR and World Bank).

Third World Network (1998) *Options for Implementing the TRIPS Agreement in Developing Countries* (Penang: Third World Network).

Tomz, M., J. L. Goldstein and D. Rivers (2007) 'Do We Really Know that WTO Increases Trade? Comment', *American Economic Review* 97(5): 2005–18.

UNCTAD (1968) *The Kennedy Round Estimated Effects on Trade Barriers* (Geneva: UNCTAD).

—— (1980) *Assessment of the Results of the Multilateral Trade Negotiations* (Geneva: UNCTAD).

—— (1996) *The TRIPS Agreement and Developing Countries* (Geneva: UNCTAD).

—— /WTO (1996) *Strengthening the Participation of Developing Countries in World Trade and The Multilateral Trading System,* TD/375 (Geneva: UNCTAD).

—— /WTO (1997) 'Post-Uruguay Round Tariff Environment for Developing Country Exports', UNCTAD/WTO Joint Study, TD/B/COM.1/14, October.

UNDP (2006) 'Trade on Human Terms', *Asia and Pacific Human Development Report 2006, Overview* (Macmillan India for UNDP).

—— (2013) *Human Development Report 2013* (New York, UNDP).

USAID (2005) 'Integrated Framework Simulation' Geneva, October.

US Congress (1999) 'House Committee on Government Reform, Subcommittee on Criminal Justice, Drug Policy and Human Resources', Testimony by J. Papovich, Assistant US Trade Representative, 22 July.

Vivas-Egui, D. (2003) *Regional and Bilateral Agreements and a TRIPS-plus World: the Free Trade Area for the Americas (FTAA)* Geneva: Quaker United Nations Office.

Wacziarg, R. and K. H. Welch (2008) 'Trade Liberalization and Growth: New Evidence', *World Bank Economic Review* 22(2): 187–231.

Whalley, J. (1987) *Dealing with the North: Developing Countries and the Global Trading System,* CSIER Research Monograph (London, Ontario: The University of Western Ontario).

Whichard, O. G. (1999) 'Measurement, Classification and Reporting of Services Activities: An International Perspective,' mimeo, US Department of Agriculture, Washington DC.

Wilson, J., T. Otsuki and B. Majumdstar (2003) 'Balancing Food Safety and Risk', *Journal of International Trade and Economic Development,* (12)4: 377–402.

Winters, L. A. (2000) 'Coherence with no "here": WTO co-operation with the World Bank and the IMF', paper presented at the CEPR/ECARES/World Bank Conference, Brussels, 14–15 July.

——, N. McCulloch and A. McKay (2004) 'Trade Liberalization and Poverty: The Empirical Evidence so far', *Journal of Economic Literature* XLII: 73–166.

Wolfe, R. (2011) 'Did the Protectionist Dog Bark?' Policy Report, Stockholm: ENTWINED.

World Bank (1998) *World Development Report: Knowledge for Development* (Washington, DC: World Bank).

—— (2000, 2004) *Global Economic Prospects* (Washington, DC: World Bank).

—— (2004) *Integrated Framework for Trade-related Technical Assistance: An Independent Evaluation of the World Bank's Approach to Global Programs OED* (Washington, DC, World Bank).

—— (2009) *Unlocking Global Trade Opportunities: The Aid for Trade Program of the World Bank Group* (Washington, DC: World Bank).

—— (2012) *World Development Indicators* (Washington, DC: World Bank).

WTO (1995) *The Results of the Uruguay Round of Multilateral Trade Negotiations: The Legal Texts* (Geneva: WTO).

—— (1995–2012) *Trade Policy Review,* for 49 individual developing countries, various dates (Geneva: WTO).

—— (1997a) 'Report of the Panel on India: Patent Protection for Pharmaceutical and Agricultural Chemical Products' WT/DS50/R, September.

—— (1997b) 'Market Access for Least Developed Countries', High Level Meeting on Integrated Initiatives for Least Developed Countries' Trade Development, WT/LDC/HL/14, November.
—— (1997c) *Trade Policy Review*, European Union, PRESs/TPRB/65.
—— (1998a) 'India – Patent Protection for Pharmaceutical and Agricultural Chemical Products', Report of the Panel, WT/DS79/R, August.
—— (1998b) 'Market Access for Exports of Goods and Services from the LDCs: Barriers and Constraints', WT/COMT/LDC/W/11/REV.1, December.
—— (1998c) 'Coherence' GC/13, October.
—— (1999a) 'Developing Countries and the Multilateral Trading System: Past and Present' Development Division, Background Document prepared for the High Level Symposium on Trade and Development, Geneva, 17–18 March.
—— (1999b) 'Third Progress Report on the Follow-up to the High Level Meeting', Subcommittee on the Least Developed Countries, WT/COMTD/LDC/W/13, February.
—— (2000a) 'Integrated Framework for Trade-Related Assistance to LDCs: The Process to Date, Concerns and Suggested Improvements', WT/COMTD/LDC/W/18.
—— (2000b) 'Disputes Status Report', July.
—— (2001a) Doha WTO Ministerial 'Ministerial Declaration', WT/MIN(01) DEC/1, November.
—— (2001b) Doha WTO Ministerial 'Declaration on the TRIPS Agreement and Public Health', WT/MIN (01) DEC/2.
—— (2001c) 'Working Party Report on the Accession of the People's Republic of China' WT/ACC/CHINA/49 and Appendices, Geneva: WTO.
—— (2003a) 'Final Report of the Evaluation of the Integrated Framework: Summary' WT/IFSC/6/Rev2/Add.1, December.
——(2003b) Council for TRIPS 'Implementation of Article 66.2 of the TRIPS Agreement' IP/C/28, 20 February 2003.
—— (2004a) *Trade Policy Review*, Canada, WT/TOR/112.
—— (2004b) *Trade Policy Review*, European Union, WT/TPR/136.
—— (2004c) *Trade Policy Review*, United States, WT/TPR/126.
—— (2006) 'Recommendations of the Aid for Trade Task Force' WT/AFT/1, July.
—— (2008) *Trade Policy Review*, Mauritius, WT/TPR/198.
—— (2009) *Report to the TPRB from the Director General on the Financial and Economic Crisis and Trade Related Developments*, WT/TPR/OV/W/1, WTO: Geneva.
—— (2010) Trade Policy Review, WAEMU, WT/TPR/236.
—— (2011a) IP/C/W/558/Add.6 20 October.
—— (2011b) IP/C/W/555/Add.1 10 October.
—— (2011c) 'The WTO and Preferential Trade: from Co-existence to Coherence', *World Trade Report*, WTO: Geneva.
—— (2011d) *Trade Policy Review*, Japan WT/TPR/243.
—— (2011e) *Trade Policy Review*, Canada WT/TPR/246.
—— (2012a) 'Members Streamline Accession for Poorest' News Item, 6 July (Geneva: WTO).
—— (2012b) *Report on G-20 Trade Measures*, 31 October (Geneva: WTO).
—— (2012c) 'Trade and Public Policies: A closer Look at Non-Tariff Measures in the 21st Century,' *World Trade Report*, WTO: Geneva.

—— (2012d) *Accessions Time Table*, December (Geneva: WTO).

—— (2012e) IP/C/W/558/Add.7 21 February.

—— (2012f) Negotiating Group on Trade Facilitation, 'Draft Consolidated Negotiating Text', TN/TF/W/165/Rev.14.

—— (2012g) Committee on Customs Valuation, *Annual Report*, G/L/1012, November.

—— (2012h) *Trade Policy Review*, East Africa Community, WT/TPR/271.

—— (2013) 'The Future of Trade: The Challenges of Convergence', Report of the Panel on Defining the Future of Trade (Geneva: WTO).

Xiong, B. and J. Beghin (2011) 'Does European Aflatoxin Regulation Hurt Groundnut Exporters from Africa?' Iowa State University Working Paper 11026, February.

Index

The manufacturer's authorised representative in the EU is Springer Nature Customer Service Centre GmbH, Europaplatz 3, 69115 Heidelberg, Germany. If you have any concerns regarding our products, please contact ProductSafety@springernature.com

Printed and bound by CPI Group (UK) Ltd, Croydon, CR0 4YY

10/10/2026

02231228-0009